The cinema of Oliver Stone

MANCHESTER
1824

Manchester University Press

The cinema of Oliver Stone

Art, authorship and activism

Ian Scott and Henry Thompson

MANCHESTER UNIVERSITY PRESS

Published by Manchester University Press
Altrincham Street, Manchester M1 7JA
www.manchesteruniversitypress.co.uk

British Library Cataloguing-in-Publication Data
A catalogue record for this book is available from the British Library

Library of Congress Cataloging-in-Publication Data applied for

ISBN 978 0 7190 9916 8 hardback
ISBN 978 1 5261 0871 5 paperback

First published 2016

Typeset by Out of House Publishing
Printed in Great Britain
by Bell & Bain Ltd, Glasgow

Contents

Figures

Preface

From the outset, the research and writing for this book have benefited from an ongoing and intimate collaboration with the filmmaker. On one level, this depth of engagement from Oliver Stone should come as no surprise. All through his career, Stone has shown willingness – and indeed a deep interest – in engaging with academic and journalistic debate about his films and their contextual significance. For him, being actively involved in the afterlife of a movie and the discussions that it generates is part and parcel of the filmmaker's responsibility. For example, he directly accepted an engagement with the American Historical Association concerning its debates over the merits of *JFK* and *Nixon*, recorded in Robert Brent Toplin's *Oliver Stone's USA*. He also was involved in detailed discussions about the academic commentary on *Alexander* outlined in Paul Cartledge and Fiona Rose-Greenland's *Responses to Oliver Stone's Alexander.*

However, Stone went even further with our project. He gave his time and energy over a significant period, thus committing his life and work to the long-term and sustained investigation of him and his films. He provided hours of interview time over many meetings, roughly within the space of five years of his working life. To assist with this process, we wrote up pre-interview notes outlining the issues to be covered at each session. In response, Stone never arrived unprepared. Invariably, he had read the notes and had his own written summary of what he wanted to cover by way of reply. His spoken responses were rich in detail – more than we could make full use of in this text – and so we have taken the decision to publish the full transcripts verbatim. In addition to this personal commitment, Stone provided full access to all of his production files, enabling us to spend many weeks working at Ixtlan's offices in Santa Monica, California, where all of the files were retrieved from storage and reviewed.

In view of the degree of access, it is a legitimate question to ask how a critical distance between authors and subject could be maintained. No doubt, Stone's previous work with scholars helped here. He understood that there would be – and always have been – differences of opinion on topics, and he seemed to rather embrace that fact, almost as though it was borne of a career where disagreement from critics had become so instinctively second nature that he welcomed it back like an old friend. His only concern was that we should work with the facts and tie any conjectures firmly back to that factual base. Stone never sought any editorial input to the project. He understood from the outset that our independence as authors would strengthen the book. The unwritten contract – such as it was – was that the faith implied in such openness and disclosure would be answered with a professional assessment done to the best of our abilities. We have sought to honour that aspiration, but leave it to the reader to judge. Stone took up the invitation to read a final version of the manuscript, which allowed him the opportunity to highlight any factual errors and to respond further on any of the debates if he wished.

Acknowledgements

This research and the writing of this book was enhanced in no small part by the help given by Richard Heffner, Professor of Communications and Public Policy at Rutgers University, USA, and one-time chair of the Classification and Rating Administration (CARA). Sadly, Dick died in December 2013, but his professional advice and knowledge of the inner workings of the film industry, as well as the personal friendship he offered, were all crucial components in the progression of this project.

Several people at Oliver Stone's production company – Ixtlan Inc. – in Santa Monica, California provided invaluable assistance with the progress of the research. Thanks are due to Morgan Marling, John Cooper, Evan Bates and Janet Lee. We owe a particular debt to Evan Bates, who supported and facilitated the project from the outset, arranging interviews and set visits; and to Janet Lee for her help with materials, permissions and seeing things through to conclusion.

A number of Oliver Stone's present and former associates were happy to give their time for interviews both on- and off-set, for which we are very grateful. Thanks are due to Bob Daly, Eric Kopeloff, Moritz Borman, Tod Maitland, Paul Graff and Christina Graff.

Abbreviations

ARRB	Assassination Records Review Board
BAFTA	British Academy of Film and Television Arts
CARA	Classification and Rating Administration
CDO	Collateralised Debt Obligation
CDS	Credit Default Swap
CIA	Central Intelligence Agency
CTE	Chronic Traumatic Encephalopathy
DEA	Drug Enforcement Agency (US)
FBI	Federal Bureau of Investigation
FPI	Film Packages International
GCHQ	Government Communications Headquarters (UK)
HBO	Home Box Office
ICE	Immigration and Customs Enforcement
IMF	International Monetary Fund
ISIS	Islamic State of Iraq and Syria
MPAA	Motion Picture Association of America
NFL	National Football League
NSA	National Security Agency
NVA	North Vietnamese Army
PCI	Paramount Communications Inc.
UA	United Artists
WGA	Writers Guild of America
WMDs	weapons of mass destruction

Introduction

'Oliver Stone is still a mystery – to me too.'[1]

'I don't want to make a silly movie. I don't want to make it for the wrong reasons. I have a storytelling sense and a sense of drama, and I want to continue.'[2]

Oliver Stone: the remaking of a maverick filmmaker

To examine the welter of publications about writer-director Oliver Stone over the last thirty years is to enter a netherworld where the divisions between fact and fiction, and truth and objectivity often blur, if not break down. Assessments of Stone populate the entire spectrum of writing – academic, popular, critical and journalistic – and run from near-deification to outright denunciation. The details reveal a filmmaker who has been exposed possibly more than any other artist in Hollywood's history to a spellbinding mixture of praise, speculation, conjecture, criticism and downright denigration. The titles alone tell their own story: *Oliver Stone's America: Dreaming the Myth Outward*; *Oliver Stone's U.S.A.: Film, History and Controversy*; and *Stone: The Controversies, Excesses and Exploits of a Radical Filmmaker*.[3] Stone is not just a director, not just an artist, not even just an auteur. Rather, he has come to represent an adjective that says something about the era of Hollywood filmmaking that he has worked in, and even more about late twentieth and early twenty-first-century American history that he has repeatedly visualised and constructed on screen. All of it has been accompanied by a running commentary virtually unheard of with regard to other filmmakers. '[H]e has attracted greater controversy and more passionate criticism than any of his contemporaries. The plaudits and condemnations come in almost equal measure,' confirm Andrew Pepper and Trevor McCrisken in their work on Hollywood's historical movies.[4]

Therefore, very few analyses of the man or his films begin without the words 'controversy', 'inaccuracy' or even 'outrage' and 'exploitation'. Albert Auster, talking of arguably Stone's two most provocative pictures, *JFK* (1991) and *Nixon* (1995), encapsulates the prevalent feeling:

> The initial reception of both films by the American media was hardly what one might call restrained or polite. Even before film critics had their say, journalists, political commentators and assorted literati weighed in with critiques of the films.[5]

Auster rightly locates that recurrent historical period of the 1960s and early 1970s as a central philosophical component of the two pictures and of Stone's revaluation of the country, right in the heart of the Cold War era. As he notes: 'Taken together, they presented Stone's mythic interpretation of American history and politics since the 1960s.'[6] It is this analysis of the personal – not to say provocative – commentary allied to historical re-enactment in Stone's pictures which has been fused together for so long in assessments of the director, that one could be forgiven for thinking it was the default position of all critics on Stone, right from the off.

In fact, Oliver Stone's career was never as outrageously contentious as this when it started, neither was it even at the putative height of his artistic and commercial powers in the decade that spanned the late 1980s and early 1990s. From unlikely writing credits for *The Hand* (1981), which he also directed, *Conan the Barbarian* (John Milius, 1982) and *8 Million Ways to Die* (Hal Ashby, 1986), to the more lauded and/or cultish work for *Midnight Express* (Alan Parker, 1978, for which he won the Academy Award for Best Adapted Screenplay), *Scarface* (Brian De Palma, 1983) and *Year of the Dragon* (Michael Cimino, 1985), Stone's early career CV gathered together solid and praiseworthy credentials that lined him up as a filmmaker with something important (and occasionally outlandish) to say. The somewhat over-the-top nature of several of the features above certainly could have their extravagance and virtuosity laid at the door of their respective directors, Milius, De Palma and Cimino: each of them an auteur, each coming out of the New Hollywood circle that emerged during the 1970s, and each with an outlook, sensibility and fascination for certain topics that Stone easily shared, and to which he subsequently devoted himself. All three were important influences on Stone's acculturation as a director. Indeed, the connection and mutual regard help explain some of the determinants that made their screenwriting protégé's career, if anything, even more flamboyant, extreme and ultimately successful, than their own.

Most obviously, Cimino's Oscar-winning *The Deer Hunter* (1978) set the benchmark for a grittier and more politically refined assessment of the Vietnam War that Stone built upon in a personal fashion, first with *Platoon* (1986), and then *Born on the Fourth of July* (1989). This latter production, which would later become the second part of Stone's trilogy about the conflict, echoed Cimino's own sense of despondency and fatigue with the war during the early 1970s, with his story hitting the screens more than a decade before Tom Cruise's Academy-nominated performance as real-life veteran, Ron Kovic.

De Palma's directorial influence should not be dismissed so easily either. For in the likes of *Dressed to Kill* (1980) and *Blow Out* (1981), there is the ghost of a homage to previous Hollywood genres and a hint of the violence and sociopathic behaviour that Stone would focus on in films such as *Natural Born Killers* (1994) and *U Turn* (1997). With Milius, there was a unifying of these themes and subjects. As a script contributor to some of the *Dirty Harry* series (1971–88), to the gangster movie *Dillinger* (1973), and as a writer on *Apocalypse Now* (1979) for Francis Ford Coppola, Milius produced a similarly conceived set of features, ideas and characters that he too wanted to bring to the screen in a particular way, just as Stone set out to do once his own career was well under way in the 1980s. Yet even in the midst of these shared dispositions, Stone's apprenticeship as a filmmaker had complex layers and a growing independent streak. Milius liked the *Conan* script but opted not to shoot it in the form that Stone had intended, and there was no collaboration between director and writer during production. In the case of *Scarface*, Stone had written the script before De Palma joined the project, although in this instance the director certainly did share his writer's vision of making the movie almost operatically violent. Nonetheless, even with these addenda, the formative influences of Milius, De Palma and Cimino are unmistakable.

That Stone's reputation and influence superseded these directors in time is not merely a story about commercial viability or, indeed, better filmmaking – although with only a few exceptions from the other three, both assertions were true – so much as it was Stone's constant and uncanny ability for a decade or more to capture the zeitgeist of the American condition and make it cinematically vivacious, exciting and vital. Stone's name became a byword for controversy because of an accumulation of issues, debates and situations that thrust his politics, personality and pictures into the spotlight. Not the least of these confluences was the era itself. Often, when people speak of Oliver Stone's cinema, they do not associate it with the 1980s – and if they do, it is only perhaps to reflect on the fact that some of his best movies were made during that decade. Stone's oeuvre is seldom seen as a commentary on, or a reflection of, the age itself; but Stone should be linked more irrevocably with the era of the 1980s than with the 1960s or 1970s. Why? Because of the condition of the country, the fallout from the previous ten years of trauma, and most importantly, the overarching presence of Ronald Reagan during the decade.

Stone's disregard for Reagan is legendary, and it informed the most scorching indictments in his filmmaking during the decade. From the condemnation of Central American foreign policy in *Salvador* (1986), to the inexorable rise of 'shock jock' celebrity culture in *Talk Radio* (1988), by way of the financial 'masters of the universe' satire at the heart of *Wall Street* (1987), Stone took potshots at every angle of Reagan's political philosophy. That the man left the White House in 1989 as one of its most popular ever incumbents, and that films such as *Born on the Fourth of July* seemed to capture for some audiences the essence of Reagan's idealism (in as misguided a way as the appropriation of Bruce Springsteen's *Born in the USA* had been during the Republican president's 1984 re-election campaign), only confirms a need to reappraise the director, the films, the politics and the era more generally, especially in light of Stone's subsequent career.

Stone's success aside, Hollywood was going through a broad commercial renaissance and expansion in the second half of the

1980s. Acquisitions of cinema chains, company mergers and an expanding breed of franchises tied into further products and merchandising all spoke of a newly-emerging global entertainment complex. While the artistic credibility of the New Hollywood cohort of filmmakers from a decade previously might have dissipated to some extent, the rehabilitation of Hollywood financially, and the soaring revenues of its most popular movies – starting with *ET* (Steven Spielberg, 1982) and continuing on through *Ghostbusters* (Ivan Reitman, 1984), *Back to the Future* (Robert Zemeckis, 1985), *Top Gun* (Tony Scott, 1986), *Fatal Attraction* (Adrian Lyne, 1987), *Rain Man* (Barry Levinson, 1988) and *Batman* (Tim Burton, 1989) – made the mix of commercial sensibility and political credibility a heady and successful concoction for directors such as Alan Parker (*Mississippi Burning*, 1988), Stanley Kubrick (*Full Metal Jacket*, 1987) and of course, Stone. *Born on the Fourth of July* ended up the forty-first highest grossing film of the 1980s, with *Platoon* only just behind in forty-third place. Together they earned more than $300 million worldwide, in addition to critical adulation.

What linked these filmmakers together was that each was acutely aware that their films could remind cinemagoers of the consequences of the political era that they were living through, as well as synonymise that legacy with the New Right agenda of the 1960s, Civil Rights and Vietnam. Social and political dislocation remained pertinent for these directors, even though their films often became caught up in the maelstrom of high-octane, entertaining, feel-good pictures that attracted young people in particular back into cinemas during the decade, and which headed much of the box-office lists generated during that time. Stone was a vital component in that appraisal. As Frank Beaver describes it, Stone's films throughout the Reagan years carried a 'subtext of urgency ... suggesting a compulsive creator with a mission.'[7]

However, by the time the 1990s were underway, Stone's brand of politically and commercially engaging cinema seemed less attuned to the emerging popular mood. Allowing the pictures alone to do the talking for him became less viable. 'Stone [went] to great lengths to try and justify the historical perspectives he has placed on film and to answer the condemnations he has received,' suggest Pepper and McCrisken.[8] Those efforts principally revolved around the mammoth accompanying books which acted as companions to *JFK* and *Nixon*. Clocking in at more than 500 pages each, the books were less often remembered for having pro- *and* anti- voices, historicism and observations concerning the presentation of Kennedy's assassination and Nixon's fall from grace and then from office, than they were for being extended bids at convincing his audience that Stone was right about the historical theses that he presented in these pictures. Did the change in decades, and hence alteration in the political atmosphere, have something to do with the way that the films were conceived and the reception around them handled? Certainly, the Clintonian, post-Cold War 1990s seem a more halcyon interlude now, looking back: a coda to the 1950s where the imminent threat of total war was replaced by the strategic anxieties of individual campaigns.

As the Cold War ended, and even allowing for interventions such as Bosnia and Somalia, the 1990s could be seen retrospectively as a staging post: the calm before the storm of 9/11 and the Bush Doctrine that followed.[9] In that temporary lull, Stone's attention did not waver, but arguably that of the American audience did; caressed first with the hubris that washed in after the first Gulf War and the embrace of Francis Fukuyama's 'end of history' thesis;[10] and later with the celebrity scandals of O. J. Simpson and Michael Jackson, together with easy political distractions such as the Monica Lewinsky story.[11] Stone's history in *Born on the Fourth of July*, *JFK* and *Nixon* was wholehearted and demanding, but the end of the Cold War had untethered the USA and left the past not as prologue – as Stone's adopted Shakespearean quote from the end of *JFK* advised – but as just that: history. Was it any wonder that he lost traction in the mood of the times? Moreover, a related and potentially even bigger issue for him was the voguish style of cinema being employed.

The force of the truth/fiction, artist/historian binaries that swirled around the director in those years, for example, lost its force as audiences adjusted to the new world order and sought different and less contested cinematic narratives away from Stone's acerbic treatise. Pepper and McCrisken do a fine job of outlining many of the scholars and critics who supported Stone's agenda in the early 1990s. They argue that his politics could be seen as visceral and aesthetic, as much as it was ideological and historically authentic. Quoting Jack Davis, they identify Stone's talent for making people 'experience history not on an intellectual level but on an emotional one'.[12] They go on to identify the danger in this approach too, which more often than not results in audiences 'feeling' history rather than 'thinking' about it – but was Stone at fault here? His media commentaries and book response with *JFK* and *Nixon* were designed to support his case, but they also seemed to suggest that he anticipated that danger, as well as a need to encourage a thinking and critical edge to the reception of his films.

The broader change that Pepper and McCrisken pointed to was real enough. As the 1990s proceeded and the new millennium dawned, reliving, feeling and experiencing the past became increasingly important to society at large, arguably more so than actually *studying* it. Indeed, who could argue that historians themselves, certainly on television and film, were not adopting a similar trick and making the study of history popular, if not populist, once more? The issue for Stone and his style of filmmaking was that much of this popular exploration of the past was being played out in Hollywood with the emphasis on not simply *feeling* the past, but *feeling good* about it: a trend solidly exemplified in popular pictures such as *The Last of the Mohicans* (Michael Mann, 1992), *Braveheart* (Mel Gibson, 1995) and *Apollo 13* (Ron Howard, 1995), as well as *The Patriot* (Roland Emmerich, 2000).

The waves of controversy rolling in for *JFK* and *Nixon* during the 1990s did not interrupt the idea that Stone should, could and did have provocative things to say about the past, and about academic as well as mainstream accounts of it. If nothing else, he strongly countered the idea that cinema was merely an entertainment medium, whatever its pretensions; ironically enough, an idea that probably sat far less easily with Hollywood executives in the 1990s than it had done a decade before. Nevertheless, there was a mismatch here. Stone's instincts were taking him in one direction towards historical enquiry and reassessment, while the country was moving somewhere else. Audiences who thought that indeed they had reached the end of history, were finding less use for contested versions of the past.

In the 2000s then, Stone's filmmaking altered along with his outlook in the wake of 9/11. That link between cultural influence through box-office vitality, political commentary by way of studio allegiance to the director's vision (Stone's relationship with

Bob Daly and Warner Bros. in the early 1990s was crucial in this regard), and just some unknown capacity to spot the trends and desires of wider society which then can be communicated through a story or historical period, were no longer as much of a vital confluence as they once were in Stone's filmmaking. *Alexander* (2004) and *World Trade Center* (2006) seemed perfectly in line with tastes and predilections for the return of the 'sword-and-sandals' historical epic and, after 2005, a harder-edged, more resonant assessment of the nation five years on from 9/11. These were productions that followed in the wake of successes such as Ridley Scott's *Gladiator* (2000) and Paul Greengrass's *United 93* (2006).[13] However, not only did these films precede Stone's, they also garnered more critical and commercial attention *and* somehow seemed more fiery and resolute than his efforts. *Gladiator*'s conventional 'honourable man seeks justice for himself and Rome' narrative was uncomplicated by any deeper historicism than a reconditioned and CGI-ed Coliseum, and played well with audiences both at home and overseas. On a reported budget of $103 million, it took $187 million at the domestic box office and a further $258 million outside the USA. Nominated in twelve categories, the film won five Oscars.

By comparison, Stone's *Alexander* offered a more complex biopic of the enigmatic progress of Alexander the Great, incorporating all of the inevitable unanswered questions that history throws up along the way. The consumption by mainstream US audiences of the original 2004 release (it was subsequently re-edited no less than three times) was complicated further by Stone's decision to confront the issue of homosexuality with his central character. Be it in spite of (or because of) such a portrayal, the film did not fare well at the US box office, taking a mere $34 million on a reported budget of $155 million. (The film's nomination for six Golden Raspberry ('Razzie') awards[14] did not help its profile either.) Overall, *Alexander* was rescued commercially by its performance outside the USA, where the reception was kinder and the picture made a further $133 million.

In the comparison of *World Trade Center* with *United 93* – the story of the final moments of the commercial airliner hijacked by terrorists that was headed for Washington, DC, but which eventually crashed in a field in Pennsylvania on 11 September 2001 – the contention was one of aesthetics more than historicism. One could have imagined Stone making a very similar film to Greengrass's with such a script and raw material. Instead, there was a perceived conventionality to his take on the attacks which, in *World Trade Center*, took the form of following in the footsteps of real-life Port Authority policemen John McLoughlin and Will Jimeno (Nicolas Cage and Michael Peña) as they battled into, got trapped in and then buried amid the collapsing towers on 9/11.[15] The film follows their rescue and eventual rehabilitation, casting its gaze across the eyes of heroic first responders battling the fires and destruction of Lower Manhattan on that day.

Not for the first time, Stone's treatment of the subject-matter wrong-footed critics and supporters alike. The narrative sub-text in *Alexander* anchored the film around a bisexual leader immersed in a Middle East military conquest when the USA was engaged militarily in Iraq. Such analogous conflict certainly suggested to many a polemical intent. By contrast, *World Trade Center* was absent of polemics at a time when the Left was beginning to question the foreign policy direction taken by the Bush administration in the half-decade since 9/11. Therefore, taken together, the two films invited the ire of social conservatives on the one hand, and the disdain of liberal supporters on the other.

The latter seemed especially bitter. *The Onion* satirical publication took to 'revealing' *World Trade Center*'s major conceit: that there was a 'single-plane' theory central to the tale of 9/11, and that Stone's film was about to unleash its story on an unsuspecting world which had not thought about the prospect of one plane crashing into everything![16] Can artists survive everything except ridicule? Was the story no more than an irreverent homage to Stone's previous power and force? After all, the director himself was no stranger to self-parody. He was perfectly happy in the 1990s to help fellow director Ivan Reitman concoct his fantasy 'presidential takeover by common man' story in *Dave* (1993), by playing himself appearing on *Larry King Live* and suggesting – rightly, of course, in the plot – that President Mitchell (Kevin Kline playing both parts) in the White House was no longer the same incumbent as he had been before his alleged collapse and hospitalisation. Time naturally mellows people and adds perspective and, notwithstanding the Reitman cameo, Stone could afford to be more generous in his position than once was the case. Nevertheless, the irreverence, together with the emergence of a new generation of political filmmakers in the early 2000s, did seem to be marginalising a director who was once the fulcrum of polemical cinematic angst in Hollywood. Stone followed *World Trade Center* with his third presidential biopic, *W.* about George W. Bush in 2008, followed by a reprise of Gordon Gekko in *Wall Street: Money Never Sleeps* (2010), and a tour around the perils of drug dealing in *Savages* (2012). All three films had things to say about their subject matter, but all did so with noticeably more muted polemics than supporters and critics alike had expected.

Indeed, Stone's career since the turn of the millennium suggests a director less easily defined than his convenient monikers ('controversial', 'angry', 'polemical', 'political filmmaker') would have one believe. If it also suggests that Stone's position as a critical and commercial purveyor of political cinema is no longer as dominant as it once was, one might ask: what is left to say about Hollywood's most vociferous filmmaker of his generation? This book does focus attention on the period from the late 1990s to the middle of the second decade of the new century. However, it does so not counterintuitively or to the exclusion of Stone's 'classic' era, but more as a coda to it: a rejoinder that adds weight and emphasis to the past, and to the overall assessment of the man and his films. It also realigns this later period (the second half of Stone's career, if you will) with the context of his early films, challenging some of the typical perceptions of commentators that have seen his work as flabbier and less insistent than the earlier years – simply not as provocative as the director was in his pomp.

Certainly, the aesthetic bravado that so infused *JFK, Nixon, The Doors* (1991) and *Natural Born Killers*, as well as the polemical responses that characterised *Salvador, Platoon* and *Born on the Fourth of July*, do seem sparser in the work after 1997. The topics seem more diverse too. From ancient historical epics to sports films, to recollections of 9/11, Stone appeared to scour the landscape of American (and world) history and culture in search of subject matter: this when polemics, rhetorical posturing and angry condemnations of US cultural, economic and political imperialism came as naturally to others as they had to him in previous times. However, as filmmakers are apt to do, Stone actually changed direction in the late 1990s – a central theme to be explored here – and self-consciously moved away from some of the bigger questions and larger dilemmas which had occupied his filmmaking for two decades.

In seeking evidence of change within his film catalogue, the variances were as much to do with treatment as theme. Stone's desire to deal in issues and events of national and international importance was self-evident from the start. With the release of *Salvador* in 1986 and consolidated by *JFK* five years later, Stone had reached a point already where he found himself in the role of spokesperson for a nebulous array of liberal and left-leaning political interests in the USA. 'This critique of the establishment is part of who I am,' he admitted in interview, and reviewers found the cloak fitted him well.[17] Critics at the time described the former film as 'thrilling', 'violent and gutsy' and 'a brand of left-wing machismo that's nearly extinct.'[18] Stone said he liked the 'anarchy' in *Salvador*, and the camera's breathless intensity and kinetic energy certainly set a tone for all that was to come, both cinematically and ideologically.

In other words it was, as Frank Beaver identifies, a 'primer' for *Platoon* and the films to follow, up to, including and beyond *JFK*.[19] That interest in national events was maintained in *World Trade Center*, *W.* and *Wall Street: Money Never Sleeps* during the 2000s; however, the drama not only muted the explicit polemics, but also muted their inference. While *Platoon* focused on the minutiae of combat, audiences and critics alike proclaimed what they saw as wider messages about the futility of that war and, indeed, all conflict. In *World Trade Center*, meanwhile, Stone deliberately swayed away from the geopolitical aspects of the story and focused his efforts on individual courage and endurance. In *W.*, his treatment of former President George W. Bush was more nuanced and less scabrous than many of his supporters might have wished for: by Stone's reading, Bush was less malevolent than he was simply a man out of his depth. 'He's Peter Sellers in *Being There*. He just doesn't belong,' he explained.[20]

Wall Street: Money Never Sleeps was less incendiary than its predecessor, and ended on a less critical note than some observers had expected, with the resurrected Gordon Gekko (Michael Douglas) from the first film seeking redemption in his new role as paternal servant and grandfather. It was a breath of optimism that seemed to negatively colour assessments of the film.[21] The treatment of drug cartels and cross-border violence was similarly restrained in *Savages*. Don Winslow's original book revolves around a kidnap and rescue set against the incursion of a Mexican drug cartel into southern California. Towards the end of the book, Winslow allows himself a brief moment of wider reflection in considering life in the 'Golden State': '[W]e made gods of wealth and health. A religion of narcissism. In the end, we worshiped only ourselves. In the end, it wasn't enough.'[22] Stone regarded this as an unnecessarily pessimistic commentary, and chose to excise the references in the final screenplay. It was a decision and strategy that infused his other films of the time: an injection of guarded optimism running alongside a visibly changed use of stylistic palette. In *U Turn*, *Alexander* and *W.*, melodramatic visual motifs in combination with narrative pathos allowed Stone to move away from the realist and hyperrealist styles of his early years, instead offering a form of expression with pretensions to more classical dramatic preoccupations, and pushing questions of personal morality more to the fore.

Nonetheless, Stone's interest in politics had lost none of its fervour. Alongside shifts in approach to drama, he grappled with more steadfast political and historical topics in documentary filmmaking. *Comandante* (2003), *Persona Non Grata* (2003), *Looking for Fidel* (2004), *South of the Border* (2010), *Castro in Winter* (2012), *Mi Amigo Hugo* (2014) and the ten-part television series, *The Untold History of the United States* (2012), all confirmed a continuing appetite for challenging the establishment's political narratives, and disrupting what Stone saw as the mainstream media's collusion in the promulgation of those narratives.

Stone's style might lead one to think that his fast-paced editing, and ability to command hours of filmed and historic footage while making it plausible and visually engrossing, would align him with filmmakers who have adopted much of his technique for their own careers. From Michael Moore and Eugene Jarecki, to Errol Morris and Alex Gibney, contemporary documentary-makers owe much to Stone's cinematic construction of images and ideology. Indeed, the ambitions of these fellow documentarians – expressed notably in *Fahrenheit 9/11* (Michael Moore, 2004) and *Fog of War* (Errol Morris, 2003; both released after *Comandante*) – ran parallel to Stone's own desire for greater government accountability. Yet in the same way that a new and distinctive style emerged in Stone's drama, so he moved in a counter-intuitive direction as regards the construction and delivery of his documentaries. Like Moore, he is present in the films, but restrained. In *Comandante* (2003), despite the stylistic continuity evident in the intercutting of archive footage, the somewhat sympathetic portrayal of Cuba's revolutionary leader Fidel Castro is more meditative and reflective than it is exhilarating and exhaustive. The argumentative force of the film lies not in its construction, but in the very act of giving Castro a hearing – a forceful statement somewhat confirmed by HBO's subsequent decision to drop the film from its schedule at short notice in spring 2003. Stone believed that the film offered some redress for what he saw as establishment bias in the mainstream media coverage of Cuba. HBO was less than convinced.

The ensuing licensing dispute between himself and the broadcaster as a result of the cancellation effectively prevented any transmission or US release: a state of affairs that received almost no coverage in the USA, and yet which brought the Bush administration's policy towards alleged 'un-American' expression and comment in the wake of 9/11, and the then nascent invasion of Iraq, into sharp relief.

HBO's own reasoning for its intervention to prevent the broadcast of *Comandante* was, in itself, revealing. HBO tried to justify the decision as an editorial issue – a need to include further material on dissident activity in Cuba, given the execution of three hijackers by the Cuban authorities in April 2003, it claimed – almost three months after the film had premiered at the Sundance Film Festival. Despite being peeved by the decision, Stone spun the request into a positive separate documentary – *Looking for Fidel* (2004) – which highlighted the dissident issue on the island.

Stone followed his work on Castro with *South of the Border*: a road trip of sorts unfolding first through an appraisal of the revival of Venezuela, then followed by a series of interviews with South American leaders giving their own impressions of the continent's economic conditions, as well as their assessment of the then Venezuelan president, Hugo Chávez. By this point, Chávez had long since taken over from Castro as the US government's Latin American nemesis; but, as with *Comandante*, the style is deliberately pensive and conventional, rather than confrontational and acerbic. As he did in *Comandante*, Stone sought an alternative image of Chávez by way of political and cultural realignment. Stone's follow-up documentary, *Castro in Winter*, made his return to that island and pursuit of the Cuban leader a notional trilogy that formed another free-wheeling, if somewhat retrospective, discussion of the themes that echoed through *Comandante*. However, the film also transcended and penetrated a little more widely the cult of the last Cold War revolutionary.

Collectively, these documentaries shared a common revisionist goal to enlighten audiences about Latin American history, as well as to shine a light on US policy in the region. What they consciously reacted against was what Stone saw as an emerging entertainment, feature-film aesthetic tied to satirical polemics visible in, for example, Moore's *Capitalism: A Love Story* (2009) and Gibney's *Enron: The Smartest Guys in the Room* (2005). Stone did not dislike these films – indeed, he has spoken with admiration for the filmmakers – but he did see a way for his well rehearsed, frenzied and kinetic presentation to take a backseat, while reintroducing audiences to Stone-as-documentarian in the traditional sense, not just dogmatist for the sake of opinion. While some of this shift in his filmmaking philosophy might look like a contrarian at play, Stone has never felt obliged to simply meet the expectations of his audience – and in that regard, he is as much at odds with the world as ever he was in the 1980s and 1990s.

Nevertheless, the shift to documentary work was not driven by aesthetics alone. As Stone himself confessed, it was another way of meeting with, and handling, his political engagement. 'The move to documentary work is an effort to put pressure where I can best put it, even if it's a reduced impact,' he explained.[23] It is true that neither *Comandante* nor *South of the Border* generated anywhere near the tumult that accompanied the production and release of a movie such as *JFK*. That high watermark of activism in his career eventually saw Stone giving evidence in Congress to the Subcommittee on Legislation and National Security in April 1992: discussions that would lead to the establishment of the Assassination Records Review Board (ARRB), and the subsequent release into the National Archives of many previously secret government documents relating to the assassination of President Kennedy.[24]

Therefore, while comparison to the later documentaries seems slight in their wider public and political impact, Stone's work in the 2000s not only continued his activism, but arguably reaffirmed basic tenets of a philosophy that possibly was more unpopular in the new century than it had been in the last.

Meanwhile, Stone's unflattering description of US President Barack Obama as a 'snake' to a group of foreign correspondents in Tokyo in August 2013, merely underscored the fact that the political Left enjoyed no conciliatory privileges either in his continuing desire to challenge aspects of the myth of American power and exceptionalism.[25] And the subsequent confirmation by Stone in June 2014 that he would film the story of National Security Agency (NSA) whistle-blower Edward Snowden – arguably the biggest political controversy of the twenty-first century so far – underlined the point. No one seemed very surprised that Stone should take up this cause; indeed, *Entertainment Weekly* simply wondered why it had taken him so long to pick the project up.[26] The leaks by Snowden to the *Guardian* and *Washington Post* concerning mass surveillance exactly a year before had sent shockwaves through Congress and the Obama administration.[27] Making a connection between Stone and the story seemed natural, and news that he was developing a film out of the Snowden revelations suggested that Stone had recaptured the zeitgeist – or maybe that it had caught up with him. A 2006 address for the David Lean Foundation delivered to the British Academy of Film and Television Arts (BAFTA) in London confirmed that Stone had been on the case long before Snowden had become the centre of attention. 'The right to any privacy at all has been sacrificed on the altar of our "national security",' he declared in the speech, already aware of the intrusion into many parts of the citizenry's private records, and accounts that would only really become newsworthy and revelatory in the early 2010s.[28]

That Stone should be so attuned to the activities going on in the darker reaches of the national security state so early, and so continuously – both at home in America and abroad – should not really be a surprise. He has been a filmmaker whose persona has always taken on that of the 'guerrilla fighter', who forged his career out of the trauma and devastation of Vietnam. That connection to his past anchors the first objective of the assessment here: that this is a critical and discursive reassessment of *all* of Oliver Stone's films and career. That the focus preys on the period from the late 1990s onwards especially, is not merely the convenience of highlighting a phase of his career that has been less detailed by critics so far. It is to lay claim to the fact that Stone has been broadly assumed, conditioned and stereotypically pigeonholed as not the same filmmaker after this time as he was in the first half of his career. We argue this to be true to an extent, but with disclaimers. Politically, socially and in terms of his belief in the power of cultural appropriation to galvanise the public to arms and to demands, he is very much the same filmmaker that he was at the beginning of his career, when those feelings in him were conditioned by the experiences of the 1960s. As the Snowden project demonstrates, they continue to inform his cinema to the present day, but aesthetics have undoubtedly shifted. By utilising many of the typical forms and functions of film studies, engaging along the way with notable theories, critical discourse, historical analysis and methodology, we seek to show how and why that changing artistic appreciation is essential to understanding not just the second phase of his career, but the whole of it. In this pursuit a number of conceptual themes are aired: the nature and role of melodrama; narrative construction and the 'happy ending'; the commercialisation of the auteur brand; and the relationship between history and drama.

A further key objective and component of the book – using Oliver Stone as a major touchstone for the changes wrought over the period – is to reassess the changing nature of the film industry, Hollywood – if not America more generally – and what filmmaking, industrial practice, forms of censorship, institutional organisations and media outlets contribute to and say about the state of cinema in America today. The story of Hollywood filmmaking since the final collapse of the studio system has been to recognise change, diversity and the establishment of new practices and functions in the industry. Film studies approaches have given some flavour to that, while primarily promoting the reading and deconstruction of the films: the work of scholars such as Linda Ruth Williams, Steve Neale and Barry Langford are all notable in this regard. Meanwhile, a number of industry historians and analysts, including for example Jon Lewis, Thomas Schatz and Ronald Brownstein, have focused on the structure of Hollywood more particularly, examining and advancing debates about finance, censorship and political influence – all issues we outline here – but not always with close recall to a particular filmmaker, or set of films working within the heart of this ever-changing system. By calling upon Stone's career, which has spanned much of the New Hollywood period and beyond, the book is in a position to comment on both his importance and the changing industry's form and function.

Nothing in Hollywood travels far without reference to money, and as a backdrop to this book's exploration of the transitions in Stone's career, it is worth noting at the outset that the second phase of it has been associated with a perceived decline in his stock as a commercial filmmaker. Yet figures suggest that this 'decline' is not realised in financial earnings or studio neglect for his abilities as an artistic, even visionary director. Total US and foreign exhibition revenues for all of Stone's directed work is in the region of $1.58 billion, of which some $700 million has been earned in the period after *Nixon* in 1995. These figures include the $167 million total earning for *Alexander*, a worldwide gross only exceeded in his career by *JFK* (see Table 1). While this overview may be slightly skewed owing to likely underreporting of the independently distributed *Platoon* (which industry insiders as well as Stone himself believe may well have earned more money not officially recorded), there is certainly evidence here of a continuing level of commercial performance during the 1990s and 2000s by which few industry professionals would be disappointed, and at which some critics would be surprised. As for studio relationships, Stone has worked with Paramount on *World Trade Center*, with Fox on *Wall Street: Money Never Sleeps*, and with Universal on *Savages*, always on his own terms. His ownership of the projects in all cases has never been in doubt. There has even been a revival of sorts in his old relationship with Warner Bros., which was responsible for his major movies of the 1980s and 1990s. In what must be something of a record, Stone, with encouragement from the studio showing a loyalty to their director that few others command, completed his fourth editorial pass at *Alexander* with a version titled *The Ultimate Cut*, bringing to an end a near-decade-long desire and struggle to shape this personal epic to the best of his abilities.

The auteur credentials that have produced loyalty and respect from studios and actors alike are augmented by other industry insiders also who know him. He has built and retained a reputation

Table 1 Oliver Stone: theatrical releases

Title	Release date	Rating	Distributor	Opening theatres	Widest theatres	Opening weekend	Opening weekend average	Domestic cume	Foreign cume	Worldwide box office
The Hand	24/4/1981	R	Warner Bros.	183	183	$566,736	$3,097	$2,447,576	–	$2,447,576
*Scarface***	9/12/1983	R	Universal	996	1,008	$4,597,536	$4,616	$44,668,798	$20,476,000	$65,144,798
Salvador	23/04/1986	R	Hemdale	–	–	–	–	$1,500,000	–	$1,500,000
Platoon	19/12/1986	R	Orion	6	1,564	$241,080	$40,180	$137,963,328	$15,000,000	$152,963,328
Wall Street	11/12/1987	R	20th Century Fox	730	989	$4,104,611	$5,623	$43,848,069	$42,158,932	$86,007,001
Talk Radio	21/12/1988	R	Universal	6	653	$50,298	$8,383	$3,628,372	$104,008	$3,732,380
Born on the Fourth of July	20/12/1989	R	Universal	4	1,434	$172,021	$43,005	$70,100,195	$90,000,000	$160,100,195
The Doors	1/3/1991	R	TriStar	840	1,236	$9,151 ,800	$10,895	$34,416,893	$31,883,000	$66,299,893
JFK	20/12/1991	R	Warner Bros.	1,164	1,395	$5,223,658	$4,488	$70,405,498	$140,000,000	$210,405,498
Heaven and Earth	25/12/1993	R	Warner Bros.	–	781	$379,807	–	$5,864,949	$18,100,000	$23,964,949
Natural Born Killers	26/8/1994	R	Warner Bros.	1,510	1,904	$11,166,687	$7,395	$50,292,625	$41,600,000	$91,892,625
Nixon	20/12/1995	R	Disney	–	977	$1,608,174	$3,129	$13,681,765	$6,400,000	$20,081,765
U Turn	3/10/1997	R	Sony	1,230	1,311	$2,730,440	$2,220	$6,682,098	$9,078,582	$15,760,680
Any Given Sunday	22/12/1999	R	Warner Bros.	2,505	2,505	$13,584,625	$5,423	$75,530,832	$27,596,000	$103,126,832
Alexander	24/11/2004	R	Warner Bros.	2,445	2,445	$13,687,087	$5,598	$34,297,191	$133,300,000	$167,597,191
World Trade Center	9/8/2006	PG13	Paramount	2,803	3,021	$18,730,762	$6,334	$70,278,893	$92,691,347	$162,970,240
W.	17/10/2008	PG13	Lionsgate	2,030	2,050	$10,505,668	$5,175	$25,534,493	$4,588,565	$30,123,058
South of the Border	25/6/2010	NR	Cinema Libra	1	12	$21,545	$21,545	$174,203	$278,131	$452,334
Wall Street: Money Never Sleeps	24/9/2010	PG13	20th Century Fox	3,565	3,597	$19,011,188	$5,333	$52,474,616	$85,246,476	$137,721,092
Savages	6/7/2012	R	Universal	2,628	2,635	$16,016,910	$6,095	$47,382,068	$33,849,451	$81,231,519
Total								$791,172,462	$792,350,492	$1,583,522,954
Average								$39,558,623	$44,019,472	$79,176,148

Source: Data provided by Ixtlan Inc., 12233 W. Olympic Blvd., Los Angeles CA 90064, USA.

as a director who is not for hire: someone who, in the words of former Warner Bros. President Bob Daly, 'follows his passion as opposed to following the dollar'.[29] Despite this, Stone has a reputation for sticking to budget. Moritz Borman, who has produced several of Stone's films, including *Alexander, World Trade Center, W.* and *Savages,* recalls how Stone's versatility and pragmatism as a filmmaker contribute to this financial diligence. During the shooting of *Alexander,* when a sandstorm threatened to delay filming the Battle of Gaugamela in Morocco, Stone simply incorporated the new backdrop into the shoot.[30]

Moreover, he has retained his reputation for long working days, especially during shoots. Eric Kopeloff, producer of *W., Wall Street: Money Never Sleeps* and *Savages,* has identified in Stone a daily commitment to getting things done however long it takes, and a drive that is intolerant of anyone not willing to put in the same amount of effort.[31] The production people who work for him do so out of an unqualified respect for someone they see as a true professional – someone for whom the role of director is not just a job. Paul Graff and Christina Graff, Stone's special effects team for *Wall Street: Money Never Sleeps* and *Savages,* and award-winners themselves for their work on TV series such as *Boardwalk Empire* (HBO, 2010–14), see Stone's modus operandi while on set as keeping people slightly on edge, as Paul Graff observes:

> He rumbles like a bowling ball and he shakes everything up and puts people out of balance – and as people regain their balance, there is energy that is harvested for the project. He never knocks somebody out or knocks them over; he just knocks them hard enough so that they are out of their comfort zone, and as they regain their balance they are struggling, slightly on edge. If you do that to a lot of people, you can lead that energy. That's Oliver Stone – shaking things up.[32]

Nevertheless, there have been some adjustments personally and professionally. Borman notes that Stone appears calmer and more reflective than in earlier years. Tod Maitland, who worked as Stone's sound mixer on *Talk Radio, Born on the Fourth of July, The Doors* and *JFK,* and then returned to the fold on *Wall Street: Money Never Sleeps* and *Savages,* concurs with Borman's assessment: 'In the early years, Stone appeared to introduce new elements during the shoot just to add to the chaos.'[33] During the same period, social activities off-set were equally high octane; but Maitland has observed the emergence of a more serene director, both on- and off-set.[34]

As these associations and assessments demonstrate, the profile that Stone has built for himself in the second half of his career – as a political documentary-maker, critic of the establishment and advocate for a wide range of Left-leaning causes – in no way has tarnished his reputation as an auteur, or his allure as a seminal director. Indeed, Stone's regular appearances on television shows such as Bill Maher's *Real Time* (HBO) merely seem to confirm the synergies between his role as a filmmaker and political commentator. Among the select list of contemporary political filmmakers – including Michael Moore, George Clooney, Paul Greengrass and Michael Winterbottom – Stone's political critique is arguably the most wide-ranging. He is someone without formal political affiliations who is not afraid to offer policy assessments of Afghanistan, Iran, Israel and Latin America, as well as broader assessments of deficiencies in US foreign policy and the fallacies of empire. If there is something of the contrarian in this persona that confounds supporters as much as it riles opponents, then these qualities seem to add to the appeal of his auteur brand, rather than weaken it.

The emergence of a filmmaker-political pundit is part of the story of Stone explored in this book. It is a development that is much more than an evolution of a new media presence for a well-known director; not just a move away from a defence of individual films and debate about related issues towards being a comfortable talk-show staple. Stone reflected on his future career as far back as the mid-1990s, identifying an important transition that would carry him through the subsequent phases of his life:

> The work has been compassionate, but I don't feel that I've been a particularly compassionate human being. That is the greatest lesson I have to learn. I was always willing to expose myself to discomfort and uncertainty, but now I'm trying to expose myself more to love and compassion. I no longer have the feeling that I have to justify my life by my work.[35]

Stone's coming to terms with his own past did not play out as merely an extended interlude and cinematic swerve between *Nixon* and *U Turn* in the 1990s; rather, it has unfolded slowly and continuously since that time. His pain at the break-up of his parents' marriage when he was fifteen, his contemplation of suicide as a teenager, his determination to reject the world at Yale University that was on offer to him, his enlisting in the US army for front line service in Vietnam in 1967, his feelings of alienation after active service, his effort to succeed in Hollywood and reconcile the elation of success and the depression of rejection, his decision to end his marriage to Elizabeth Stone in 1993 and his response to the pressure induced by criticism of *JFK*, *Heaven and Earth* (1993), *Natural Born Killers* and *Nixon* have not been simply airbrushed out of his psychology. However, these elements of a life and career have been shifted out of their earlier alignment. They no longer generate the same propensity to illuminate only the darkness within him. In conversation during the research for this book, Stone reflected on his early career success, observing that: 'With few exceptions there is a point where a man's life reaches a zenith and he doesn't know it, and no matter what he does after that he can never approach that again.'[36] Yet he qualified this acknowledgement of the passing of the artist's quintessential 'moment in the sun' by further ruminating that: 'I'm still the same person, and the work endures, and I hope that people will eventually notice it.'[37]

Undoubtedly, Stone's outlook has been leavened both by his engagement with Buddhism and a new marriage to Sun-jung Jung in 1996. While Stone's personal work schedule, his continuing willingness to face combative questioning about his documentary work and his broader political opinions seem to attest to an acceptance of – even desire for – pressure, this gradual personal realignment means that the scrutiny that was in earlier years self-directed via his films, has become more genuinely focused on the machinations of the political world that he sees around him. All of this has nurtured new routes towards personal and professional expression, and invited a new mix of influences to come to bear on Stone's dramatic work. Those influences are investigated in this book.

So, while on the surface one might be left to wonder whether Stone's second-half career is as vital or insistent as that which went before, and therefore how worthy of discussion it might be, we believe it is potentially more worthy, precisely because of the changes and evolution which have gone into his filmmaking during the two decades after the release and reception of *Nixon* – a film he has long felt personally connected to and which, after its commercial failure, prompted a re-evaluation in him.

On one level, and for some critics, the collection of films in the second half of his career might add up to a filmmaker not quite capturing the zeitgeist or polemical force of previous times. *Alexander, World Trade Center, W., Wall Street: Money Never Sleeps* and *Savages* were all subject to such assessment. However, with lesser productivity and alternative directions to pursue, Stone arguably has forged a new path that is more resonant and challenging than ever it was in the halcyon 1980s and early 1990s; and all this even while the decision to film *Snowden* (2016) allowed media commentators to dust off their favourite descriptors again, inevitably embracing words such as 'contentious', 'controversial' and 'politicised'.

Despite such obvious and convenient markers for his personal, professional and political stances, Stone's career development actually has followed particular and very tailored liminal concepts, and thus this book is organised around five key and interrelated themes for his work: war, politics, money, love and corporations. Each theme foregrounds a subset of Stone's filmography, as well as drawing on distinct aspects of his personal and professional development, including production practices and industry relations. Each theme also highlights particular questions and perspectives in film theory and textual analysis, and draws out equally pertinent aspects to do with the operation of Hollywood and the broader entertainment industry. The allocation of films to chapters is not arbitrary, but neither is it definitive. Inevitably, films are subject to multiple readings. *Alexander*, for example, could be readily incorporated into readings that foreground politics, war *and* love. The choice here to privilege that film within the discussion of love merely denotes the particular resonances that this aspect of the film has for the overall argument being advanced about Stone's development as a filmmaker. In pragmatically responding to that preference in argument, the book also picks up the film in shorter references elsewhere, as required. The same rubric is applied to many of Stone's other feature films and broader work.

Chapter 1 is about war, and the fire from which Stone emerged. The experience of combat in the jungle of Vietnam radically changed the worldview of the young romantic, and provided the motivation that drove his early career in film. The chapter takes

Platoon as its starting point, before considering how ideas of 'just war' and the 'War on Terror' have informed the construction and reception of later films such as *World Trade Center* and *W.* Chapter 2 follows the logic of Stone's development from war into his engagement with American politics. A review of *JFK* provides the essential platform from which to understand Stone's evolving critique of the political establishment, honed in a series of documentaries that include *Comandante, South of the Border* and the *Untold History* series and in later feature films such as *W.* The chapter also deals with questions of the representation of history and the debate – we might say 'argument' – between a range of historians and filmmakers about how cinema might best deal with the relationship between drama and history, concluding with an appreciation of how Stone's critique of the security state articulated over several years has influenced, and finally found expression in, the decision to dramatise the Snowden story.

Chapter 3 deals with money, and begins by revisiting the original *Wall Street* (1987) before exploring how both *Wall Street: Money Never Sleeps* and *Savages* have allowed Stone to offer critical perspectives on the American Dream in the twenty-first century – and where (if anywhere) it fits into the American psyche. With retribution rather than justice at their moral core, these two later films blur the lines between Stone's personal optimism and his pessimism about the state of the financial markets and 'War on Drugs', as only two examples of the American twenty-first-century condition. In Chapter 4 the focus shifts to that largely unexplored aspect of Stone's filmography: the theme of love. This analysis draws on several of Stone's early films including *Wall Street* and *Heaven and Earth*, before a detailed exploration of *U Turn, Alexander* and *W.* is undertaken. Stone's use of pathos and melodrama is discussed, as is the prominence of the roles offered to, and underappreciated importance of, female actors in his films. Chapter 5 on corporations begins by exploring Stone's longstanding critique of the media industry, with reference first to *Talk Radio* and then *Any Given Sunday* (1999).

We then trace the evolution of a broader assessment within Stone's work that has been increasingly concerned not just with media corporations and their relationship with government, but also with the ways in which the post-9/11 rhetoric about national security has seen ever-closer ties between defence, information technology (IT) corporations and the government. This has led Stone inevitably to critique and explore the close links between US political ambitions of global dominance – the extension of the 'American Century'[38] – and the international commercial ambitions of US corporations. The chapter explores the evidence for this development with a further discussion of Stone's documentary work, as well as revisiting the narratives in *W.*, *Wall Street: Money Never Sleeps* and *Savages* before returning to the *Untold History* series: a piece of work that stands as the most comprehensive statement yet of Stone's position on the condition of the USA in the middle of the second decade of the twenty-first century.

All five chapters then describe an auteur, an industry and a political culture that have been in constant flux. For Stone, the period since the mid-1990s has been one of personal change and a less self-critical outlook on his career, if not life; an aesthetic shift to include melodramatic flourishes alongside the established realist and hyperrealist cinematography; and a professional diversification into documentary work. In all of this, a distinct 'auteur' brand has taken shape as an increasingly detailed political critique has emerged: one that has moved from the film-specific platform established with the likes of *Salvador* and *JFK*, to a much broader locus that has rounded on the 'American Century', the myths of empire and American exceptionalism. In the same period, the industry itself has become increasingly corporatised and – many would contend – averse to contentious content on screen. Somehow despite such moves, Stone has remained within the movie colony as a contrarian working on his own terms. What seems increasingly certain in assessing Stone's whole career is that his 'auteurist presence' is a unique one in Hollywood. He is unquestionably the foremost political filmmaker of the last thirty years, and for that reason alone his career, films and dramatic history are an important critical legacy of the way that concerned social and political filmmaking has shifted, and how Hollywood has adapted to those evolutionary tendencies. Oliver Stone has seared his name into the national consciousness in a way that few artists in any era, let alone the present one, could hope to emulate. The following pages demonstrate how and why that ubiquity aligned itself with the most provocative filmmaker of recent generations.

Notes

1 Chris Salewicz, *Oliver Stone: The Making of His Movies* (London: Orion Books, 1997), p. 118.
2 Interview with Oliver Stone, Santa Monica, CA, 19 August 2013.
3 Susan Mackey-Kallis, *Oliver Stone's America: Dreaming the Myth Outward* (Boulder, CO: Westview Press, 1995); Robert Brent Toplin (ed) *Oliver Stone's U.S.A.: Film, History and Controversy* (Lawrence, KS: University of Kansas Press, 2000); James Riordan, *Stone: The Controversies, Excesses and Exploits of a Radical Filmmaker* (New York: Hyperion, 1995).
4 Andrew Pepper and Trevor McCrisken, *American History and Contemporary Hollywood Film* (Edinburgh: Edinburgh University Press, 2005), p. 131.
5 Albert Auster, 'Oliver Stone's Presidential Films' in Philip John Davies and Paul Wells (eds) *American Film and Politics from Reagan to Bush Jr* (Manchester: Manchester University Press, 2002), p. 65.
6 Auster, 'Oliver Stone's Presidential Films', p. 67.
7 Frank Beaver, *Oliver Stone: Wakeup Cinema* (New York: Twayne, 1994), p. 181.
8 Pepper and McCrisken, *American History*, p. 132.
9 The 'Bush Doctrine' refers to a range of foreign policy principles adopted under George W. Bush's presidency. The term was first used by vice-president Dick Cheney in a speech in 2003. See U.S. Department of Defense, 'Vice President Tells West Point Cadets "Bush Doctrine" is Serious', *DoD News* (3 June 2003). Available at http://archive.defense.gov/news/newsarticle.aspx?id=28921 (accessed 1 March 2016).
10 Francis Fukuyama, *The End of History and the Last Man* (London: Penguin, 2012; first published 1992).
11 In October 1995, former professional footballer and actor O. J. Simpson was acquitted of murdering his wife Nicole Brown Simpson, and her friend, waiter Ronald Lyle Goldman, in June 1994. In late 1993 singer–songwriter Michael Jackson had faced allegations of child sexual abuse. Reports in 1998 of an extra-marital relationship between Monica Lewinsky and President Bill Clinton eventually led to impeachment hearings. All three cases received enormous media coverage.
12 Pepper and McCrisken, *American History*, p. 155.
13 *United 93* was released in April 2006, three months before *World Trade Center*.
14 The first Golden Raspberry Awards ('Razzies') were hosted in 1981 by publicist J. B. Wilson as a tongue-in-cheek way to recognise the worst in Hollywood cinema. The Razzies have continued annually, one day before the Oscars.
15 David Holloway, *9/11 and the War on Terror* (Edinburgh: Edinburgh University Press, 2008), p. 86.

16 'New Oliver Stone 9/11 Film Introduces 'Single Plane' Theory', *The Onion* (8 August 2006). Available at http://theonion.com/articles/new-oliver-stone-911-film-introduces-single-plane,2017/ (accessed 6 December 2015).
17 Interview with Oliver Stone, Santa Monica, CA, 19 August 2013.
18 Beaver, *Oliver Stone*, pp. 79, 81.
19 *Ibid.*, pp. 80–1.
20 Interview with Oliver Stone, Santa Monica, CA, 8 December 2011.
21 Lisa Schwarzbaum, 'Wall Street: Money Never Sleeps', *Entertainment Weekly* (25 September 2010). Available at http://ew.com/ew/article/0,,20428073,00.html (accessed 6 December 2015).
22 Don Winslow, *Savages* (London: Arrow Books, 2010), p. 291.
23 Interview with Stone, 8 December 2011.
24 Final Report of the Assassination Records Review Board (30 September 1998). Available at http://archives.gov/research/jfk/review-board/report/arrb-final-report.pdf (accessed 1 March 2016). Also Congressional Record, 102nd Congress (1991–2), 25 June 1992, H5307. Available at http://thomas.loc.gov/home/LegislativeData.php?&n=Record (accessed 6 December 2015).
25 Maria Puente, 'Director Oliver Stone Says Obama Is a "Snake"', *USA Today* (16 August 2013). Available at http://usatoday.com/story/life/people/2013/08/16/director-oliver-stone-says-obama-is-a-snake/2665239/ (accessed 6 December 2015).
26 Nicole Sperling, 'Oliver Stone's Next Target: Edward Snowden', *Entertainment Weekly* (2 June 2014). Available at http://insidemovies.ew.com/2014/06/02/oliver-stone-edward-snowden/ (accessed 6 December 2015).
27 Xan Brooks, 'Edward Snowden NSA Whistleblowing Story to Be Filmed by Oliver Stone', *Guardian* (2 June 2014). Available at http://theguardian.com/film/2014/jun/02/edward-snowden-nsa-film-oliver-stone (accessed 6 December 2015).
28 Oliver Stone, 'David Lean Foundation Speech', 6 September 2006. Available at www.bafta.org/sites/default/files/uploads/transcripts/2006_david_lean_lecture_by_oliver_stone.pdf (accessed 6 December 2015).
29 Interview with Bob Daly, Santa Monica, CA, 18 October 2010.
30 Telephone interview with Moritz Borman, 18 August 2011.
31 Interview with Eric Kopeloff, Santa Monica, CA, 21 October 2010.
32 Interview with Paul Graff and Christina Graff, Venice, CA, 8 December 2011.
33 Maitland also believes that 'Stone's abilities as a director stem in part from his being immersed in the real world, as compared to other Hollywood directors who tend to live in a bubble.' He suggests that it is this exposure to outside people that helps Stone shape his characters. Interview with Tod Maitland, Santa Susana, CA, 11 August 2011.

34 Interview with Tod Maitland, Santa Susana, CA, 11 August 2011.
35 In Riordan, *Stone*, p. 521.
36 Interview with Oliver Stone, Santa Monica, CA, 7 December 2011.
37 *Ibid.*
38 Henry R. Luce, 'The American Century', *Life* (17 February 1941), pp. 61–5.

1
War

Introduction

> This I feel. A curse. Mother said it more than once, 'You could be killed over there, Oliver,' as if I were incompetent, not man enough to take care of myself; I hated her motherlove arrogance. Did I listen? Did it make sense? Mothers are cowards. Curses passed down the vaginal passageways deep to man. True as true can be. I told her that I didn't really want to go back to Yale, I was an adventurer, just like her and went to Vietnam instead. But I wonder what she'll say when she finds out about this. My limbs stiffening, waiting in this groin wound of a rotten field in Vietnam.[1]

Oliver Stone penned these words, not as part of some reflective memoir of his experiences as a soldier in the Vietnam War, but immediately upon return from his first trip to Saigon in 1965 where, during a year away from his studies at Yale University, he had done nothing more dangerous than work as an English teacher in a Catholic school. US forces had begun arriving in Vietnam during that year as part of a dramatic escalation, although the ground war that would engulf American foreign policy for the next decade was not yet properly underway. Gripped with the desire to make his mark as a writer, the trip to Asia provided the raw material for Stone's first writing project: a semi-autobiographical novel that lay dormant for many years before being published in the 1990s as *A Child's Night Dream*.

The themes of suicide and death reverberate through the pages of this early writing, and it is not hard to see how the American post-Second World War psychoses of power, responsibility, guilt and redemption dictate much of Stone's thinking. Midway through the book, Stone imagines scenes of jungle combat between Americans and the North Vietnamese Army (NVA) almost as though he was wishing a destiny for himself and his nation that was already tilting towards a frightening reality. Indeed, these self-absorbed imaginings of an impressionable young student were transformed at the end of 1967 on Stone's entry into the US army, into the unforgiving reality of a stripped back infantryman who quickly had to adjust to the speed of combat, chaos of friendly fire and freezing effects of fear. The manuscript had played its part in this transformation. Its rejection for publication, along with associated criticism from his father Lou (Figure 1) about the wisdom of seeking a career as a writer, had catapulted Stone into volunteering for the army: an impulsive move fused with anger and feelings of rejection that would expose him to fourteen months of front line jungle combat.

By any standard, Stone has been a product of war: intrigued by it, physically and psychologically marked by it, propelled to action by

Figure 1 Lou and Oliver Stone, Hong Kong, February 1968

it, and galvanised in opposition to it. The world he grew up in – a post-war America that conspired against communism abroad, and ran scared of its shadow at home – was forged in the call to war that newspaper editor Henry Luce entreated Americans to embrace in his 1941 article, 'The American Century':

> In the field of national policy, the fundamental trouble with America has been, and is, that whereas their nation became in the 20th century the most powerful and the most vital nation in the world, nevertheless Americans were unable to accommodate themselves spiritually and practically to that fact. Hence they have failed to play their part as a world power – a failure which has had disastrous consequences for themselves and for all mankind. And the cure is this: to accept wholeheartedly our duty and our opportunity as the most powerful and vital nation in the world and in consequence to exert upon the world the full impact of our influence, for such purposes as we see fit and by such means as we see fit.[2]

To use Luce's own phrase, there is much 'brassy trumpeting' of the American condition throughout his piece. In noting that the twentieth century was America's moment of maturation, he suggested that the country was already the intellectual, scientific and artistic capital of the world. Within the hyperbole also lay the threads of an American foreign policy that, from the end of the Second World War, would have such a profound effect on the baby boomer generation to which Oliver Stone belonged. Luce lamented the 'moral and practical bankruptcy of any and all forms of isolationism', and called both to the Republican Party to shake itself free of its historical aversion to engagement, and to all Americans to support Franklin D. Roosevelt in a way that would ensure that his third term in office would be marked by a break from the isolationism of the previous eight years. The point for Luce at least was that America already had become the 'powerhouse of the ideals of Freedom and Justice' throughout the world – and it was now time to fully embrace that pre-eminence.[3]

After the Second World War, Luce's philosophy emerged in key policy statements such as the Truman Doctrine, NSC-68[4] and anti-communist ideology more generally, conditioning America to its late-twentieth century wars and infusing the central tenets of Oliver Stone's life. Unsurprisingly, his 'Vietnam trilogy' has received some of the most intensive scrutiny among all his films, and the pictures certainly do parade Stone's preoccupations with political judgement, Cold War consensus and, of course, the nature of conflict, as much as they do his cinematic pretensions. Yet few studies have really addressed these planks of his cinematic oeuvre, much less Stone's engagement and viewpoint with the wider military and cultural consequences of the 'American Century', let alone its later manifestation suggested by the 'War on Terror'.

Stone's early life and career were dominated by the effects of Vietnam. Much later with *Nixon* (1995), Stone was still piecing together his personal and cinematic treatise on what the country and the conflict meant to himself and his fellow Americans – and his work has returned to that territory and its wider Cold War ramifications time and again. However, there has been a shift too. His post-9/11 films, *Alexander* (2004), *World Trade Center* (2006), *W.* (2008) and *Savages* (2012) also had plenty to say about war, but for the most part they said it in a more understated manner. It has been left to Stone's emerging documentary work in the 2000s to air his forthrightness. The ambitious ten-hour series, *The Untold History of the United States*, which began airing in the USA on Showtime in November 2012, and in Britain on Sky Atlantic in May 2013, was co-written with Associate Professor of English at American University, Peter Kuznick. The series and accompanying book[5] challenged conventional Cold War history and emphasised themes and facts which the authors believe had been excised or downplayed in a host of studies of the twentieth century. The themes of empire and perpetual war were important reference points in this reassessment. Therefore, as a project, *Untold History* was nothing less than a repudiation of Luce's prophecy and the corresponding call to arms and psychological hold that his 'American Century' concept had had on the nation's psyche for more than seventy years.

Despite the vehemence of this repudiation, Stone's public declarations and cinematic position on war and empire have never simply aspired to isolationism. He is not a pacifist. He does not advocate disengagement from the threat of international terrorism in the modern age, but he does see the US administration's tendency towards militaristic solutions as ultimately self-defeating. Its intelligence gathering, as events in the 2010s gave testimony to, covered an ever-increasing multitude of confusing sins. Of course,

Stone's past as a combat veteran looms large in his politics and attitude to conflict, and it is easily forgotten that this has made him a difficult target for critics who normally would lambast their adversary for a pretender's ignorance in such matters. With Stone, his military record cannot even begin to entertain such criticism.[6] Neither boastful nor contrite about this past, he has used it to construct a critique of foreign policy that no one else in Hollywood could come close to emulating.

Indeed, war is the central mantra of almost all that Stone does, in his films and life. The battle to craft images and meaning is no easier, or less challenging, than it was when he started making films, and his dogged application to the task belies nothing less than a personality forged in war. Off-set, his perspective has been affected more than any other filmmaker by a society long geared for conflict: a country that has come to know war almost as an extension of its being, from the Cold War to the 'War on Terror'. Why that should be so has been Stone's rallying call from the moment he stepped back on American soil in November 1968, and it has become an increasingly urgent question for him in the years since 9/11.

In this chapter we take as our premise that Stone's perspective on war provides a firm footing from which to interpret not just his films or the wider Hollywood machinery, but to think more carefully about the American polity and its constant, historical and reiterating focus on the mantra of war. Thus Stone's later films are examined as part of the response to 9/11 and how America has confronted twenty-first-century war, including *World Trade Center* (2006) and *W.* (2008) as well as the *Untold History* (2012) documentary series. As a first step towards that exploration, this chapter begins by revisiting *Platoon* (1986). As anchor, motivator, point of national recognition and window into Stone's preoccupations, the film remains a crucial component in any retrospective.

Platoon

In July 1976, Stone began work on a screenplay that, in time, would concretise not just his perspective on Vietnam, but his position as a filmmaker in Hollywood. It was populated almost entirely with a cast of characters and events from his period of active service in 1967–68, and the retelling was as much an act of personal catharsis as it was any desire to speak the truth about the situation there. The immediate effect of the war on Stone was not some damascene conversion to liberal politics, but the germination of an angry disillusionment felt by many returning veterans from South-East Asia, exemplified in the 1971 march in Washington, DC by Vietnam Veterans Against the War.[7] Having abandoned attempts to record his experiences on paper – a task rendered impossible in jungle conditions – Stone had taken belatedly to photographing the country as a personal record of his time there (Figure 2). The combination of his writing and the stark imagery that he managed to capture on film triggered his imagination, and produced a dawning realisation that photography provided a bridge between internal writing processes and the outside world.[8]

Stone arrived back in the USA in November 1968, to a country changed by the war in a manner later brought to life in *Born on the Fourth of July* (1989). The clichés and stereotypes have now taken a hold in the popular imagination, but for Stone, the fallout and rehabilitation were all too real. He took a road trip through California and on into Mexico. Upon his return, he was arrested in San Diego for possession of drugs: a habit that had become near enough a way of life in his bid to put the experience of combat behind him. Stone spent two weeks in jail before managing to extricate himself with help from his father. All the while he accumulated all the firsthand evidence he could ever want to write a story of similar entrapment and extreme conditions. The jail, like Vietnam, was a breeding ground of experience for Stone that he somehow already knew how to process, and later transfer to paper and the screen. Within a decade many of the experiences of that two-week stint in a San Diego prison would help him re-enter the mind of a prisoner, as he shaped the screenplay for the award-winning *Midnight Express* (Alan Parker, 1978).

A month after returning to New York from the west coast, Stone was again living in impoverished conditions, but he had begun making short movies with a borrowed Super 8 camera. This led him to write *Break*, his first screenplay and the first one that tried to express something of the experiences of Vietnam. *Break* had much of the essence of *Platoon* played out to the sound of The Doors.[9] In other words, it was an early amalgam

Figure 2 Oliver Stone, Vietnam

of the thoughts and subject matter that in time, Stone would be able to commit to his movies. Thanks to the G.I. Bill,[10] he then found himself able to enrol in film school.[11] Luckily for Stone, New York University had not only one of the most progressive and well-regarded programmes in America; it also had, in Martin Scorsese, a tutor who himself was trying to get on the ladder of film. Scorsese became a mentor to Stone, and saw in him a kindred spirit who was equally fractious, similarly questioning, and who wanted to turn his camera on the extraneous conditions of an America that had fallen apart in the six short years since the Kennedy assassination.[12]

Unsurprisingly then, one of Stone's first attempts at filmmaking while at New York University was *Last Year in Viet Nam* (1971), which sought to capture some of the raw disillusionment of the war at home. Film was beginning to have a galvanising effect, zoning in on Stone's emotional reflexes and allowing him an outlet for the post-traumatic anxieties that were whirling around in his head. Classmates including future writing partner Stanley Weiser later reflected on a young man who was undoubtedly on the brink and even had a 'dark, dangerous edge to him'.[13] Stone himself realised that such descriptions, while possibly true, really went to the heart of the dislocation that Americans felt towards Vietnam. 'We'd taken a fork in the road,' he said of himself and fellow veterans, but did not realise how a big a diversion it was.[14] Stone sought solace by finding a routine and then a relationship with a Lebanese-born Moroccan attaché, Najwa Sarkis, which brought stability to his life at a time when he found himself committing to his studies and discovering a talent that promised to offer a real career prospect for him.

By September 1971, Stone was married to Sarkis, had graduated from New York University, and was now working on another screenplay. *Once Too Much* still centred on Vietnam with, as he later remarked, 'an eerie parallel to Ron Kovic's *Born on the Fourth of July*.'[15] Mexico featured as a setting, just as it had for Stone on his return – but so did a tragic, downbeat ending resulting in death and loss. The war was becoming an enduring concern from which Stone could never shake himself free, even in everyday life, but he had not yet found the story that he really wanted to tell. He knew that, unlike John Wayne's *The Green Berets* (1968), he was not seeking a jingoistic redemption, but everything else had not yet fallen into place. It would not be until summer 1976, when he tried to crystallise his experiences once more, that a new screenplay emerged, titled *The Platoon*.

By this time, Stone had separated from Sarkis, and despite financial difficulties, was beginning to reintegrate with civilian life. Nevertheless, Vietnam remained an obsession. The final American retreat from the rooftop of the embassy in Saigon in April 1975 had been played out on television, and Stone was on a personal mission not simply to tell his story, but to bring to the attention of the whole American public the futility of this and all wars. From the Tet Offensive, through the bombing of Cambodia to the Paris peace accords, the mindset that had allowed so many Americans to blithely continue accepting political bromides about communism, and then watch death and destruction nightly on their television sets had, in Stone's eyes, reached its nadir in that last desperate evacuation that offered no answer to the inevitable question of what it had all been for.

The new screenplay was finished before the end of summer 1976, and immediately attracted interest from producer Marty Bregman. While Bregman could not find a studio willing to fund the film, one consequence of circulating the script within Hollywood was that

Columbia Pictures offered Stone the opportunity to write *Midnight Express*. Another consequence was that Bregman introduced Stone to Ron Kovic in July 1978, and asked him to write a story based on Kovic's bestselling memoir of two years before: *Born on the Fourth of July*.[16] That screenplay was completed too, a shooting schedule was arranged, but the deal fell through late in the day. By now, Hollywood was discovering the feel-good blockbuster mentality led by one of Stone's contemporaries, Steven Spielberg, and Vietnam was a subject that few studios wanted to tackle. Subsequent to their university days, Scorsese had got on the ladder of directing too and had managed to make a low-budget version of his own 'Vietnam screenplay', the gritty, unforgiving but critically acclaimed *Taxi Driver* (1976). However, Scorsese was swimming against the tide of an industry moving towards *Rocky* (John G. Avildsen, 1976), *Star Wars* (George Lucas, 1977) and *Grease* (Randal Kleiser, 1978), underlining the resolve that Stone would need to make his story, or film anyone else's.

Ironically, the filmmaker that helped break the taboo about Vietnam was also the one that persuaded Stone to keep trying with his own script. In 1984, Michael Cimino offered Stone a screenwriting job adapting Robert Daley's book, *Year of the Dragon*, which had a former Vietnam veteran as its central protagonist. Just as Stone was touting *The Platoon* and meeting up with Kovic back in 1978, Cimino was putting the finishing touches to *The Deer Hunter* (1978): a breakthrough movie for which he received huge commercial and critical acclaim. However, Cimino's reputation then quickly took a huge hit with the now-infamous *Heaven's Gate* (1980), a film that was every bit as lavish and extravagant with its budget and shooting schedule as with what appeared on screen.[17] In five short years, Cimino went from the next great American director to virtually a jobbing filmmaker-for-hire. As a result he negotiated with Stone for a reduced fee for the *Year of the Dragon* screenplay, in exchange for which Cimino promised Stone that he would persuade producer Dino de Laurentiis to back *Platoon* as his next project. Through no fault of Cimino's, the deal quickly faltered.

De Laurentiis was unable to find a distributor to work with him, and in summer 1984, after Stone had scouted locations in the Philippines, the project was halted. The central problem of finding a distributor was a very tangible one, and it revealed much of the industry's continuing attitudes towards any kind of contentious treatment of Vietnam or any recent history. Sagas of returning veterans had seen success for Cimino as well as for Hal Ashby in *Coming Home* (1978), and Francis Ford Coppola in his mesmeric *Apocalypse Now* (1979); but the trend had not really taken hold and doing a new, more realistic Vietnam story was proving a tough sell. Stone became directly involved in the *Platoon* dispute when he wrote to Eric Pleskow at Orion Pictures in August 1984:

> Your refusal to distribute 'Platoon', even with Dino guaranteeing your losses, stuns me. Your contention that the film's political content is leftist and contrary to present rightist tendencies in the country seems to me erroneous in perception.[18]

Notwithstanding Stone's frustration, in fact industry chieftains such as Pleskow were not wide of the mark in their reading of current national sentiment. With Ronald Reagan as president, as William Palmer notes, the early 1980s had been marked by a distinct shift in the reading and understanding of the Vietnam War. Films such as *The Deer Hunter* and *Apocalypse Now* were harsh and unyielding but they unwittingly contributed towards a new national discourse, led by Reagan and featuring John Rambo as its Hollywood poster boy, that was tasked with reimagining the war not as defeat, but at worst as a noble cause, and at best as a misconstrued success.[19] In the face of changing national moods, Stone was confronted with the possibility of the project sitting with De Laurentiis *ad infinitum* but without sufficient leverage to get it made. The producer's refusal to proceed, and a dispute over money that Stone had spent already on the scouting trip to the Philippines, pushed him towards legal resolution in the Los Angeles Superior Court.[20]

The court action petitioned for De Laurentiis to be prevented from using the completed *Year of the Dragon* screenplay or Stone's name, and sought $5 million damages and $5 million punitive damages. Stone's trump card was that *Year of the Dragon* was only a few months away from release, and a pending court case put that release and the associated investment in jeopardy. The swiftly arranged agreement was dated 20 December 1984 and confirmed a payment from De Laurentiis to Stone of $100,000, plus expenses of $25,000 already received. More important by far was the agreement that Stone would assume full title to *Platoon*. The final detail of that agreement was honoured on the last day of February 1985, with a request from the De Laurentiis Corporation to the Motion Picture Association of America (MPAA) to withdraw its registration of the title *Platoon*. Stone registered his claim with the MPAA one week later.[21]

Thus, war was elemental within Stone's emerging career and in the battle to forge a reputation and shake up the staid Hollywood routine, as he saw it. With a battle won against one of the industry's leading figures, Stone's fortunes were set to change dramatically. The unlikely saviour was a man called John Daly, an independent film producer who ran a small British company called Hemdale. While the De Laurentiis agreement was being brought to an end, Stone signed an agreement on 5 February 1985 with Arnold Kopelson's Film Packages International (FPI) to produce *Platoon*. Daly liked the screenplay he had seen, and on 18 September he confirmed to Stone that Hemdale was prepared to commit $5.5 million for the making of *Platoon*. Daly also liked something else he had seen: a screenplay about the war in El Salvador that Stone had written in the early months of 1985, based on notes from a journalist and friend, Richard Boyle. Plans to shoot *Salvador* (1986) had been built on a budget part-funded by Stone taking a loan against his New York home, but the project had stalled after initial collaboration from officials within the Salvadoran government had been withdrawn.

After Daly's confirmation of the support for *Salvador*, Stone opted to shoot that picture first, as previously planned, in Mexico. Upon completion, he moved directly on to *Platoon* in early 1986, with a return to the Philippines and a training camp for the actors. Supervised by Marine Captain Dale Dye, actors Charlie Sheen (Private Chris Taylor), Tom Berenger (Staff Sergeant Bob Barnes) Willem Dafoe (Sergeant Elias Grodin) and their colleagues spent two weeks living in the jungle, and at the end of this baptism, filming started immediately.

The narrative follows Taylor's arrival in Vietnam and his experience as a fresh recruit. He quickly finds that there are two very distinct groups within the platoon, one assembled around Staff Sergeant Barnes, who are white, working class and socially conservative; and the other around Sergeant Grodin, who are a mix of black and white, pot-smoking, members or fellow travellers of the counterculture. The tensions that build between Barnes and Grodin were taken more or less straight from Stone's own experiences with his combat platoon, and operations such as the night ambush and hamlet scenes were close to what he had seen. Following a confrontation between Barnes and Grodin during an assault on a village, Barnes takes the opportunity in a later firefight to shoot Grodin. The latter survives, only to be killed by the NVA in open ground as the rescue helicopter saving the rest of the company pulls away. In the realisation of what has just happened Taylor resolves to kill Barnes. Following a confrontation between the two men in the final night battle scene, Taylor shoots Barnes dead.

The Barnes–Grodin battle of wills was there from the earliest versions of the screenplay, although the Christian symbolism which signposts the broader moral struggle underpinning the action was a later refinement. In the June 1977 treatment, the struggle between the two men found a resolution through Barnes giving platoon member Angel the discreet order to kill Grodin. By April 1985, the battle, now infused with religious sentiment, was much more clearly a fight for Taylor's soul: the child born of two fathers. *Platoon*'s central moral dilemma now questioned whether Taylor was simply taking the place of Barnes in seeking retribution for the death of Grodin as the narrative reaches its climax. Taylor's closing voiceover attempts no justification for the killing, but it does disavow Barnes's dubious mantle. Through Taylor, Stone voiced his own redemptive wish 'to teach to others what we know and to try with what's left of our lives to find a goodness and meaning to this life'.[22]

The desire expressed in Taylor's elegiac voiceover not to make the same mistakes over again was a mantra that Stone personally retained and, as we will explore later, one that became a key undercurrent in his later critiques of the US administration and the 'War on Terror'. The media reaction to *Platoon* covered the full spectrum of appreciation, from barbed criticism to veneration. It was a range of commentary that Stone would come to know well over the next decade. Pauline Kael of *The New Yorker* thought that Stone was on Barnes' side and simply getting high on war.[23] Others, such as Roger Ebert at the *Chicago Sun-Times*, saw the necessity of such a film in helping Americans understand the loss of life in the war.[24] Some criticism surely would have been more stinging, had it not been for Stone's status as a veteran – for this was no personal, psychedelic exploration of violence. Rather, *Platoon* orchestrated its violence in often random, almost nonsensical patterns that attuned it to the rhythm and discontinuities of fighting. Extended periods of inactivity and routine patrols are followed by swift bouts of extreme and discordant confrontation, searching for an enemy that was, as Taylor opines, within the GIs themselves most often. Amid this 'swirling confusion' and 'surreal experience', as Lawrence Lichty and Raymond Carroll would have it, Stone tried to fashion a broader critique of US power and institutional breakdown.[25] The real violence, he wanted to say, was arranged by government and exacted upon a series of nation states whose crime had been to show ideological tendencies incompatible with American global, hegemonic aims. The Academy, at least, was sure that he had hit the mark, and recognised his efforts with the Oscar for Best Director.

What was lost in the hyperbole and subsequent huge public embrace of the film – and what, to a significant degree, has remained understated in later assessments of Stone – was the importance of *Salvador* as a companion piece to *Platoon* in the overall narrative of his career. Stone had grabbed people's attention with his visceral depiction of war, testified to by reports of veterans leaving cinemas in tears, having been so affected by the Vietnam he presented on-screen (Figure 3). Moreover, the enormous financial success of the film moved Stone into a different league in Hollywood. What was less well observed was the political critique that was abundant in the earlier film. *Salvador*'s critical depiction opened the way towards new appreciations of Central America and the USA's role in the region. For example, following Stone's film, his erstwhile producer Ed Pressman – at the same time as working on *Wall Street* – helped British director Alex Cox realise his punkish biopic, *Walker* (1987), which compressed American meddling in Nicaragua in the 1980s with imperialist William Walker's adventures there a century earlier.[26]

Equally influential then, in their own ways, *Salvador* and *Platoon* laid the foundations for Stone's subsequent assault on

Figure 3 Oliver Stone, First Cavalry Unit, Vietnam, August 1968

the establishment. With a much higher profile, *Platoon* was the all-encompassing battle; but *Salvador* helped order that battle. Together, they established a foothold for Stone's political intent. The targets became Wall Street, the media and the entertainment industry, but Stone never really left Vietnam after that initial foothold had been carved out. Three years after *Platoon*, it was no surprise that he would return to the conflict with a film that mixed the personal, the political and the generational all together.

Born on the Fourth of July and *Heaven on Earth*

As well as anchoring his career, *Platoon*'s core contrast between Barnes and Grodin also prefigured the transition that Stone would later experience: from the full-on combative turbulence that had infused more or less everything from *Salvador* to *Natural Born Killers* (1995), to a more reflective self – one searching less for answers to personal questions, than for explanations about the broader condition of the country. In the midst of that personal transition, the nation, with Hollywood in tow, reasserted its hegemony in the post-Vietnam era. American global strategy was made manifest in a series of interventions in Haiti, Panama, Somalia and the Balkans in the late 1980s and early 1990s. Most notable was the incursion into Kuwait and Iraq, where live-action news feeds of missiles closing in on their targets became the visual motif of this new panoptic military ascendancy. The advocates of this reinvented interventionist stance also found a supporting cultural narrative in the discourses fuelled by the substantial fiftieth anniversary commemorations of the D-Day landings during the decade. The 'good war' doctrine had its historical antecedents and modern day equivalency, the argument suggested.

However in 1989, when Stone released *Born on the Fourth of July*, the possibilities for a different kind of American late century seemed more feasible. The film was an obvious companion piece to *Platoon*, and even shared similar funding difficulties. Stone had planned to shoot the film in 1979 after his initial meeting and work with Kovic, but that option had fallen through. More surprising for Stone was the discovery some ten years later, following in the wake of *Platoon* and *Full Metal Jacket* (Stanley Kubrick, 1987), that few in Hollywood seemed prepared to contemplate a further Vietnam movie. However, as with *Platoon*, Stone's persistence eventually carried him through: senior executives at Universal saw the potential, and provided backing.

The plot explored the personal trauma endured by Kovic and his family as they came to terms with his injuries sustained during the war. Over ten years in gestation, the story never lost its resonance for Stone. Kovic had been a marine and volunteer like him who had signed up entirely in support of his government, and who then had been radicalised by his experiences. Becoming a vehement opponent of the war, Kovic was the real deal for Stone: a committed patriot who had embraced the 'American Century' philosophy, only to find a country largely indifferent to the personal price he had paid – and the price was significant. Stone acknowledged in particular that the way he dealt with Kovic's impotence made it a difficult film for many Americans to watch.[27]

However, critics were once again impressed. Vincent Canby at the *New York Times* wrote that this was the 'most ambitious non-documentary film yet made about the entire Vietnam experience', concluding that it did a better job than *Coming Home* (Hal Ashby, 1978) or *The Deer Hunter* (Michael Cimino, 1979).[28] The public agreed. The film grossed more than $70 million at the US box office ($160 million worldwide), and was nominated for eight

Oscars, with Stone taking the Best Director award, and David Brenner and Joe Hutshing winning for Best Editing. From the nostalgic confines of small town Massapequa in the 1950s, to the sensory assault on Kovic of the war, to the Bronx veterans' hospital that he was returned to, and his later odyssey through the southwest and Mexico, then on to the anti-war political campaigns of the 1970s, Kovic's Homeric journey is wholly intended as the journey of America through turbulent times. As nostalgic and sentimental as the early scenes were – and a number of critics accused Stone of 'bombast'[29] – the contrast with Kovic's later predicament and his railing at the world could not be sharper or tauter. In *Born on the Fourth of July*, Stone found a way to make his Vietnam experience universal: a moral of the Cold War era, a lesson for American futures. The film was much acclaimed and has stood the test of time. However, American military actions in Iraq just a year later belied any lessons learned, and in fact would bring a reversal in popular assessments of war and America's place in the world.

Born on the Fourth of July had captured something in the national psyche, and a fascination with the American condition among audiences further afield, that confirmed Stone's 'Midas touch' during these years. In conjunction with *Platoon*, the two films had exposed the 'Vietnam Syndrome'[30] on film for a nation still prepared for self-examination, and the result was compelling and traumatic for all concerned – but Stone was not done with the subject. The two movies had been about America; in other words, what Vietnam War films had been solely about for more than twenty years. However, Stone had not told the story of the Vietnamese yet. In 1993, his trilogy was completed with *Heaven and Earth*, a film directly addressing the consequences of the conflict for the Vietnamese population, but Stone found himself in territory that the audience did not wish to travel to with him. The photography is lush, and the performance of the central character Le Ly Hayslip (Hiep Thi Le) is full of pathos as she undertakes a journey that sees the disintegration of her family, community, country and, ultimately, life. Bound still by the all-enveloping influence of America, Le Ly's story is complicated by her love for gunnery sergeant, Steve Butler (Tommy Lee Jones). Their life in America promises idyllic recompense for the horrors of the war, but Butler's memories are too immediate, and the nightmares too overpowering. Tragedy ensues, and the film finds only crumbs of hope in a future of uncertainty for Le Ly and her family at the end.

In the space between *Born on the Fourth of July* and *Heaven and Earth*, the first Gulf War had driven a wedge into the American psyche. During the period of formal hostilities, German reunification had been concluded in October 1990. The troubling lessons from Vietnam had been overwritten with a sense of self-confidence that laid the foundations for a new, more assertive US foreign policy stance, upon which groups such as the Project for the New American Century would expound later. War, it seemed, was no longer about existential threat, but had become something of a video game. America was now ready, even eager, to forget Vietnam completely and, along with it, any cautionary lessons about empire. The goal, as Colin Harrison argues assessing that decade of the 1990s, was 'the restoration of national pride, erasing the memory of a previous ignominious defeat'.[31] Stone's invitation to empathise with the plight of a nation which had paid heavily for its role as a proxy during the Cold War was dismissed out of hand. The film grossed less than $6 million at the US box office, and was Stone's first true commercially disappointing return.

The three films provided a series of perspectives on war that acknowledged heroism and sacrifice in a multitude of guises, but which remained unequivocal in their anti-war sentiment. Often, Stone was criticised for this, but the juxtaposition of the themes is natural and important. Heroism only meant survival, and Stone's own experiences had told him that. 'Good wars' were never really good, only necessary. One of Stone's resonant quotes from Edmund Burke – used as the opening prologue in *JFK* (1991) – pointed out how evil triumphs when good men do nothing. Stone's 'good' men and women in these films were Taylor, Kovic, and Le Ly: each one confronting violence, each overcoming adversity, and each learning the lesson that life's constant fight is to find peace in the flames of war – even long after that war is over. If *Heaven and Earth* appeared darker than its companions, more corrupted as a piece by the implacability of Vietnam, it was because Stone's own political perspective on the war and all that followed it had hardened, just as the country was settling into a less questioning and more self-satisfied cultural zeitgeist.

The contrasting reception that each of the movies had, but especially the last of the trilogy, charted the gulf that was opening up between Stone and some of his audience. The country was heading back to the conservative-centre ground in the 1990s, with Hollywood in tow. Economic growth was mounting under the new Clinton administration, the post-Cold War dividend seemed open to speculation, and mainstream cultural predilections were finding favour in the disposable history of *Forrest Gump* (Robert Zemeckis, 1994), the vanquishing of aliens in *Independence Day* (Roland Emmerich, 1996) and more generally in the blockbuster franchises of *Jurassic Park* (1993–2015) and *Batman* (1989–2012). The shift was confirmed for Stone by both the commercial failure of *Nixon* (1995) as well as the controversy generated by *Natural Born Killers*.

In fact, *Natural Born Killers* was not entirely on its own as cultural commentary in these years. In the approach to, and aftermath of, the Rodney King episode in Los Angeles in 1991–92,[32] and the riots that followed, grainier and more culturally synonymous product was arising that took 'war' back home. From Spike Lee's *Do the Right Thing* (1989) and John Singleton's *Boyz n the Hood* (1991), through Joel Schumacher's *Falling Down* (1993) to the violence of Quentin Tarantino's *Reservoir Dogs* (1992) and *Pulp Fiction* (1994), American society, race, class, social position and exclusion were being exposed in forms that were as visceral as Stone's cinema, but with themes that he had rarely approached in his career thus far. What was clear was that broader questions about conflict, empire and US foreign policy failure were no longer as interesting to producers or mainstream audiences. However, events within a decade gave Stone a way back in to put his position on 'war'.

The 'War on Terror'

American interest in war was revived during the 1990s as part of a collective recollection of just war, defence of freedom and justice that accompanied the fiftieth anniversary D-Day commemorations: sentiments that would slide seamlessly into the post-9/11 narrative on global terror. The groundwork for this new discourse had been mapped out by the Project for the New American Century, in a report on American global military dominance published in September 2000 that later attracted notoriety for its comment that military transformation would be slow unless some catalysing 'Pearl Harbor' event were to befall the USA.[33] One year later, the prophetic assertion came to devastating and tragic fruition.

Hollywood caught the emerging national mood very quickly. As Carl Boggs and Tom Pollard rightly point out, the film colony had used the late 1970s and 1980s as a moment to critically evaluate recent US military history and philosophy. By the 1990s its focus had changed to the Second World War, with its subscript of 'just war' and ripe populist and popular cultural sentiment, typified by Steven Spielberg's award-winning *Saving Private Ryan* (1998). Patriotically and historically mangled though it may have been, Michael Bay's *Pearl Harbor* (2001) was no less popular, and revisited cinemas to much fanfare in the aftermath of 9/11.[34]

In the immediate 9/11 moment, a number of other films also began to engage with complex narratives that promulgated the 'good war', dedicated to notions of liberation, freedom, nation-building and moral superiority, and which inadvertently or otherwise became de rigueur as cultural bulwarks of the Bush administration's agenda. Using classical moorings, the nobility and romance of conflict was reaffirmed in *Troy* (Wolfgang Petersen, 2004), *Kingdom of Heaven* (Ridley Scott, 2005) and *300* (Noam Murro, 2006). Just war sentiments and heightened realism were visible in Clint Eastwood's retelling of the battle for Iwo Jima in *Flags of our Fathers* and *Letters from Iwo Jima* (both 2006), while Sam Mendes' first Gulf War story, *Jarhead* (2005), conveyed the tedium of war in all its stilted fashion. Several Hollywood directors tried to grapple more directly with political aspects of the 'War on Terror', including Stephen Gaghan with *Syriana* (2005), Gavin Hood's *Rendition* (2007), Ridley Scott investigating CIA intelligence-gathering in *Body of Lies* (2008), and Paul Greengrass deconstructing the controversial search for weapons of mass destruction (WMDs) in *Green Zone* (2010). Of these, the only film to recover its budget at the US box office was *Syriana*: a surprisingly ambitious narrative effort that used multiple storylines and characters to construct a web of infiltration and deceit, linking US foreign policy to the worldwide battle and demand for oil reserves. These films engaged with terrorism, the psychological effects of combat and the role of intelligence agencies, but they also provided a crucial backdrop to Stone's work during the same period.

Stone's on-screen response both to 9/11 and the resurgence of Luce's 'American Century' vision in the project for a new century were seen to varying degrees in *Alexander* (2004), *World Trade Center* and *W. Alexander* had been conceived prior to 9/11, although the heated debate that it aroused was less about the film's post-9/11 allegorical tone than it was about the portrayal of the eponymous military campaigner as bisexual. Exploring the psychology of a young man who had quickly asserted his authority as a fighting general, the film follows an ascendency that was consolidated with the taking of Persia in 331 BCE. After embarking on the Persian expedition, Alexander never returned to his homeland and, in the absence of reliable historical sources, his exact motivations and goals can only be speculated. He died in Babylon in 323 BCE with his ultimate vision unknown.[35] While Stone was drawing in no way a direct comparison between George W. Bush and Alexander, the latter's campaign in Persia obviously called to mind the implications of the Iraq invasion in 2003, as the director later reflected. In a response to a letter from Jack Valenti in December 2004, about the reception of *Alexander* in the USA, Stone asked simply:

> What is going on with America? I can't help but feel it is, in its way, isolated from history. I haven't seen any commentary on the film that brings out the eerie parallels in that Alexander did what George Bush is trying to do first and better.[36]

A number of US reviewers never found their way to contemporary events through the film either, but that was not true of everyone. The *New York Times* first saw the picture as alluding to Stone himself, offering no direct equation with Iraq.[37] However, writing in the same paper two days later, Emily Eakin observed that:

> For a politically ascendant America at war far from home, the story of the region's most famous conqueror has irresistible allure. Liberator, dictator, uniter, divider, visionary, murderer, empire-builder, oppressor, idealist, feminist, multiculturalist, sexist, racist, gay, straight, bisexual: Alexander is today all this and more. Infinitely malleable and all-encompassing, auspicious allegory and cautionary tale, his story is tailor-made for the new world order.[38]

Whether he took such plaudits to heart or not, Stone did plot a direct dramatic engagement with the post 9/11 crisis after

Alexander, and it came first with *World Trade Center* and then *W.* If reviewers missed or were simply uninterested in *Alexander*'s political allusion, the anticipation felt by the time that *World Trade Center* went into production five years on from 9/11 was clear for all to see.

World Trade Center

The 9/11 Commission Report was issued on 22 July 2004. Running to some 567 pages, it attempted to provide a full account of:

> the facts and circumstances relating to the terrorist attacks of 11 September, 2001 including those relating to intelligence and law enforcement agencies, diplomacy, immigration issues and border control, the flow of assets to terrorist organisations, commercial aviation, the role of congressional oversight and resource allocation, and other areas determined by the Commission.[39]

The Commission's forty-one recommendations dealt with foreign relations and the need to show moral leadership to the rest of the world, as well as more specific findings related to emergency response, border security and reporting lines within the various intelligence agencies. In measured, even muted language, the Commission recommended that the 'War on Terror' could not concern itself merely with military responses, concluding that 'if we favour one tool while neglecting others, we leave ourselves vulnerable and weaken our national effort'.[40]

The message about moral leadership was thrown into sharp relief immediately on publication. Just a few weeks earlier in May 2004, investigative journalist Seymour Hersh had published a detailed account of the treatment of detainees by the US army at the Abu Ghraib detention centre in Baghdad: a series of revelations that produced international outrage and a major public relations crisis for the Bush administration.[41]

The balanced response that the Commission was seeking appeared lost on the administration, but nevertheless, the report's core content was compelling. At its heart was a detailed and harrowing account of events inside the towers of the World Trade Center from the time at which the first plane struck the North Tower, to the point 102 minutes later when both towers had collapsed in on themselves. The Commission's account included details of the efforts of the first responders on the scene, including personnel from the Fire Department, Port Authority and Police Department.

The Commission's narrative of that morning was also the central pivot in Stone's *World Trade Center*, released in the USA almost two years later on 9 August 2006. *World Trade Center* took as its focus the true story of the survival of two Port Authority police officers: John McLoughlin (Nicolas Cage) and Will Jimeno (Michael Peña). They entered the North Tower lobby just as the South Tower collapsed and were trapped in the debris. Two of their colleagues were killed during this incident, and a third died after the North Tower in which they were trapped also later collapsed. Eventually, McLoughlin and Jimeno were found and rescued several hours later.

Support from the Port Authority Police Department was secured in August 2005, and filming commenced in mid-October with a budget set at $63 million. To avoid any potential upset during filming, much of the work was done in Los Angeles, with only limited location shooting over a four-week period in Manhattan. In terms of dramatic structure, Stone organised the narrative around several scenes with McLoughlin and Jimeno trapped in the collapsed buildings, intercut with family and friends scenes and the efforts of rescuers. Each scene in the hole was shorter than its predecessor, a conscious effort to avoid overloading the audience with darkness on the screen. Cutting to the families allowed for moments piecing together their lives, but the sense of confusion and fear about what has happened is retained in scenes involving the rescuers, as it is increasingly with the families. Details from McLoughlin's and Jimeno's accounts of the entire incident were used wherever possible, and these included Jimeno's telling recollection of a vision of Christ at one point.

Inevitably, the filming raised many contentious issues. Stone was drawn to the rescue, and wanted to tell that story without getting dragged into the wider political debates about 9/11 then in full swing. He was also alert to media reports about his involvement in a 9/11 film – and not without justification. In May 2003, conservative websites had been debating a boycott of Disney as a result of the announcement that Miramax (then owned by Disney) would support Michael Moore's planned documentary *Fahrenheit 9/11* (2004). Disney buckled, and Moore's film was only rescued by Harvey and Bob Weinstein who bought out Disney's interest and then, with help from Lionsgate, successfully distributed the film. Stone was all too aware then that a movie of that day had pressures of recollection, authenticity and vested interest with which to contend.

Stone saw in *World Trade Center* a story that was personal, courageous, committed and that did not need political controversies to get in the way of McLoughlin and Jimeno's astonishing feat of survival. Stone sidestepped the wider political debate and opted for as much authenticity as the film could muster. He was wary of sentimentality, and it was a fine line to walk. Both McLoughlin and Jimeno were involved in script reviews that ensured accuracy, but they inevitably brought their own sensitivities, which occasionally lessened some aspects of the dramatic tension. For example, in a January 2006 script review, Jimeno was concerned about the impact of a particular scene on the widow of a former colleague, and asked for two script changes.[42]

The release and marketing of the film brought further worries. Initially, Paramount Studios had proposed 11 August (8/11) for release, apparently to avoid any suggestion that they were exploiting the actual date of the attack. Stone objected, seeing that choice as equally insensitive, and the release date was brought forward by two days. The general vigilance concerning the risks of bad publicity even extended to a decision to avoid a suggestion, first made by Moritz Borman, that the production team might capitalise on the publicity for *United 93* (Paul Greengrass, 2006) by arranging a television debate between Stone and Greengrass. Fellow producer Michael Shamberg felt that rather than seeking closer association, the differences between each movie were better emphasised.[43]

Stone's dramatic line for his movie reaped some dividends in the mainstream and conservative press. In a pre-release article, the *Wall Street Journal* described the film as 'not the usual Stone conspiracy project'.[44] A review carried by *USA Today* commented that *World Trade Center* was 'a powerful film without any discernible agenda'.[45] The *Los Angeles Times* gave some insight into what the 'absence of agenda' issue might mean, when it surmised that the film had been embraced by right-wing commentators because of its pro-American, pro-family, pro-faith, pro-male orientation.[46] Stone's decision to focus on a story about individual endurance and heroism, rather than offering any explicit wider political perspective, had wrong-footed some critics for sure. A *Washington Times* editorial typified the response. Recalling earlier descriptions of Stone in the paper as a 'conspiracy-addled director with a soft spot for dictators', they now announced: 'It is with the greatest regret that we recall those words. For with "World Trade Center", Mr. Stone has made a truly great movie.'[47] David Edelstein, writing in *New York* magazine, seemed to sum up the incongruous responses from many observers. Stone was praised for the understated nature of the film: 'No speed-freak editing. No lefty tub-thumping. No conspiracy theories. Just a celebration of American valor in the face of devastation.'[48] However, the same article concluded by observing that Stone had chosen a strange time to be apolitical, confirming the real burden that the mainstream American media had placed on the director's shoulders. Stone's glowing reviews for a straight-line picture seemed tinged with disappointment that the conspiracist bogeyman had not behaved to type.

Other details in the press coverage of *World Trade Center* posed different issues for Stone. Several reviewers questioned the veracity of details within the rescue sequence at the end of the film.[49] Indeed, in the immediate aftermath and later, conflicting reports remained of who exactly did what and at what point. Of more concern to Stone were suggestions that in effect he had worked as a hired hand for Paramount, reined in by some of the other contributors about how the film's plot should progress. In the *New York Times* review, A. O. Scott suggested that Andrea Berloff's screenplay had 'impose[d] a salutary discipline on some of the director's wilder impulses'.[50]

In fact, Stone had raised the issue of writing credits with Shamberg and co-producer Stacey Sher. In a letter dated 13 July 2006, Stone reported that in recent interviews with the *New York Times, Dateline* and *Newsweek* he had been asked questions that indicated someone had spoken to the journalists beforehand, giving them the perception that Stone had loved the screenplay so much that he shot it as it was. Stone made clear in the letter that he was not happy about this suggestion of being a 'hired director'. He added that while he was content not to pursue writing credits or money, and while he was keen to support the career of a new writer, he wanted to state clearly that he was closely involved in reworking the script a year before release.[51] The production files suggest that Berloff's original script had a detailed grasp of the material, while Stone's input in several revisions of the screenplay were to do with dramatic structuring, including merging scenes to provide key narrative information in shorter times. Revisions had been made as far back as November 2004 as well as summer 2005, and a final version dated 14 September 2005 was used by Paramount for legal clearance.[52]

As the file designation for this copy of the screenplay in Ixtlan's production files indicates, this was not the only screenplay that Stone was working on that summer. During this period he held meetings with writer Kevin Elders on a project titled *War on Terror*. On the face of it, this looked more like the kind of film that Stone might have been expected to make. *War on Terror* told the story of the investigation of a terrorist cell in the USA, focusing on the arrest and disappearance of a dentist. The story's political perspective was everything that *World Trade Center* was not, looking in depth at CIA actions after 9/11 and the US government's difficulties in Afghanistan and Iraq. The screenplay also touched on the Patriot Act of 2001, and the US's relationship with Iran. Stone and Elders held script meetings in August 2005, and Elders provided a revised draft of the story at the end of September. Stone eventually sent a finished version of the document to Brian Lourd at Creative Artists Agency in February 2006, seeking guidance on who might be interested in funding such a project – there was no one. Stone understood that the story offered an ideological challenge to the Bush administration's orthodoxy. However, at the beginning of 2006, the criticism and unease about American foreign policy was still not sufficient enough to entice backers into pledging support for such a film, while there remained a lack of popular and establishment criticism. A year later, much would change, but Stone had already shot *World Trade Center* and moved on.

In this period Stone acquired the rights to *Jawbreaker*, a book by Gary Bernsten,[53] a CIA operative responsible for coordinating some of the agency's efforts in Afghanistan and the initial hunt for Osama Bin Laden. Stone described Bernsten as a 'real hard-core, right-wing operative', but he was interested in the story for what it said about the Pentagon's failure to support the CIA at Tora Bora, where initially Bin Laden was believed to be.[54] The story of an all-American hero resonated here, but so too did controversies surrounding government failure and inaction. However, unlike *War on Terror*, *Jawbreaker* looked for a time like it might get studio backing from Paramount. Stone later reflected that he probably would have made a hero out of Bernsten and possibly been criticised for that.[55] In the end, no deal was done and the Bin Laden manhunt would take another five years, while Hollywood's dramatisation of that tale would arrive in 2012 with Kathryn Bigelow's *Zero Dark Thirty*. Stone saw dramatic possibilities in all three screenplays that he looked at in 2005, but emotion and politics ran high at the time, and Stone thought that *World Trade Center* was the story he could tell best at that moment, even if it did seem to be anchored within mainstream national narratives about 9/11.

Certainly, the ideological centre of gravity in *World Trade Center* embraced many of the attributes highlighted by the *Los Angeles Times* review: pro-American, pro-family, pro-faith and pro-male. The rescue scene in which one of the marines, Dave Karnes (Michael Shannon), declares that good men would be needed to avenge the attack was read by some as jingoism sanctioned by Stone. There was also religious symbolism, with the recital of prayers by McLoughlin as well as Jimeno's vision and his mother-in-law's praying. These elements led David Holloway to see the film in the wider context of 9/11 representations as 'mawkish and cliché-ridden'.[56] However, Stone had committed to working with the recorded details as verified by the people who were there. Karnes did return to Iraq for two tours of duty. Jimeno did recount some kind of vision. Undoubtedly the buried Port Authority officers are male, but their wives Donna McLoughlin (Maria Bello) and Allison Jimeno (Maggie Gyllenhaal) are neither sidelined as a result of this concentrated action in the rubble of the towers, nor are they simpering women – as Stone often was accused of sanctioning. Both performances seem to project the same kind of courage that Stone was looking for in the portrayal of the lead characters. Far from constructing a conventional paternalistic discourse, Stone reminded critics and audiences that conservatives did not have an exclusive franchise on pro-American, pro-family values. *Platoon* had made essentially the same point. Stone did not want to politicise the film, but he felt that the story of the day naturally led to the question of what happened afterwards with the 'War on Terror'.

In one way, the picture operates similarly to *Platoon* as a war film. It was just that Stone saw *World Trade Center* as a working-class view of a different kind of combat. The audience is thrust into the epicentre of the action, but without the narrative conventions of some structured rescue operation to provide context and exposition. Instead, the various family and rescue stories are pieced together slowly. Jimeno and McLoughlin are removed from the hole, but no larger examination of the day is brought forth. Thus, views are constricted in a similar manner to *Platoon*: a close-quarters depiction of pain, courage and fear without the all-enveloping geopolitical causation. Taylor's and McLoughlin's voiceovers at the end of each film sought goodness and meaning to the events portrayed, stressing how compassion and community can still outshine madness and destruction. Two different environments with the same essential meaning; but what had changed between the two films was an embedded neo-conservative ideology forged in the Reagan-era of the 1980s, now led by George W. Bush's administration.

W.

The front page of the *New York Times* on 5 November 2008 ran a single word headline: 'Obama', and subtitled it 'Racial Barrier Falls in Heavy Turnout'.[57] Barack Obama's election as the forty-fourth president had electrified metropolitan centres on the east and west coasts. The election marked the conclusion of George W. Bush's eight years in the White House: eight years that seemed as contentious as they were long. As Jeffrey Toobin recounts, the administration began in a tumult of vote recounts in Florida, and the eventual intervention of the Supreme Court to assert that Bush had a legal and constitutional claim on the office.[58] Any semblance of subsequent calm that might have begun to settle on the presidency after that noisy start was removed forever, not just by the attacks on the World Trade Center and the Pentagon, but by the subsequent controversies over Guantanamo Bay, Abu Ghraib and elsewhere, the misuse of intelligence in the run-up to the invasion of Iraq, and fabrication of the public case for WMDs, as well as the reconstruction debacle that unfolded in Iraq after the fall of Saddam Hussein. Through it all, Bush had retained the presidency in 2004. However, when domestic controversy intervened – namely the sluggish, some said absent, reaction to Hurricane Katrina in August 2005, which destroyed large swathes of New Orleans and Louisiana – Bush's approval ratings plummeted in his second term, driven further down by the insurgency in Iraq that made the US mission anything but accomplished from 2005 to 2008.

In the midst of the administration's decline, in April 2007, a draft screenplay titled *Bush* had been completed by Stone and his long-term collaborator, Stanley Weiser. The two had been classmates at New York University, and Weiser had later worked with Stone on *Wall Street*. In spring 2007, Stone's mind was wandering towards the legacy of Bush and what sort of a place America had come to be in the six years since 9/11. However, cinematically it was not his prime focus. Stone was actually concluding preparations for the shooting of *Pinkville*, a story about the massacre of Vietnamese civilians by US forces at Mỹ Lai in March 1968. Once more, Vietnam was back on the director's radar, haunting his thoughts, the images and pictures of American action towards combat detainees in Iraq in particular drawing him back to the controversies of another age: his age.

Stone's commitment to the whole project was undeniable, but it collapsed for lack of funding only weeks before principal photography was due to start in late 2007.[59] Drawing on the official army investigation and report by Lt General W. R. Peers published in 1979, *Pinkville* had obvious personal claims to Stone's attention, but the story now had contemporary resonance in the wake of the pictures from Baghdad's Abu Ghraib prison, which accompanied Seymour Hersh's reporting in 2004.[60] As with *War on Terror*, the project spoke to Stone's core interests and was sure to carry political resonance in the wake of the scandal. Several revisions of the script were undertaken in summer and autumn 2007. With funding from United Artists (UA), filming was scheduled to start in December 2007 with Bruce Willis in the lead role. When Willis, unhappy with aspects of the script, pulled out shortly before commencement of shooting, the project was suspended. A replacement in the form of Nicolas Cage was found; however, UA had sustained a poor performance with another war project – *Lions for Lambs* (Robert Redford, 2007) – and pulled the funding for the project, whereupon Weiser pressed his case with Stone to work on the Bush script.[61] The director consented. He turned his attention to securing finance for the Bush project, which would be titled *W.*, and began in earnest to fine-tune the screenplay.

Stone's involvement in the *W.* script followed a familiar pattern when he was not the original writer. Painstaking reworkings were incorporated to help ensure that the dramatic construction would work. In some situations, this meant small deviations from the historical record. While Ari Fleischer (Rob Corddry) who was President Bush's press secretary was replaced by Scott McClellan in July 2003, Stone opted to retain the Fleischer character in scenes after 2003 for reasons of continuity. The same commitment to dramatic cogency was clearly evident in script review sessions between Stone and Weiser. In one Stone was concerned that a scene involving Laura Bush (Elizabeth Banks) was 'on the edge of exposition'. Weiser countered that 'this really happened', to which Stone replied: 'I'm talking about the dialogue as a movie, about the way they sound as actors. It may be true, but it doesn't fucking matter.'[62] As ever, Stone was searching for tone: he and Weiser did recognise that fear had been a key element in Bush's first term, and advancing that theme was crucial for the screenplay.[63]

Like *Pinkville*, securing finance and agreeing a marketing strategy for *W.* proved difficult. On 1 March 2007 a collaboration agreement was signed between Stone and Moritz Borman with a third signatory – Paul Rassam, a producer who had worked on *Alexander* – added in September. With the help of producer Bill Block, finance for production was confirmed. However, none of the main studios were interested in distributing the film, and the team eventually secured support from Lionsgate. Although known for the horror franchises *Saw* (2003–10) and *Hostel* (2005–11), Lionsgate had found more mainstream recognition with the Oscar-winning *Crash* (Paul Haggis, 2004), and proved to be a supportive partner.

The key marketing objective set for *W.* was to get the film into cinemas before the presidential election in November 2008. In line with this objective, a forty-four-day shoot was scheduled from 12 May to 9 July 2008 in Shreveport, Louisiana, with a total budget of $25 million. Lionsgate's efforts were not helped by an early unauthorised publication of part of the script. The *Hollywood Reporter* carried a story on 7 April 2008, confirming that it had sent script materials to four biographers of George W. Bush for comment.[64]

The unauthorised publication led to legal threats from the production office to several media outlets, including the *Los Angeles Times* blog and *Hollywood Reporter*. Another potential difficulty for Lionsgate was highlighted by *Entertainment Weekly* in its coverage of the making of *W.*[65] Richard Nixon had died almost a year before Stone's biopic of him commenced shooting in May 1995, and more than twenty years had passed since Nixon's resignation from the presidency in August 1974. By comparison, George W. Bush was not only still a serving president, but his legacy and the future of the Republican Party's grip on power was very much in the balance in summer 2008. The possibility that Stone's verdict on Bush might be in cinemas before the November 2008 election ensured close and potentially damaging scrutiny of the proposed film from the media, if not the Republican Party and its supporters.

The *New York Post*'s headline on 13 May 2008, 'Foreign Bucks to Bash Bush', called attention to the overseas funding for the film quoting *Fox News* contributor Monica Crowley as saying: 'Oliver Stone's movies are routinely and predictably packed with lies'.[66] Just like *JFK*, sections of the media were formulating opinions about the film even before it was finished. However, Stone's comments in an *Entertainment Weekly* piece the same month hardly assuaged his critics about the film's ideological stance:

> Bush may turn out to be the worst president in history ... I think history is going to be very tough on him. But that doesn't mean he isn't a great story. It's almost Capraesque, the story of a guy who had very limited talents in life except for the ability to sell himself.[67]

Adding to questions over the politics was the reception of films that had begun to take an increasingly reactionary stance towards the administration after 2005. The Iraq War had been largely box office poison, and by summer 2008 it appeared doubtful as to how a lame-duck president would draw filmgoers to the multiplexes, no matter how intriguing the story might be. When *W.* did arrive in cinemas, this issue was compounded by reviews that suggested there was actually a *lack* of controversy. *Variety's* Todd McCarthy commented that the film offered 'a relatively even-handed, restrained treatment of recent politics'.[68] Polite – the film and the review – was not exactly what Lionsgate wanted. The company's president, Tom Ortenberg, was quoted in a January 2009 *New Yorker* article as saying: 'Who wants to see an even-handed editorial think piece from Oliver Stone?'[69]

While Stone had been at pains to emphasise in the media that he really was no fan of the president – he suggested to Rachel Maddow on MSNBC that Bush was not deep and complicated but narrow-minded and provincial, and that part of the Bush legacy would probably be a presidential library with nothing in it – the film seemed strangely restrained to some reviewers.[70] It suited Ortenberg as much as the *New York Post* to play up Stone's image as a controversial filmmaker, yet evidence mounted in review after review that while the film was admired, supporters and critics alike still were not entirely satisfied. Stone was seeking an alternative portrayal here, much as he had done with *Nixon* thirteen years beforehand. While there was no eulogy, Stone was conscious of steering the picture away from the fast-moving and cartoonish polemics of Michael Moore's *Fahrenheit 9/11*: that caricature, however accurate, had been done. Stone really wanted to know how Bush had ever got to the White House in the first place, and who and what were the controlling forces behind the presidential façade.

The film picks up the administration's story in 2002, after 9/11 but before the invasion of Iraq. Through a series of flashbacks it slowly teases out an understanding of George W. Bush through an examination of his relationships with his father (James Cromwell) and his wife Laura (Elizabeth Banks). Taking us from college days, through dead-end jobs to ownership of the Texas Rangers baseball team and spiritual revival, Stone builds a parallel reading of Bush that criss-crosses his past with the administration's descent into war, and which runs at a tangent to liberal stereotypes of the man – less a condemnation than a plea for empathy.

W. premiered at the Austin Film Festival on 16 October 2008, and went on wider US distribution the following day. Given the press attention during production, the box office response was relatively moderate, with the film taking $25.5 million in the USA. Stone observed that:

> We took the tack of national security. McCain pulled even in the polls in August 2008, and then the economy became the main issue in September. This became the one issue in the election, and at that point our movie became irrelevant to the debate that ensued between Obama and McCain.[71]

While *W.* is most easily categorised as Stone's third presidential biopic, its treatment of subject matter and relative absence of polemic marks a divide between earlier and later projects. Like *JFK* and *Nixon*, *W.* uses the presidential motif to draw us into the hinterland of personal and political intrigue that was part of the history of the period. However, the picture takes a distinctly more personal approach to its subject matter than either of its companion pieces. The film does not ignore the larger historical and political context of Iraq, but that is not its focus, only the *deus ex machina*. In *JFK* and *Nixon*, Stone identified a strong protagonist and allowed each of them to show the audience the context.[72] With *W.* the purpose was less to use the protagonist as guide than fundamentally look at the protagonist themselves. As Stone commented, it was a lighter film made about what he saw as a lighter man: a more compassionate picture than many observers expected, but one bathed in pathos. That was its criticism. You did not have to feel anger at Bush, only pity at seeing a man hopelessly out of his political depth.[73]

W., then, is a film about American politics and the country's participation in the 'War on Terror', but it is also a psychological deconstruction of a man caught in the shadow of his father, just as Richard Nixon was somewhat enveloped by the apparitional presence of his mother in the earlier picture. In seeking to understand the war within Bush, Stone was inviting comprehension rather more than judgement. In that sense, *W.* is curiously sympathetic about the human condition as much as it is about power at the highest level. If Richard Nixon at the very least colluded in the malfeasance of his underlings, Bush is simply sidestepped in as much of a way as Colin Powell (Jeffrey Wright) is in the film. If there was a deeper nuanced message, then a degree of compassion – not necessarily for Bush – was the headline. Stone's choice of ending – Bush's quizzical look skyward for the baseball that will never arrive – was not intended to obscure the difficulties of his time, merely plant Bush in a no-man's land of unfulfilled promises, moral crises and unsustained legacy.

As with the opening scenes of *Nixon*, Stone envisioned Bush as a salesman, a little like Andy Griffith's character Larry 'Lonesome' Rhodes in Elia Kazan's *A Face in the Crowd* (1957). He sold a war, not very well, but he sold himself far better. Iraq may have been about oil for Dick Cheney and about draining the swamp of terrorists for

Donald Rumsfeld, but it was a kind of catharsis for Bush; a final remaking of himself in the material world that built on, and was driven by, his spiritual rebirth as an evangelical Christian. Importantly, Stone's construction of Bush in three acts – the young rebel, the middle-age patrician through marriage and political achievement (as governor of Texas), and finally the president – did not have him changed by these progressions. Emotionally and psychologically scarred by his formative years, Bush in office nevertheless displayed many of the same traits to which his younger self succumbed.

Therefore, Stone's dramatic history in *World Trade Center* and *W.* privileged character above outright polemical commentary. The result was partly to do with circumstance, partly with Hollywood conservatism, and in part to do with Stone's own cinematic evolution. Had Stone's filmography in this period included *War on Terror*, *Jawbreaker* and/or *Pinkville*, then undoubtedly the overall direction and assessment of his work would have looked different. Studio conservatism may have stayed his hand to a degree, but it was not as if, through *Syriana*, *Green Zone* and others, Hollywood was ignoring the question of American political and diplomatic enquiry. In any case, *W.* had different ambitions and focus, and Stone's polemics were being more consciously directed now at documentaries.

Soon after completing *W.*, Stone began to orchestrate a decidedly polemical critique of the entire Luce vision of the 'American Century', both in media appearances and in the construction of his mammoth documentary undertaking, *The Untold History of the United States* (2012). Again, Vietnam was crucial to the discourse of this project – not just for Stone, but for the country as a whole.

Untold History

President Barack Obama made a symbolic appearance at the Vietnam Veterans' Memorial on Memorial Day, 28 May 2012. The date marked the launch of a thirteen-year project approved by Congress to trace and commemorate the war. During his speech, the president commented that:

> One of the most painful chapters in our history was Vietnam – most particularly how we treated our troops who served there. You

were often blamed for a war you didn't start, when you should have been commended for serving your country with valor. You were sometimes blamed for misdeeds of a few, when the honorable service of the many should have been praised. You came home and sometimes were denigrated, when you should have been celebrated. It was a national shame, a disgrace that should have never happened. And that's why here today we resolve that it will not happen again.[74]

In these comments, as elsewhere in the speech, the intersections with current political and foreign policy preoccupations were not hard to spot. After more than a decade of engagement in the 'War on Terror' started by his processor, President Obama was tacitly acknowledging that American veterans of both Iraq and Afghanistan were returning to a country that was seriously divided on the wisdom of the entire campaign, and the supporting doctrine of a 'War on Terror'. However, his references to Vietnam were also an important acknowledgement of the way in which that war continued to resonate with Americans. Notwithstanding the Reagan era recast as a noble venture, and the Project for the New American Century global mission into the Middle East in particular, Vietnam retains a talismanic power. It continues to embody and disseminate cultural, social and political narratives about the period and the longer ideological and moral superiority prescribed by Henry Luce back in the Second World War.

Leading filmmakers such as Michael Cimino (*The Deer Hunter*, 1978), Norman Jewison (*In Country*, 1989), Francis Ford Coppola (*Apocalypse Now*, 1979), John Irvin (*Hamburger Hill*, 1987), Stanley Kubrick (*Full Metal Jacket*, 1987) and Brian De Palma (*Casualties of War*, 1989) may have had their say on Vietnam, but then they moved on to other topics without a second glance. Stone never left the jungles, hamlets, cities and horrors of the war behind. In the 2000s he had not made a 'Vietnam' movie in fifteen years, but his personal experience, contemporary events, and his continuing media presence propagating ideas, comments and reactions buried him in the conflict almost as much as the 1970s and 1980s had done.

For example, the lessons from Vietnam for the Iraqi and Afghanistan campaigns were drawn out in a long interview with Stone conducted by Bill Moyers, and aired on PBS's *Bill Moyers*

Journal, on 4 December 2009.[75] The interview, intercut with key scenes from *Platoon* and *Born on the Fourth of July*, referenced aspects of the war such as friendly fire and the stress of battle. Moyers began by noting that the president had contended that Afghanistan was *not* like Vietnam. Was that right, and had the director lessons from that war to pass on to the president?[76] Stone reminded the audience of the age-old dictum: invading a country without local knowledge of customs and traditions will not win hearts and minds, and he thought that such a position appeared diametrically opposed to the strategy being enacted by the president. Stone's prediction was that US actions ran the risk of awakening nationalist sentiments within the Pashtun tribes, who would make common cause with the Taliban, resulting in the USA being sucked into a full-scale war – a war that would be likely to go beyond the borders of Afghanistan. Less than five years later, many of Stone's fears became a reality. The emergence of ISIS in Syria and Iraq, their assault on the Kurdish region of that territory, and US dalliances with a military return to lands in which they had spent ten years trying to assert their influence, all reinforced Stone's master narrative of ignorance and complicity in the rise of local, ethnic and ideological insurgency.

The Moyers interview provided an important insight into Stone's thinking around where broader, post-war American history was now heading. The *Untold History* series already was starting to take some shape on paper. This interview and other media appearances not only showcased the emerging argument, but acted as a spur to further thinking and debate with co-writer and historian Peter Kuznick about the scope and direction of the documentary series. Stone's conception of the USA was of a nation driven by New Century thinking that could not entirely escape the old Cold War and bipolar diplomacy. As the 2010s loomed, America's president could not extricate his nation's foreign policy from some of the fundamentals of the Luce-centred 'American Century' tropes that had fashioned the country's reactions for so long. Stone's desire to get to the bottom of why this version of history had taken such a hold on American policy was evidenced in the enormous effort that went into the work with Kuznick.

Explored in ten hours of footage and approximately 750 pages of accompanying text, the *Untold History* project had a long gestation period. In 1996 Stone and Kuznick had discussed a film treatment about US vice-president Henry Wallace and his ouster from the Democratic ticket at the 1944 Democratic Party conference. Although that film never made it off the page, Stone found himself drawn back to the story a decade later, while discussing with Kuznick the idea of a short documentary about Truman and the H-bomb; the larger project emerging from that discussion. Beginning with the US entry into the Second World War and then following US foreign policy through the Cold War, Vietnam, Nixon and *détente* to Reagan, the series culminates with an episode looking at the US administration's first war of the twenty-first century: the 'War on Terror'.

The series drew together much of Stone's preoccupation with American history. Originally titled *An Inconvenient History: A Counter History of the United States,* the budget of $5.2 million was to cover all ten chapters. The original structure for the series started with a chapter on Hiroshima, followed by one on Luce and Wallace, after which the story of the Cold War and its aftermath would be traced.[77] A later revision began with the Second World War, followed by a chapter specifically on the atom bomb, whereupon the narrative would step back in the following two chapters to consider events at the turn of the century through to the Great Depression and the New Deal, before picking up the post-war story from Korea to Afghanistan, with the final chapter titled 'War on Terror'.

The shooting of *W.* delayed plans to air the series in October 2010, and these were further disrupted by Stone's belated acceptance of the offer to direct a follow-up to *Wall Street.* All this took place while he prepared and shot his *South of the Border* documentary. *South of the Border* premiered at the Venice Film Festival in September 2009, just two days before the commencement of principal photography on *Wall Street: Money Never Sleeps,* by which point the shooting of *Castro in Winter* had also been completed. Stone's high-pressure production schedule at this time confirmed his energy for the projects, and reminds one of the intensity of his late-1980s heyday.

By December 2009, Kuznick and Stone had drafts for the first six chapters of *Untold History,* although there were already concerns about some of the content and the direction that the work was taking. Stone felt that the chapters were becoming bloated and overly complex, a criticism that Kuznick accepted.[78] What was becoming apparent was a developing professional tension in terms of approach and objectives. Ultimately, Stone was looking for something that would work as a television programme, whereas Kuznick was seeking a much more detailed account of the events. It was a classic juxtaposition of a historian's eye for detail, and a filmmaker's unbending desire to get to the story. A resolution was found in the decision to publish a companion book with the series.

Through 2010, Stone juggled *Untold History* between other projects. Showtime agreed to postpone the planned October 2010 airing, giving Stone and Kuznick more time as the chapters expanded to twelve, and progress on the companion book continued apace. Beyond the concerns about detail, Stone was very alert to how the series might be presented and received by audiences.

Indicative of this depth of concern were protracted discussions over the title of the series. In August 2010, Stone wrote to Kuznick saying he wanted to change the title from *Secret History of the United States* – the working title at that point – to *The Untold History of the United States*. He was concerned about the connotations of 'secret' in so far as it invited potential criticisms from the more literally minded about where the secrets were, when in fact what the series was doing was presenting a different point of view with established facts. In spring 2011, there was further discussion about the title, and several alternatives were considered and rejected. A proposal from Stone in January 2011 to call the series *Empire: The Forgotten History of the United States* was questioned by producer Fernando Sulichin, because of the polarising nature of the word 'empire'. In March 2011, Stone discussed possible titles with David Nevins, the president of Showtime. Stone was concerned that calling the series *Oliver Stone's Forgotten History of the United States* would foreground his name in a way that might be unhelpful, while Nevins in turn was worried about what 'forgotten' might suggest to audiences. Nevins had been a supporter of the *Untold History* option for some months previous to this and, as it turned out, this title prevailed.

In parallel with these discussions about the title, steps were taken to test the materials at private screenings with invited historians and other professionals. On 18 March 2011, a screening was organised at the Tribeca Film Center for several historians, including Sean Wilentz, Professor of History at Princeton University.

Wilentz would later emerge as one of the leading critics of the book and the series. Other private screenings for academics and media people followed. The need to secure a degree of professional endorsement for the line of argument pursued in the book and series was something exercising Stone and Kuznick from an early phase of the work. However, this task was complicated, not least by a particular media storm over comments that Stone made in an interview published in the *Sunday Times* in July 2010,[79] in which he described Hitler as a 'Frankenstein' but that the monster also needed a Dr Frankenstein: the implication being that others both inside and outside Germany, including American industrialists, assisted with Hitler's rise to power.

Stone also bluntly suggested that Hitler may have done more damage to the Russian people than he did to the Jews. The American Jewish Committee was quick to claim that Stone had effectively 'outed' himself as an anti-Semite.[80] A swift apology on the same day was an effort to quell the online storm that had quickly gathered, but Stone's penchant for never working from scripts – he seldom has any paperwork with him at all –has left him exposed sometimes, as here, to unsolicited comments. Quickly retreating from them has not always done the trick.

Despite Stone's apology, the story inevitably resurfaced. In a *New York Post* article in March 2011, Alan Dershowitz made reference to the remarks in the context of a story on anti-Semitism that, in reality, was recycling several earlier celebrity stories on the subject.[81] Stone responded via his producer Edward Pressman, but the incident illustrated the challenges of media management generated by the director's sometimes combative, off-the-cuff remarks. A more unusual and final pre-launch effort to support the reception of the series took place at the private Wellfleet Harbor conference in September 2012, at which one of the episodes was shown.[82] This was the first film presented in the forty-seven-year history of the group, and seen as an opportunity to create a positive buzz with key thinkers.

Following a successful showing of the first three chapters at the New York Film Festival in October 2012, the series finally aired on Showtime commencing on 12 November 2012, just two weeks after publication of the accompanying book. The plan to complete twelve episodes had been revised in spring 2011, bringing the final series in at ten episodes, with the two pre-Second World War episodes removed from the broadcast schedule but retained for the DVD box set.

Stone gave several interviews to online news shows, including *The Young Turks* and MOXnews.com, and made appearances at public meetings, including the Penny Stamps School of Art and Design at the University of Michigan, as part of the 'Distinguished Speakers' series with journalist Bob Woodruff, where he stated his motivations for the programmes.[83] In these appearances, Stone talked about the atomic bomb, the shadow that it cast on post-war life in the USA, and the way in which he believed that had Truman not ascended to the presidency, American history might have been very different. This line of thinking, in turn, had led to a re-evaluation of what Stone described as a series of American-concentric myths about the winning of the Second World War, the bomb and the Cold War. He reasserted his contention that there are a series of arguments about US foreign policy that are not being heard, and he was looking to position the book and the series as a contribution to the wider debate about twentieth (and now twenty-first-)century US history. Pedagogically, Stone also tied his thoughts to a concern about what high-school children – including his daughter – were being taught of this history, and why.

Figure 4 Oliver Stone and Peter Kuznick, Hiroshima, 2013

The introduction to the first chapter of the book goes to the heart of this point. Stone and Kuznick refer to the 'tyranny of now': the tendency of news to offer no historical context to current events (Figure 4). As part of the narrative, Stone proposed to foreground a forgotten set of heroes: people who had been lost to history because they did not conform; arguing that despite profound mistakes, the country still had an opportunity to rehabilitate such people. One of Stone and Kuznick's central claims in the series was that Roosevelt's death on 12 April 1945 allowed the manoeuvrings at the 1944 Democratic Convention in Chicago, where Henry Wallace was defeated by Truman for the vice-presidential nomination, to exert a decisive and terrible effect on the course of the war and the peace to follow. Truman served only eighty-two days as vice-president before his ascendancy to the Oval Office. Stone and Kuznick's portrayal of Wallace's defeat is decidedly Capraesque. Having distinguished himself as Secretary of Agriculture and credited with a revival of the American farming industry in the wake of the Great Depression, Wallace nevertheless represented the radical wing of the Democrat Party that some activists feared. Therefore, the convention outcome derailed any possibility that his 1943 riposte to Luce, *The Century of the Common Man*, would ever become post-war policy.[84]

Beyond the lionisation of Wallace, Stone and Kuznick took a highly critical perspective on Truman: that despite being diligent in his efforts to succeed in both business and politics, and gifted to a degree, crucial personal limitations left him particularly ill-suited to the complex task of dealing with the Soviets in the implementation of the Yalta Agreement, and the conclusion of the war in the Pacific. After the war, this emerging interventionist and anti-Soviet stance was given a policy mooring in President Truman's 12 March 1947 speech to Congress: the Truman Doctrine. The argument runs that the subsequent division and remilitarisation of Germany, the expansion of overseas military bases and establishment of NATO, the testing of larger atomic weapons and, subsequently, a series of foreign covert interventions led by the CIA, were not just immediate manifestations of the Doctrine in the Cold War era, but the harbinger of a mindset of empire that propelled the administration and military not just into Vietnam, but inexorably on into Iraq and Afghanistan.

The on-screen polemics were articulated in a decidedly low-key manner. Stone delivered the narrative at a relatively slow pace, as a more or less continuous voiceover, broken only by the occasional segment of archive speech or actor-read voiceover. There are no talking-head inputs other than Stone's initial introduction to the series at the beginning of Chapter 1, and a few words at the end of Chapter 10. The voiceover and extensive use of archive film footage certainly carry overtones of a classic of the genre, *The World at War* (1973–74). Moreover, even with the addition of film clips, the overall effect is a distinct disavowal of the kind of entertainment values deployed by, for example Michael Moore and Alex Gibney, in favour of a presentation that is self-consciously didactic in construction and tone. Whether the style suited modern high-school audiences or even general viewers – all of which Stone aimed to pull in – is open to speculation, and certainly worthy of further examination. Showtime's own audience analysis indicated that the series maintained its first night audience levels throughout the series, and Stone and Kuznick, with the help of Eric Singer, a colleague of Kuznick's at American University, augmented the appeal to high-school audiences by later providing detailed lesson plans supporting each episode.[85]

The final chapter of *Untold History* concluded on a note of hope, but one tinged with disappointment. The moments when history might have taken the USA towards a more humane and humble outlook on the world but did not, might prepare people for a better understanding of the past, thought Stone, and a better response when another opportunity arrives in the future. Stone gave the final word to President Kennedy and his commencement address at American University in 1963.[86] It was the rhetoric of hope in what was otherwise a relentless indictment of US foreign policy.

Stone's media profile ensured reaction both from journalists and academics. A *New York Times Magazine* article about the series published in November 2012 was headlined 'Oliver Stone Rewrites History – Again'[87] Aside from the commentary on the *Untold History* series, Andrew Goldman's article revisited the *JFK* saga in a way that suggested Stone's film continued to grate. In February 2013, after the series had aired in America, Sean Wilentz wrote in the *New York Review of Books* that Stone and Kuznick effectively cherry-picked their facts throughout the programmes to support their interpretations.[88] Wilentz was challenging a broader development in historical analysis that historians such as Robert Rosenstone had raised years before, not least in a debate with Stone at the 1997 American Historical Association meeting. On the changes in historical analysis in the previous fifty years, Rosenstone described an emerging view of history as a moral story about the past in which the truth resided 'not in the verifiability of individual pieces of data but in the overall narrative'.[89] Rosenstone's point was that history is a contentious business which does not simply possess an accumulation of settled facts. The implication was that some of the criticism of Stone had been academically proprietorial. He was accused of presenting himself as a historian, and Wilentz's criticisms drew on that unease. Yet Stone had moved ever closer to documentary traditions and with it historical accountability, but here he was, still being held up to feature film criticisms and contentions.

Following the series, Stone continued expounding the programme's views in a series of engagements. In August 2013, before taking part in a speaking tour of Japan, he joined in with protesters on Jeju island in South Korea who were opposing the construction of a naval base. After the Edward Snowden disclosures about mass surveillance by the NSA and its British counterpart GCHQ (Government Communications Headquarters) broke, Stone drew on these revelations to push further his argument about the overreach of the American empire.[90] Stone and Kuznick wrote a joint piece for the *Huffington Post* in which they quoted Samuel P. Huntington and captured all that Stone's assessment of war and the American empire had come to mean for him: 'The West won the world not by the superiority of its ideas, values or religion ... but rather by its superiority in applying organised violence. Westerners often forget this fact; non-Westerners never do.'[91]

Conclusion

In *World Trade Center* and *W.* as well as the *Untold History* series and other documentaries during this period, notably *South of the Border*, Stone provided a mix of melodramatic and polemic assessment of America as it wrestled with the 'War on Terror' and its place in the world after 9/11. Stone's own production files show that some explicitly political materials were considered for production, but could not be executed for a number of reasons. Against that backdrop, *World Trade Center* and *W.* stand as testaments to the changed environment in Hollywood and in the country post-9/11 to what was possible in those circumstances, as well as being confirming statements of Stone's own realignment. *World Trade Center* has several parallels with *Platoon*, both in its narrative subtext about individual courage and in its concluding message about goodness. Both films had mixed receptions from critics, and both captured something of the zeitgeist of the era. Of course, two things had changed in the interim. The zeitgeist had slipped its liberal moorings in favour of a neo-conservative berth, and Stone's chosen tool to upbraid the establishment had changed from drama to documentary. It was a conscious choice intended to maintain the momentum of political critique, yet critics either stuck with their reticence towards the feature films, and/or failed to spot the more approachable criticism directed out of the documentaries.

Most of all, critics did not appreciate how much Stone's work had been embedded by thoughts of 'war'; literal, metaphoric and symbolic. The message of war in *Platoon* was a cry to learn from the past, and *Untold History* paraded the same signs about the possibilities for a better world. However, what *Platoon, World Trade Center* and *W.* all truly emphasise is the understanding that ultimately, war is rooted in the battle within ourselves, within individual conscience and within our soul. Henry Luce's 'American Century' required that self-interest and power trumped all other concerns, and war was the necessary consequence of such ideals. Stone's filmmaking career, rightly or wrongly, consistently and antithetically battled those feelings about war in favour of understanding, compassion and humility.

Notes

1 Oliver Stone, *A Child's Night Dream* (New York: St. Martin's Press, 1997), p. 85.

2 Henry R. Luce, 'The American Century', *Life* (17 February 1941), p. 63.

3 Luce, 'American Century', p. 65.

4 The Truman Doctrine, announced to Congress by President Truman in 1947, outlined a broad foreign policy objective to counter Soviet expansion. NSC-68 (National Security Council Report 68) – a top secret document produced in 1950 – envisaged militarisation as the primary means to counter Soviet expansion. NSC-68 set the tone for US foreign policy throughout the Cold War and, arguably, the same approach continues to the present day.
5 Oliver Stone and Peter Kuznick, *The Untold History of the United States* (New York: Ebury, 2012).
6 For his Vietnam War service, Stone received the Air Medal (awarded for 25 or more air combat assaults), the Army Commendation Medal, the Bronze Star (for heroism in ground combat) and the Purple Heart, having been wounded twice.
7 John Morton Blum, *Years of Discord: American Politics and Society 1961–1974* (New York and London: W.W. Norton & Co., 1991), p. 387.
8 James Riordan, *Stone: The Controversies, Excesses, and Exploits of a Radical Filmmaker* (London: Aurum, 1995), p. 60.
9 Riordan, *Stone*, p. 526.
10 The GI Bill passed by Congress in 1944 offered a range of benefits, including educational entitlements, to returning military personnel. Similar entitlements have been provided for veterans from later conflicts including Korea, Vietnam and Iraq.
11 *Ibid.*, p. 70.
12 Riordan, *Stone*, pp. 71–2.
13 Ibid, p. 73.
14 Chris Salewicz, *Oliver Stone: The Making of His Movies* (London: Orion, 1997), p. 25.
15 Riordan, *Stone*, p. 75.
16 Ron Kovic, *Born on the Fourth of July* (New York: Pocket Books, 1977; first published 1976).
17 Steven Bach, *Final Cut: Dreams and Disaster in the Making of Heaven's Gate* (London and Boston, MA: Faber and Faber, 1985).
18 *Platoon*, Platoon Personal Misc file, Early Projects Box 31, Ixtlan Production Files (hereafter I-PF), Los Angeles, CA.
19 William J. Palmer, *The Films of the Eighties: A Social History* (Carbondale, IL: Southern Illinois University Press, 1995), p. 21.
20 *Platoon*, Platoon History file, Early Projects-Box 34, I-PF. Los Angeles Superior Court reference C526895, filed 14 December 1984.
21 *Platoon*, Platoon Budget file, Early Projects-Box 34, I-PF.
22 *Platoon*, 1986.
23 Pauline Kael, 'The Current Cinema: Little Shocks, Big Shocks', *New Yorker* (12 January 1987), pp. 94–6.
24 Roger Ebert, 'Platoon', *Chicago Sun-Times* (30 December 1986). Available at http://rogerebert.com/reviews/platoon-1986 (accessed 7 December 2015).

25 Lawrence W. Lichty and Raymond L. Carroll, 'Fragments of War: Oliver Stone's *Platoon*' in Peter C. Rollins and John E. Connor (eds) *Why We Fought* (Lexington, KY: University of Kentucky Press, 2008), p. 398.

26 Tony Shaw, *Hollywood's Cold War* (Edinburgh: Edinburgh University Press, 2007), pp. 278–9.

27 Interview with Oliver Stone, Santa Monica, CA, 19 January 2010.

28 Vincent Canby, 'Born on the Fourth of July', *New York Times* (20 December 1989). Available at http://nytimes.com/movie/review?res=950DE6DA1F38F933A15751C1A96F948260 (accessed 7 December 2015).

29 See for example Sheila Benson, 'Oliver Stone Goes to War Again', *Los Angeles Times* (20 December, 1989). Available at: http://articles.latimes.com/1989-12-20/entertainment/ca-482_1_ron-kovic (accessed 1 March 2016).

30 The 'Vietnam Syndrome' in US political discourse references the perceived reluctance (inferring weakness) of the wider public in the late 1970s and 1980s to support foreign military action following the Vietnam War. Presidential contender Ronald Reagan used the term in an address to the Veterans of Foreign Wars in August 1980. See http://presidency.ucsb.edu/ws/?pid=85202 (accessed 1 March 2016).

31 Colin Harrison, *American Culture in the 1990s* (Edinburgh: Edinburgh University Press, 2010), p. 98.

32 The acquittal of four Los Angeles police officers of assault following the videotaped arrest and beating of motorist Rodney King sparked the 1992 Los Angeles riots, in which fifty-five people lost their lives.

33 Project for the New American Century, 'Rebuilding America's Defenses: Strategy, Forces and Resources for a New Century' September 2000, p. 51. Available at https://wikispooks.com/w/images/3/37/RebuildingAmericasDefenses.pdf (accessed 7 December 2015).

34 Carl Boggs and Tom Pollard, *The Hollywood War Machine: US Militarism and Popular Culture* (Boulder, CO and London: Paradigm Press, 2007), pp. 144–68.

35 Paul Cartledge and Fiona Rose-Greenland, 'Introduction' in Paul Cartledge and Fiona Rose-Greenland (eds) *Responses to Oliver Stone's Alexander: Film, History and Cultural Studies* (Madison, WI: University of Wisconsin Press, 2010), pp. 3–12.

36 *Alexander the Great*, Letters ATG file, ATG-Box 24, I-PF.

37 Manohla Dargis, 'With No More Parents to Conquer, He Wept', *New York Times* (24 November 2004). Available at http://nytimes.com/2004/11/24/movies/24alex.html?_r=0 (accessed 7 December 2015).

38 Emily Eakin, 'Ancient Conqueror, Modern Devotees', *New York Times* (26 November 2004). Available at http://www.nytimes.com/2004/11/26/books/ancient-conqueror-modern-devotees.html (accessed 7 December 2015).
39 Thomas Kean, (ed) *The 9/11 Commission Report: Final Report of the National Commission on Terrorist Attacks upon the United States* (New York and London: W.W. Norton and Co., 2004), p. xv.
40 Kean, *9/11 Commission Report*, p. 364.
41 Seymour Hersh, 'Torture at Abu Ghraib', *New Yorker* (10 May 2004), pp. 42–7.
42 *World Trade Center*, WTC changes file, Box WTC files: 2005–2006 I-PF.
43 *World Trade Center*, WTC Publicity March 06 file, Box WTC Misc #13, I-PF.
44 Sam Schechner and John Lippman, 'Hollywood's Popcorn Recipe', *Wall Street Journal* (7 April 2006). Available at http://www.wsj.com/articles/SB114437101313419558 (accessed 7 December 2015).
45 Claudia Puig, 'Intimate "Trade Center" Tells Larger Tale', *USA Today* (8 August 2006). Available at http://usatoday30.usatoday.com/life/movies/reviews/2006-08-08-wtc-review_x.htm (accessed 7 December 2015).
46 Editorial, 'Oliver Stone's Tribute' *Washington Times* (23 July 2006). Available at http://www.washingtontimes.com/news/2006/jul/23/20060723-093638-8062r/ (accessed 1 March 2016).
47 Ibid.
48 David Edelstein, 'Up from the Ashes', *New York* magazine (14 August 2006). Available at http://nymag.com/movies/reviews/18855/ (accessed 7 December 2015).
49 Rebecca Liss, 'Oliver Stone's World Trade Center Fiction: How the rescue really happened', *Slate* (9 August 2006). Available at http://slate.com/articles/news_and_politics/life_and_art/2006/08/oliver_stones_world_trade_center_fiction.html (accessed 7 December 2015).
50 A. O. Scott, 'Pinned Under the Weight of History and Skyscrapers in "World Trade Center"', *New York Times* (9 August 2006). Available at http://nytimes.com/2006/08/09/movies/09worl.html (accessed 7 December 2015).
51 *World Trade Center*, WTC budget-business file, Box WTC Letters, I-PF.
52 *World Trade Center*, War on Terror file, Box WTC Misc #14, I-PF.
53 Gary Bernsten and Ralph Pezzullo, *Jawbreaker: The Attack on Bin Laden and Al-Qaedda: A Personal Account by the CIA's Key Field Commander* (New York: Crown Publications, 2005).
54 Interview with Oliver Stone, Santa Monica, CA, 7 December 2011.

55 *Ibid.*
56 David Holloway, *9/11 and the War on Terror* (Edinburgh: Edinburgh University Press, 2008), p. 86.
57 Later editions substituted 'heavy turnout' and replaced it with 'decisive victory'. See: https://nytimes.com/images/2008/11/05/nytfrontpage/scan.jpg (accessed 1 March 2016).
58 Jeffrey Toobin, *The Nine: Inside the Secret World of the Supreme Court* (New York: Anchor Books, 2007), pp. 165–208.
59 *Pinkville*, Scripts file, I-PF.
60 Seymour M. Hersh, 'Torture at Abu Ghraib' *New Yorker* (10 May 2004), pp. 42–7. (Hersh had been the first American journalist to report on Mỹ Lai in November 1969.)
61 Interview with Oliver Stone, Santa Monica, CA, 7 December 2013.
62 *W.*, Script Research Bush file, Box W Script and Research, I-PF.
63 *W.*, Bush Research Cont. 1 file, Box Annotations and Research, I-PF.
64 Stephen Galloway and Matthew Belloni, 'Bush Biographers Mixed on Script for Oliver Stone's "W" ', *Hollywood Reporter* (7 April 2008). Available at http://hollywoodreporter.com/news/bush-biographers-mixed-script-oliver-108789 (accessed 7 December 2015).
65 Benjamin Svetkey, 'First Look: "W" – Oliver Stone's Bush Biopic', *Entertainment Weekly* (12 May 2008). Available at http://ew.com/ew/article/0,,20198476,00.html (accessed 7 December 2015).
66 *New York Post* (13 May 2008). 'Foreign Bucks to Bash Bush'. Available at http://pagesix.com/2008/05/13/foreign-bucks-to-bash-bush/?_ga=1.267338062.1328634931.1311780894 (accessed 7 December 2015).
67 Stvetkey, 'First Look: "W" '.
68 Todd McCarthy, 'Review: "W."', *Variety* (7 October 2008). Available at http://variety.com/2008/film/reviews/w-3-1200471810/ (accessed 7 December 2015).
69 Tad Friend, 'The Cobra', *New Yorker* (19 January 2009), pp. 41–9.
70 Oliver Stone, *The Rachel Maddow Show*, NSNBC (14 October 2008). Available at http://nbcnews.com/id/27196799/ns/msnbc-rachel_maddow_show/ (accessed 7 December 2015).
71 Interview with Oliver Stone, Santa Monica, CA, 7 December 2011.
72 Oliver Stone, 'Stone on Stone's Image' in Robert Brent Toplin (ed), *Oliver Stone's U.S.A.: Film, History and Controversy* (Lawrence, KS: University of Kansas Press, 2000), p. 46.
73 Interview with Stone, 7 December 2011.
74 President Barack Obama, The White House, Office of the Press Secretary, 'Remarks by the President at the Commemoration Ceremony of the 50th Anniversary of the Vietnam War',

Washington, DC (28 May 2012). Available at http://whitehouse.gov/the-press-office/2012/05/28/remarks-president-commemoration-ceremony-50th-anniversary-vietnam-war (accessed 7 December 2015).

75 *Bill Moyers Journal*, PBS (4 December 2009). Available at http://pbs.org/moyers/journal/12042009/profile.htm (accessed 1 March 2016).

76 The White House, Office of the Press Secretary, 'Remarks by the President in Address to the Nation on the Way Forward in Afghanistan and Pakistan' (1 December 2009). Available at www.whitehouse.gov/the-press-office/remarks-president-address-nation-way-forward-afghanistan-and-pakistan (accessed 7 December 2015).

77 *Untold History*, Writing and Research file, Untold History-History chs 123, I-PF.

78 *Untold History*, Letters file, Untold History-General, I-PF.

79 Camilla Long, 'Oliver Stone: Lobbing grenades in all directions' *Sunday Times* (25 July 2010). Available at http://thesundaytimes.co.uk/sto/newsreview/features/article352668.ece (accessed 1 March 2016).

80 Brooks Barnes, 'Oliver Stone Controversy', *New York Times* (26 July 2010). Available at http://mediadecoder.blogs.nytimes.com/2010/07/26/oliver-stone-controversy/ (accessed 7 December 2015).

81 Alan M. Dershowitz, 'Why the Jews?', *New York Post* (6 March 2011). Available at http://nypost.com/2011/03/06/why-the-jews/ (accessed 7 December 2015).

82 *Untold History*, Letters History 2, Sept 2012 file, UH-OS Letters, I-PF.

83 Oliver Stone, interview by Bob Woodruff for Penny Stamps Distinguished Speaker Series, University of Michigan (25 October 2012). Available at http://youtube.com/watch?v=qovSevftixo (accessed 7 December 2015).

84 Henry A. Wallace, *The Century of the Common Man* (New York: Reynal & Hitchcock, 1943).

85 *Untold History of the United States*, 'Lesson Plans'. Available at www.untoldhistory.com/#for-educators (accessed 7 December 2015).

86 John F. Kennedy, 'Commencement Address at American University', 10 June 1963. Available at http://jfklibrary.org/Asset-Viewer/BWC7I4C9QUmLG9J6I8oy8w.aspx (accessed 7 December 2015).

87 Andrew Goldman, 'Oliver Stone Rewrites History – Again', *New York Times Magazine* (22 November 2012). Available at http://www.nytimes.com/2012/11/25/magazine/oliver-stone-rewrites-history-again.html (accessed 7 December 2015).

88 Sean Wilentz, 'Cherry-Picking Our History', *New York Review of Books* (21 February 2013). Available at www.nybooks.com/articles/2013/02/21/oliver-stone-cherry-picking-our-history/ (accessed 1 March 2016).

89 Robert Rosenstone, 'Oliver Stone as Historian', in Brent Toplin (ed), *Oliver Stone's U.S.A.*, p. 28.

90 Oliver Stone and Peter Kuznick, 'The U.S. and Japan: Partners in Falsification', *Huffington Post* (10 September 2013). Available at http://huffingtonpost.com/oliver-stone/the-us-and-japan-partners_b_3902034.html (accessed 7 December 2015).

91 *Ibid.*

2
Politics

Introduction

> The problem in America is that we don't apologise, and we don't learn. The protests against the Iraq War worldwide were enormous. I don't think Americans got a sense of the protest or the damage in Iraq at all. The protests were not that big a story in the USA. The American press report on every story from an American viewpoint. It is what comes naturally to them. It's not done out of malice; they don't know any better.[1]

In his introduction to an episode of the PBS programme *Open Mind*, recorded in January 1992, host Richard Heffner began by commending historian Charles Beard to his viewers, noting that Beard's views on the limitations of recorded history suggested that it must be understood 'as but an *act of faith* hopefully well and truthfully documented, of course, but essentially only what the purported historian (whether film maker, academic reporter, what have you) thinks of what someone else thinks, or saw, or heard, or believed'.[2]

In reaching back to one of America's most distinguished historians, Heffner was inviting his audience to take a step away from the media storm that was assailing his guest on the show that day, and instead to re-examine their assumptions about how history is made, how politics is portrayed, and how print media are the purveyors of a very particular process of recollection. The guest was Oliver Stone, and he was there to discuss his new release, *JFK* (1991). Centred on the 1969 trial of New Orleans businessman Clay Shaw by Louisiana District Attorney Jim Garrison, the thrust of the movie was that Shaw and others had been involved in a conspiracy to assassinate President John F. Kennedy in Dallas on 22 November 1963. Although he was by no means the first person to make the point, Stone sought to argue in the film that the Warren Commission's investigation into the assassination, and its conclusion that Kennedy had been killed by a lone gunman, was essentially a myth. Hence the film's assertion had ignited a media firestorm behind a director who was perceived to be not just imagining history, not just recreating it, but actually rewriting history to his own satisfaction.

That supposed rewriting took shape through the development of several fore-stories in the film concerning the background to Lee Harvey Oswald's life, events at Dealey Plaza, Dallas, Texas on that fateful day, and a character otherwise known as 'X', but ostensibly based on Air Force Colonel L. Fletcher Prouty, around whom Stone built what he described as a 'counter-myth' to the Kennedy assassination. The counter-myth was that the American people needed to consider the possibility that Kennedy had been removed by a *coup d'état* ordered by unknown members of the institutional establishment, and carried out by people within the security services.

The opprobrium that followed was nearly unprecedented, and might have broken other directors of less physical and mental resolve than Stone. Writing in the *Washington Post* – a paper that had carried a critique of the film while it was still in production – Rita Kempley asserted that Stone's talent was to bend the truth with mirrors[3] – and that was one of the more generous reviews. Jonathan Rosenbaum, in the *Chicago Reader*, called it 'three hours of bombast'.[4] Vincent Canby, in the *New York Times*, stated that 'the film's insurmountable problem is the vast amount of material it fails to make coherent sense of'.[5] One critic offering an endorsement was *Newsweek* reviewer David Ansen, who took to congratulating Stone for taking on the subject and making people think, as well as generally testing the waters in America at the time of what was acceptable, appropriate or even entertained by a pliant public fed on a discourse of triumph, tragedy and redemption in the post-war era.[6] The 'American Century' that Luce had talked so vividly of in 1941 was alive and well in this cultural narrative: punctured, but not fatally so, by successive military escapades and assassinations, and reimagined in a most potent and redemptive form in JFK's own presidency. In Stone's version of this post-war story, as his film laid out in its opening ten-minute montage sequence, Luce's 'American Century', the 'triumphal purpose of freedom' whose goal was the fabled 'American Dream', had become nothing so much as an American nightmare. Fed on lies, deception and misinformation, the Kennedy assassination was, for Stone, the beginning of a fall from grace that was as long as it was wide.

Years later in the *Untold History of the United States* book and documentary series that he assembled with historian Peter Kuznick, Stone equated the assassination to the bestselling novel by Fletcher Knebel and Charles W. Bailey II, *Seven Days in May*,[7] of which Kennedy had had an advance copy. The military coup at the heart of that story – made into a film less than a year later by director John Frankenheimer – has Kennedy being quoted as saying: 'It's possible, it could happen in this country.'[8] The inference was clear. The counter-myth to the lone gunman, the 'beyond the reach and influence of institutional forces' story that few could either believe or stomach, was still in place in Stone's mind – and part of a wider history that was not so much forgotten, as never told correctly in the first place. Referring to the Cuban missile crisis and Vietnam among many of the mitigating dilemmas, Stone highlighted a number of Warren Commission supporters including Lyndon B. Johnson, Robert Kennedy and Texas governor John Connolly – who had been injured in the shooting – who all expressed private doubt at the Commission's 1964 findings.

For Stone then, this matter – as with many of his considerations of America's past – was never just about cinema as history, nor the responsibilities of the filmmaker to history. *JFK* was about the true nature of political and historical enquiry, about the best ways of communicating alternative or counter-mythic tales of the recent past and/or the lost and impenetrable state of society. Stone's champions in this regard – critics and colleagues such as Classification and Rating Administration (CARA) head Richard Heffner – always have known that what he wanted to do was not test the resolve of history or the political culture, but the will of people to accept – even if they did not agree with – alternative views of history, and thus challenge what the meaning of the past could (and should) be for all of us as cinemagoers and citizens.

Therefore, history for Stone has always been a matter of communicating with, and examining, the political establishment. In his writing for other directors, *Midnight Express* (Alan Parker, 1978), along with *Scarface* (Brian De Palma, 1983) and *Year of the Dragon* (Michael Cimino, 1985), the work constituted a pre-political phase in which Stone honed his ability to deliver a particularly visceral style of storytelling that was of itself cinematic. The political agendas, if not absent, were restrained, while the social commentary, controversial as it was in the case of these films, nevertheless was integral to the personal stories of the central characters. Billy Hayes (Brad Davis) in *Midnight Express*, Tony Montana (Al Pacino) in *Scarface* and Stanley White (Mickey Rourke) in *Year of the Dragon* are all victims of their own drug and violence-induced excesses. The reality was that in these early collaborations with De Palma, Cimino and John Milius, any political angles that Stone saw opportunities to explore in the writing were diluted very quickly by his junior position vis-à-vis the director.

In *Scarface*, for example – a film that would provide street credibility when he later talked to death squad hitmen in preparation for *Salvador* (1986) – Stone saw Tony Montana as essentially left-wing and a rebel, not some one-dimensional narcissistic and nihilistic hoodlum.[9] Others, as Welsh and Whaley note, saw nothing more than a right-wing political bias lurking in the shadows, although that inference disintegrated in the face of what was to follow.[10] With *Salvador*, Stone's examination of Reagan-era foreign policy in Central America shifted gears and confirmed a radical intent in his work. The visceral writing found an outlet in Stone's directing that was at least as combative and aggressive in its focus as his screenplays had been up to this point. Moreover, having directorial control, he discovered, gave a much-needed clarity to his evolution as a filmmaker. *Salvador* provided the subject matter as well as the artistic chance to proffer political ideas and critiques, with an individual shooting style that began to hone his fabled visual immediacy.

Unlike the firsthand experience in Vietnam, Stone's education concerning Central American politics was gifted to him by an old friend, Richard Boyle, in dramatic fashion. A journalist whom he had known for a number of years, Boyle persuaded Stone to go on a trip to El Salvador in early 1985 to prepare the first draft of a screenplay about the violence that Boyle had seen there. What

Stone saw shocked him – the consequences of the civil war, as well as the social and economic reach of Cold War policy – but he knew that there was exciting material for a film too.[11] However, following the trip, there was still no way to finance the film.[12] In March 1985, Stone's father Lou was hospitalised, and within a few days passed away. It had been Lou Stone's scepticism about his son's ability to write that had fuelled the fires of Stone's military stint in Vietnam. He later recalled that the reconciliation he had with his father was not all that he would have wished for, but his father's encouragement and entreaty acknowledged the consistent demand for great stories and great storytellers.[13] In the aftermath of his father's death, Stone's tribute was to believe in himself, in the writing, and in a renewed determination to secure a deal for *Platoon* (1986) and complete *Salvador*.

The trip to Central America cut through Stone's lingering Republican leanings. The making of *Salvador* marked the point where he felt confident enough to begin to tackle a major political subject, and it is instructive to note the amount of energy that he ultimately committed to the project. This was no lightweight dalliance with the idea of a political film that might add some gravitas to his filmmaking credentials. Stone had been changed by what he saw in El Salvador, and was committed to putting the country's story on screen. Yet, while Orion Pictures had first option on distributing *Salvador*, its CEO Mike Medavoy chose to pass, citing the film as just too violent and bloody – if anything, it was *too* committed.

Into Orion's shoes stepped small British company, Hemdale. Hemdale had bankrolled the production already and now, with limited resources available, championed its distribution. Alas, it could not prevent the picture being dropped after a brief appearance in cinemas in March 1986; however, by now the fledgling video market had taken shape in the USA, with films subject to rental and sell-through options that could give renewed life to neglected product. So it was that during 1986, *Salvador*'s appearance in these developing video charts suddenly propelled the film and its director into the spotlight of a wider audience, including influential critics such as Pauline Kael. Not everyone was entirely sure what they were looking at: was *Salvador* a contributor to the macho 1980s posturing that had been so successful for the *Rambo* series, or was it in the vein of Ford Coppola's *Apocalypse Now*? Kael herself wrote in *The New Yorker* that it might be a little of both. *Salvador* suggested a new political energy for Stone, she thought, but its ideology still seemed simplistic. 'It shapes the issues so that we're seeing the primal battle for good and evil,' she observed. '[But] what he has here is a right-wing macho vision joined to a left-leaning polemic.'[14]

Kael's endorsement was hardly ringing, but she correctly identified the way in which Stone was attempting to mix a growing 1980s penchant for big-screen masculine attitudinising *à la Rambo*, while all the while welding it to an agenda that was questioning and critical, not institutionally reinforcing and conservatively minded. Boyle (James Woods) and Doctor Rock's (Jim Belushi) emergence into the country's political and social meltdown is swift and uncompromising, punctured by on-street executions, and ultimately recall to the (actual) assassination of Archbishop Óscar Romero, gunned down while holding mass in San Salvador in 1980. Boyle spots the story and exposure to be had of American complicity in a nation's collapse, but gets personally caught in the maelstrom when he falls for Maria, a woman he then attempts to help escape from the country.

Perhaps *Salvador* lacked subtlety, but its key ingredients – leftist politics, gritty visual pyrotechnics and committed central characters – provided a film template that would define Stone's political agenda for much of his career. In other words, his interest in developing a broader political critique of recent American history had found its initial register with *Salvador*.

The film's release may have been restricted, but it did pique the interest of some who remained ignorant of the US administration's efforts to support regimes in Central America that were considered friendly to American interests, while engaging in subversion towards those governments that were perceived as hostile. Unfortunately – both for the film's backers and those who wanted the issues aired – the film came out some seven months before the Iran–Contra affair first started to percolate into the public domain in November 1986, and so missed aligning itself with some of the biggest debates of the decade that started to pile criticism on Ronald Reagan's combative foreign policy. *Salvador* tackled a foreign policy doctrine that had grown in force throughout the Cold War period, and which was seeing the results of containment finally come home to roost in regions such as Central America. Five years on, Stone's next overt political critique, *JFK* (1991), gripped its audience – critics, the public and political class alike – with an immediacy that made *Salvador*'s polemics look sluggish.

Salvador had impressed some critics with its brutal realism of the injustices inherent in that country and how it was being used as a pawn in a wider ideological battle. *JFK*, meanwhile, attempted nothing less than a re-imagining of post-war American history. Stone's emergent cinematic thesis had found a subject that was already mapping out the new rules of political controversy in cinema, even before the director unveiled his alternative vision of the nation's most visceral twentieth-century event.

Therefore, this chapter traces the evolution of Stone's political consciousness and his articulation of America's twentieth-century outlook by revisiting *JFK*, the film that placed Stone centre-stage in this assault on establishment doctrine and routine. It then considers how that critique was honed in his subsequent documentary work, in particular *Comandante* (2003) and *South of the Border* (2010). The chapter also revisits the debate about drama-as-history, as well as locating Stone's documentary work within that genre's tradition and trends over recent years, including the increasing presence of feature film aesthetics and entertainment values.

JFK

By the time *JFK* hit US cinemas in late 1991, Stone's political filmmaking was the subject of op-ed pages in major national newspapers, not simply the province of independently-minded film critics. The initial reception to the counter-mythic rendering of Kennedy's death constructed two opposing ranks almost immediately. In one corner stood the media – primarily print journalists, but supported by a few television commentators – who jumped on the 'controversies' and 'inaccuracies' as they saw it in the film with relish. In the opposing corner were the American (and later world) cinemagoing audience, who lapped up the conspiracy messages in the storyline, and who rankled the media still further – not just through their acceptance of Stone's version of events as the absolute gospel, but in their assertion that Stone was a more reliable witness than the US government.

JFK was released just five days before Christmas 1991 in the USA, in the face of vitriolic commentary from a range of mainstream publications including the *New York Times* and *Washington Post* – which had begun their critique while the film was still in production – and *Newsweek* magazine. In the pages of the *New York Times*, Tom Wicker wondered if Stone's film conspired against reason.[15] *Newsweek*'s headline, 'Twisted History' was backed up by an unattributed assertion that 'Oliver Stone's *JFK* is not just an entertainment; it's a piece of propaganda for a huge conspiracy theory of the Kennedy murder'.[16] Drawing upon District Attorney Garrison's personal account of his attempts to secure a conviction in the case, the film pieces together his inquiry into pro-Cuban activism in his home city of New Orleans in the years up to Kennedy's death, leading him to Lee Harvey Oswald by way of Clay Shaw, FBI employee, New Orleans policeman and private investigator Guy Banister, pilot David Ferrie and other assorted malcontents.[17] Inspired in the film by a meeting with an unnamed government official who tells Garrison on a trip to Washington, DC of some of the unexplained events in government circles going on before, and on the day of, the assassination, Garrison unsuccessfully pursues a conviction against alleged CIA operative Shaw (Tommy Lee Jones), revealing a major plot and unseen evidence, backed by Abraham Zapruder's 8 mm home film footage, in the long closing court scenes of the picture.

The headlines might have been less than convinced by Stone's approach projected through Garrison – with assistance from Jim Marrs' book, *Crossfire: The Plot That Killed Kennedy*[18] – but the film nevertheless found favour with a swathe of filmgoers and went on to make more than $70 million at the US box office. However, outside the USA its commercial performance was unprecedented for a three-hour movie about American political history. Total worldwide takings topped $210 million, but that still was not enough for the naysayers back home.

Ironically enough, at least part of the explanation for the public's endorsement of the film and their broadly solid support of Stone could be found in these same media outlets that were directing fire at the director's agenda. For example, in a May 1991 *Washington Post* article, George Lardner Jr – a leading critic of Stone and the film – noted that a survey conducted earlier the same month by the newspaper had found that 56 per cent of Americans thought the assassination was a conspiracy, and that only 19 per cent were prepared to accept that Oswald – the gunman identified by the Warren Commission as President Kennedy's killer – had acted alone.[19] Similarly, in a February 1992 *New York Times* report about CBS news anchor Dan Rather – a long-time supporter of the Warren Commission and another erstwhile critic of Stone's film – the paper reported the finding from a joint *Times*–CBS survey that 77 per cent of the 1,281 people polled within the previous two weeks believed that people other than Oswald had been involved in the assassination.[20] Therefore, far from throwing doubt on Stone's thesis, the initial reviews and commentaries about *JFK* were actually confirming a public scepticism that was already in place before the film had seen the light of day. All the media's aggressive rebuttal of the film was doing was showing audiences that the media themselves were in cahoots with the establishment concerning the assassination and Warren Commission findings.

That predisposition had been arrived at through a complex process: of assimilation of the Warren Report itself and then of a stream of media commentaries, books and television programmes arranged on both sides of the argument over a long period before Stone intervened. Then there were official governmental reports that some commentators seemed reluctant to pigeonhole with the film, let alone the wider public perception. For example, the House Select Committee on Assassinations summary report on 2 January 1979 did reaffirm the Warren Commission findings about Oswald. Nevertheless, on the basis of acoustic evidence presented to the committee, they went on to say:

> The committee believes, on the basis of the evidence available to it, that the President John F. Kennedy was probably assassinated as a result of a conspiracy. The committee is unable to identify the other gunman or the extent of the conspiracy.[21]

Thus, by the time of *JFK*'s release, the public had been already exposed to counter-arguments, conjecture and the spectacle of two not-wholly consistent government reports on the assassination a decade-and-a-half apart. Indeed, all the information had been circling as common cultural currency in the conspiracy debate since the shooting, resulting in a level of doubt among the public which, some political insiders mistakenly believed, had been assuaged by the passage of time. Unlike *Salvador* five years earlier, *JFK* met the public's gaze head-on with its subject and concerns, and challenged them to accept, believe in, or just generally consider the possibility that the assassination offered stark evidence of a multitude of establishment sins. In one film, Stone suddenly found himself capturing the zeitgeist of an era, and he reaped the benefits and whirlwind all at the same time.

As the fallout from the film's release began to bite, Richard Heffner's questioning during the *Open Mind* interview confirmed where Stone had taken film as political medium in the post-Reagan, supposedly newly-enlightened 1990s. Heffner suggested that part of the negative reaction from the press – the 'Lords of Print' as he called them – derived from their own fear of the increasingly persuasive power of film.

Heffner asked whether this capability to combine fact and speculation left the American public at the mercy of whoever happened to be the most skilled custodian of these powers of persuasion. Stone conceded the point, but countered that he and the research team had exercised a self-appointed responsibility to the facts and done 'the best we could'.[22] While audiences may well have been impressed by the imagery, the mix of original and shot footage, the varieties in film stock and the use made of the iconic (and by then also infamous) Zapruder footage taken in Dealey Plaza as the motorcade passed by, the picture's real attraction was – as Heffner's questions suggested – probably elsewhere. What the film offered was not a persuasive narrative that essentially closed the argument to the satisfaction of all – the press response to the film bore witness to that – but rather an organising narrative for those already concerned about the veracity of the Warren Commission findings, and who had seen fragments of so many of the visual metaphors with which Stone filled the screen. For those who had been confused about the cumulative and conflicting stories and explanations offered in the years after the Commission's report was issued, here was a scrapbook of imagery and ideas anchored around the Zapruder footage, coalesced into a thesis that postulated duplicity, if not outright institutional lying.

Just as Garrison had first brought the Zapruder film into the public domain during the trial of Clay Shaw in 1969, so Stone utilised Garrison's story in *JFK* to provide a renewed level of public scrutiny for the killing, again through Zapruder's handheld camera. The final frames of the 26.6 seconds of colour imagery exhibited during the long courtroom denouement, which show the president recoiling backwards from the fatal headshot, confirmed for many the core of Stone's thesis: that the bullet that pushed Kennedy backwards could not have come from behind him – specifically from the book depository building on the corner of Elm Street – but from slightly ahead of the motorcade and, most obviously, from the grassy knoll just a few yards to the side of where Zapruder was filming, on the west side of the plaza. For the film to establish that fact, as many asserted that it did, there had to be more than one assassin. For there to be more than one rifle shooter in Dealey Plaza that day – whether Lee Harvey Oswald was holding a gun at that moment or not in the book depository – there had to have been a conspiracy, as the 1979 Congressional report asserted.

The exploration of characters, plots and history in the film added up to this central contention. Therefore, the conclusion that many observers could not shy away from was the fact that the history of America on that fateful day in November 1963 had been recorded in official documents wrongly, misrepresented as something else, propagandised to be and mean one thing, when in fact it did add up to something entirely different. However – as the argument here is at pains to point out – all these questions and assertions, the whole debate that surrounded *JFK* the film, the mocking and measured comments, the affirmation and denunciation that Stone enjoyed and endured in equal measure, was not just because his picture was perceived, rightly or wrongly, as a rewrite of history.

The media firestorm that raged for months, and indeed years, after the release occurred because *JFK* and Stone were perceived (correctly) to have a political agenda: one that sought to expose corruption, malfeasance and pervasive control within the corridors of power. Therefore, *JFK* did not just challenge history; it challenged the robustness of the American democratic experiment, and the central tenets on which the republic had been built since 1776. Its conclusion was that the institutions of the USA had been found wanting, and that they were denying the American people redress and redemption.

Nonetheless, in defending his film and hence defending an all-encompassing counter-myth to the Warren Commission, Stone also was making a crucial transition in his career. By 1991 he was being viewed, in the words of *Time*'s reporter Richard Zoglin, as 'filmdom's most flamboyant interpreter of the 1960s': a reference to the central historical setting of *Platoon* (1986), *Born on the Fourth of July* (1989) and *The Doors* (1991).[23] These films, together with *Midnight Express* (1978), *Wall Street* (1987) and *Salvador* saw *Chicago Sun-Times* critic Roger Ebert detecting an angry director wanting to set the record straight.[24] What made *JFK* a watershed for Stone was that his effort to set that record straight had moved far beyond the critique of Hollywood's rendering of the reality of Vietnam that underscored *Platoon* and *Born on the Fourth of July*; indeed, far further than the esoteric and driven polemics on foreign policy in *Salvador* or the business ethics in *Wall Street*. In the wake of *JFK*, Stone's mission was no longer just about acting as commentator for and about the 1960s and early 1970s, broadly exposing an unwinnable and ultimately unpalatable war that was hugely unpopular by its close.

Just two years after *JFK*'s release, in 1993, the op-ed pages had become vituperative. Oliver Stone had become Hollywood's *enfant terrible*, a jumbled mass of angry, polemical anti-Americanism that was only interested in his own agenda and his own self-aggrandisement – or so his critics said. Californian House Representative Bob Dornan went so far as to describe Stone in 1992 as an 'America hating, freedom hating acerbic director', and claimed in the same Congressional debate that he was a 'man that pours acid literally into the thought processes of young people across this country'.[25]

As this line and level of scorn suggests, Oliver Stone became the media's, the establishment's and some of the public's *bête noire*, not because he was a historical filmmaker intent on portraying different or alternative perspectives of the past – others had done that before and since without this level of attack. It was because he was a 'political' filmmaker who wanted to challenge convention and kick against the system in every conceivable way. Politics that had once informed and intrigued Stone's writing now became the soul of his filmmaking, and everyone understood that fact. *JFK* was not the beginning point for this fascination – his career had been mapping that path already, long before Garrison, Zapruder, Dealey Plaza and magic bullets – what the film did do was assert the primacy of that wider political perspective.

The seriousness of Stone's political development was realised not just in his advocacy of the release of government files pertaining to the assassination, but in the fact that, whatever the reviews of the film seemed to say, the man himself was receiving a serious hearing on the subject from the very political establishment that he was critiquing. Following a special screening of the film for members of Congress in 1991, Stone met with a number of senior politicians at the beginning of March 1992. Included in these meetings was Senator David Boren, chair of the Senate Intelligence Committee, as well as House Representative Louis Stokes, who formerly had headed the self-same House Select Committee on Assassinations that had signalled an official acknowledgement of a likely conspiracy at Dealey Plaza.[26] At the meetings, plans were discussed for establishing an ARRB, with the aim of making public many of the government files relating to Kennedy's assassination that had remained closed since 1963. The ARRB started its work in 1994, and by November 1998 it had released some 33,000 previously restricted files into the National Archives. In December 1997, the ARRB released files that supported one of Stone's key contentions in the film: that by October 1963, President Kennedy had initiated a drawdown of US military advisors in Vietnam, with the clear implication that had he remained in office, the military build-up in the mid-1960s would not have taken place.[27] After the closure of the ARRB, the accumulation of relevant records by the National Archives and Records Administration continued, building to a total of some five million pages of material.[28]

While many files were withheld and some of the released files had sections redacted, the result seemed a remarkable achievement for a filmmaker – one whose career at that point, while on the up-and-up, was not long-standing or especially revered. In so doing, Stone was absorbing his own art and acting on the advice given to Garrison by 'X' in the pivotal moment of *JFK*, when Donald Sutherland's character tells the district attorney that he must continue with his investigation and 'stir the shitstorm', in the hope of creating a critical mass that will force the truth into the open.

That storm abated as the years went on, but a resurgence seems likely by 2017 – the date set by the ARRB for the declassification and release of *all* the remaining documents in the National Archives. Yet one should be reminded that the legislation underpinning the ARRB left open the possibility that the then president could certify documents for a further period of restriction. Tentative closure maybe but, like Stone's movie, the truth still threatened to remain frustratingly beyond the public's grasp.

However, just as an aspiring politician's career is reinforced by electoral victory in campaign after campaign, so a filmmaker's influence in Hollywood is consolidated by box office success. *JFK* passed so far beyond mere commercial film success, and beyond the usual time-constrained spotlight for a film, that it was easy to forget that its maker did not benefit from any such consolidation. The inexorable rise that critical attention had set in train with *Salvador* was consolidated with a series of commercial, often well-received successes which had made Stone the leading filmmaker of the age by 1992. After this, he was buffeted by highly publicised public and private controversies: put simply, the films fared less well. *Heaven and Earth* (1993) and *Nixon* (1995) kept him on track with films that returned once again to his favourite haunts: namely Vietnam, politics and the 1960s more generally. While both aesthetically and ideologically these films had things to commend them, commercially they were major disappointments.

Added to this was the swirl of media criticism directed at the film sandwiched between these two pictures which, while faring much better at the box office, at one point threatened to be even more controversial than *JFK*. Starring Woody Harrelson and Juliette Lewis, *Natural Born Killers* (1994) was a violent, MTV-age, modern-day Bonnie and Clyde-type road movie that initially looked like it would combine the talents of Stone and the original writer and newly-established Hollywood wunderkind, Quentin Tarantino. Stone brought a whole new generation of young film-watchers into his orbit with the picture, attracted by what they perceived to be *Natural Born Killers*' wildly nihilistic pretensions; but it also quickly made him *persona non grata* in some Hollywood circles and beyond. In *Variety*, Todd McCarthy observed that the film's style 'may be akin to a shotgun blast, but it still manages to hit the bull's eye'.[29] However, the arguments with Richard Heffner at CARA about the rating for the film, and the discomfort that the subject matter personally caused to Warner Bros.' chair Bob Daly, left their marks on Stone.[30] It was a film that Hollywood found hard to accept, even with its commercial success.[31]

Meanwhile, Tarantino accepted full payment for an original screenplay that was typically uncompromising and resonant of his debut cult hit, *Reservoir Dogs* (1992) from two years before, as well as his much-touted script for what became Tony Scott's *True Romance* (1993). With the critical wind blowing in his direction, Tarantino's profile allowed him to get away with stating to Stone and everyone else who cared to listen that he disapproved of the rewrite of *his* script for Stone's movie.[32] Together with the turmoil in his personal life, which resulted in the collapse of his marriage to Elizabeth Stone in 1993, the spat with Tarantino and the reaction to *Natural Born Killers* provided reams of commentary in the media, but not all of it of the kind that Stone wished for, and he was catapulted into a period of depression and reassessment.

Natural Born Killers had been Stone's idea of a satirical comment on 'the replacement of values with media and its love of violence',[33] prompted in part by media fixation on the O. J. Simpson arrest and trials for the murder of his ex-wife, Nicole Brown Simpson and Ronald Goldman that were going on in the same period. It was the end of a first-stage political development in Stone's cinema that had been anchored by *JFK*. How those sociopolitical themes played out, and what they meant for the renewal of his ideological consciousness from here on in, are worthy of reflection at this juncture.

Politics as cultural authority

Arguably, politics has been the worst of all pursuits for filmmakers throughout Hollywood's history. The triumphant and insightful, not to say commercially successful, films in this genre often are perceived to be few and far between. For every *Mr. Smith Goes to Washington* (1939) there is a *State of the Union* (1948); for every *The Manchurian Candidate* (1962), a *Seven Days in May* (1964); and for every *JFK* there is a *Nixon*. However, each of these combinations are instructive: the first pair were directed by Frank Capra, the second by John Frankenheimer, and the third by Stone. Yet there are arguments to support not only the rehabilitation, but the advancement, of the second film in each couplet above their more famous and acclaimed sibling. Capra's *State of the Union* gave a rare post-war insight into the machinations of politics in the late 1940s and the 'Beltway',[34] insider mentality that had long taken a hold of Washington. Frankenheimer's *Seven Days in May* was an all-too-realistic appraisal of the ways in which a *coup d'état* emanating out of the military could be executed in the USA; while Stone's was an altogether more complex political biopic that squared off the megalomania with the masterly politician in Richard Nixon.

What does such a contrast prove, and why make the comparison? Because seemingly, it is iconography, symbolism, controversy and repetition that wins the day when it comes to remembering significant political pictures: a set of cinematic traits that are more prominent than in any other generic category of filmmaking. While good, *State of the Union* had nothing of Capra's flare for political imagery that showcased *Mr. Smith* nine years earlier in 1939; John Frankenheimer's *Seven Days in May* lacked the direct political controversy and deep-seated fears of infiltration that his *Manchurian Candidate* bought to the table in 1962, as well as having nothing like its controversial 'shelving' in the light of the Kennedy assassination a year after release; and *Nixon* had none of the historical attack and incendiary claims to which *JFK* could lay claim. The result has been that each lesser-regarded work, in the eyes of critics and fans at least, became the poorer relation. Arguably, the latter films were just not as entertaining, vibrant or pulsatingly exciting at times as their better-known companions. Nonetheless, the second three are just as important in many ways – if not even greater landmark presentations than their famous counterparts – and this says a great deal about the role of politics, and the state of political filmmaking in Hollywood, in Stone's time and earlier.

In order to be truly successful, iconic political movies somehow must embody a contest for 'cultural authority', to use Luc Herman's phrase.[35] Herman's comment referred back to *JFK* and the battle that ensued between Stone's version of events and the 'official' account that stuck to long-established precepts. However, when he also states that Stone 'succeeded in having his product of popular culture taken seriously as a vehicle of truth,' he intimates that for which many, if not all, political movies strive.[36] Yes, they are entertainment, they should have driving and credible narratives, and they should seek to encourage great performances from their players – but more than any other types of film, they also should bridge the distance between popular reconstruction and ideological examination. Political films of whatever hue should *want* to be taken seriously, the argument suggests: they should *want* to endorse, contest and unpick the political establishment in all its forms. If any *modus operandi* ought to fit the cinema of Oliver Stone, then surely this was it.

In their survey of American political films, Terry Christensen and Peter Haas note a slow evolution in Hollywood's handling of political representation.[37] While pre-war Hollywood trumpeted the Capraesque theme of heroes fighting the system with a little help from the 'people', post-Second World War depictions acknowledged ever-growing limitations on successful individual action: a binary separation that Capra's *Mr. Smith* and *State of the Union* represent very nicely.

The power of the system to corrupt individuals evoked in *All the King's Men* (Robert Rossen, 1949) and *Advise and Consent* (Otto Preminger, 1962) then took a much darker turn in several New Hollywood-era productions, including *The Candidate* (Michael Ritchie, 1972), *Executive Action* (David Miller, 1973), *The Parallax View* (Alan J. Pakula, 1974), *Three Days of the Condor* (Sydney Pollack, 1975) and *All the President's Men* (Alan J. Pakula, 1976). These films reflected profound changes in politics during the decade of their making, but they also mirrored alterations going on in the film industry, including the abolition of the Production Code in 1968, and the move towards – for a while at least – an increasing focus on auteurist directorial power in American cinema. Ultimately the films provided evidence of an increasing cinematic engagement with questions of unchecked institutional authority; although, as Richard Maltby notes, more pragmatic and commercial motives also were in evidence. In *The Candidate*, for example, Maltby suggests that the film's effectiveness as a political critique was challenged by the producers' self-conscious use of Robert Redford's star persona as Bill McKay in the lead role.[38] Michael Ritchie's film exposed the growing media infiltration of politics resulting in a greater emphasis on personality and style in electoral campaigns, and yet the film unabashedly used its star's own charismatic power to advance both the celebrity culture and personal appeal that supposedly it was criticising.

While *Executive Action* and in particular *The Parallax View* were examples of Hollywood's willingness to grapple with the spectre of dark and unyielding institutional corruption, neither film performed well at the box office. Indeed, *Executive Action* generated such negative press coverage because of its suggestion of a business and political cabal involved in the Kennedy assassination that it was quickly withdrawn from exhibition. In other words, 'cultural authority' in these films waxed and waned according to commercial and critical reaction. Only one film during the decade truly reinforced Herman's theory, transforming itself from commercial success into a mainstream discourse about the fate of American politics. That film was Alan J. Pakula's follow-up to *The Parallax View*: his adaptation of Bob Woodward and Carl Bernstein's *All the President's Men* (1974).

All the President's Men took more than $70 million at the American box office on release, and subsequently realised more than $30 million in video and DVD rental and sales. The film's success could be attributed to a number of factors, not least the changing dimensions of the rating system in the post-Production Code era. CARA initially gave the film an 'R' because of some sporadic profanity in the dialogue, only for Richard Heffner as chair of CARA to argue for the film's wider social significance, and successfully petition the industry's in-house appeals board that an exception should be made for it. Heffner's case was accepted and the film was re-rated and released as a 'PG', thus allowing it access to a far greater audience.[39]

CARA set a marker with Pakula's Watergate story that stretched the cultural and political significance of films about American public and institutional life. Common factors such as loyalty, betrayal, conspiracy and malfeasance, allied to a strong star presence and fashioned by real events, ensured that *All the President's Men* would remain iconic and vital as a political film long after its time, and others of the time clung to its coat-tails. *Three Days of the Condor*, *The Parallax View* and especially Francis Ford Coppola's prescient *The Conversation* (1974) continued to garner decent reviews and attract new audiences as video release, backed up by DVD and then Blu-ray, ensured a recurring presence for these films among fans and critics, that solidified them as a coterie of so-called conspiracy or 'paranoia' movies during the decade.[40]

These films and their filmmakers undoubtedly had a profound influence on the cinematic as well as ideological leanings of Stone as he entered the industry at the end of the 1970s. Together with a raft of other movies in different genres, Hollywood's post-studio-era pretensions broke the shackles of rigid control and consensus. It was ironic, then, that as a new decade dawned, the social and political conventions that Hollywood was absorbing and replicating shifted back towards their Production Code-era moorings. This trend found prominent expression in a distinctly conservative tranche of military and war films including *First Blood* (Ted Kotcheff, 1982), *Red Dawn* (John Milius, 1984) and *Top Gun* (Tony Scott, 1986), which were a long way removed from the New Hollywood-era selection above. Stone was one of several niche directors who sought to strike a different tone and maintain some of the agendas set by Pakula and Coppola a decade earlier. Alongside him, Warren Beatty, Constantin Costa-Gavras and Mike Nichols all made important contributions to Hollywood's more daring liberal wing, with movies such as *Reds* (1981), *Missing* (1982) and *Silkwood* (1983). The Russian Revolution, South American politics and corporate and political cover-ups seemed unlikely subjects for critical let alone commercial successes during the decade, but each of the directors bucked the ideological trend going on around them with critical appreciation and financial returns.

Clearly, Ronald Reagan's political rise and presidential reshaping of America's relations with the world was crucial in all this. Stone's emerging filmography in the 1980s owed much to the former actor, union leader and California governor's realignment of conservative politics during these years. *Salvador* pointed to a much longer, in-bred Cold War philosophy that US ambassador Thomas Kelly (Michael Murphy) in the picture inhabits. However, it also pointedly cited Reagan's administration as being on an ideological crusade to rid the region of all of America's perceived enemies. Stone's personal reference point for these on-screen political observations became the destruction of Camelot and the death of John F. Kennedy: the point at which, as he saw it, institutional power first eclipsed the presidential embodiment of the American spirit. While Stone drew directly on that transition as a source of motivation in films such as *Platoon* and *JFK*, several of his other 1980s productions in the wake of *Salvador* – including *Wall Street* and *Talk Radio* (1988) – were further barely disguised critiques of the Reagan era, marking the point at which the presidential motif had been fully absorbed into the institutional and corporate latticework around it.

Paradoxically, Stone's own Republican political inheritance from his father was being transformed by the same forces that were taking the mainstream Republican Party to the political Right. Richard Nixon's silent majority had been repulsed by the mayhem they witnessed on American university campuses; overwhelmed, as they saw it, by counterculture 'love-ins' and anti-Vietnam protests. Thus it was only fitting that the coming of age of a re-energised Republican Party, embodied in Reagan's make-believe world of politics-as-presentation, should be met by the coming of age of a cultural critic whose views had been forged in the Vietnamese jungle, fighting the supposed threat that exercised Reagan and his supporters above all else.

In tackling the fallout from this era, Stone used some fairly typical cinematic conventions to broach his subject matter, not dissimilar to those appropriated by Hollywood's great political director of the 1930s, Frank Capra. The most striking use of this Hollywood convention is in the clean-cut, Capraesque motif that Stone employs in *JFK*. The director himself acknowledged the connection while defending his on-screen construction of New Orleans District Attorney, Jim Garrison.[41] Aspects of Garrison's life, including a divorce and second marriage and his ambivalent media profile in New Orleans, are omitted from the movie. Stone argued that this was no more than dramatic licence; but the use of Kevin Costner in the Garrison role clearly allowed Stone to create a particularly attractive hero to 'guide and anchor the audience' as he put it, unencumbered by personal flaws or failings.[42]

In popular hits of the time such as *Bull Durham* (Ron Shelton, 1988) and *Field of Dreams* (Phil Alden Robinson, 1989), America's mythic relationship with baseball acted as a testament to Costner's wholesome appeal as an actor, while his portrayal of Soviet agent Yuri in Roger Donaldson's *No Way Out* (1987), and Elliott Ness in Brian De Palma's interpretation of *The Untouchables* (1987), attracted critics to the actor's brooding presence and moral circumference as a leading man. When *Dances with Wolves* was released in November 1990, Costner, in his first directorial role as well as playing the lead, Lieutenant John Dunbar, projected a classic American western hero that proved to be gold dust at the box office and a huge critical success. The film took seven Oscars, including those for Best Picture and Best Director. Stone could scarcely have picked a safer pair of hands to lead Americans through the maze of *JFK*.

Costner's portrayal of Garrison was the lynchpin of the film, yet then and subsequently it has been a performance not always universally appreciated. Perhaps for all that happened next in Costner's Hollywood career, maybe because its 'lone hero' poise was too conventional, possibly because Garrison's book *On the Trail of the Assassins*, far from being an insider's account, slowly became part of the literary conspiracists' sideshow arsenal, the performance was never recognised as it might have been. Whatever the reasons, the role of Garrison became part of myriad negative aspects of Stone's *JFK* experience. In addition, the poor returns for *Heaven and Earth* and the furore that surrounded *Natural Born Killers* precipitated a revision of his reputation among critics and some fans, suddenly wary of a filmmaker who previously and seamlessly had combined a commercial 'Midas touch' with an instinctive feel for the zeitgeist. The reversals did not stop there. When in 1995 Stone broached the subject of Richard Nixon for a biopic, the commercial and critical backlash set the film up for failure almost before it had been completed – yet for him and a few other voices, it remains arguably his best film in many ways.

In contrast to Pakula's *All the President's Men*, Stone's much more complex rendering of Nixon – and his decision to focus on the president as protagonist, rather than just using him as a symbolic or occasionally iconic release valve – made it more difficult to apply a Capraesque motif *à la JFK*. Garrison, and previous leading characters such as Ron Kovic and Le Ly Hayslip, provided focal points of reference and were adaptable to being individuals in extraordinary situations coping with pressures and dilemmas into which the audience could be drawn.

In the three hours and twelve minutes of *Nixon* (1995), Stone opted to have all the film's politics, visions, history and reputation bundled up in the controversial (not to say, antagonistic) life of

Richard Milhous Nixon, persuasively played by Anthony Hopkins. The film delves into the president's relationship with his mother, Hannah (Mary Steenburgen) and his wife Pat (Joan Allen), as well as his connections to those in pursuit of particular agendas during the Kennedy era; extending to his oversight, while vice-president, of CIA activities in Cuba and the possibility that a CIA operation against the Cubans somehow ultimately had been turned upon Kennedy. Inevitably, Nixon's political ambitions suffuse all this. Structured around his recollections over the course of one evening while listening to a crucial section of the notorious taped conversations in the White House, *Nixon* conveys tragic elements throughout that are both gripping and depleting. 'There's something almost majestic about the process,' wrote Roger Ebert. 'As Nixon goes down in this film, there is no gloating, but a watery sigh, as of a great ship sinking.'[43] Despite more positive reactions like this, the film failed to connect with American audiences, taking only $13.5 million at the US box office against a budget of $50 million, making it the biggest single commercial failure in Stone's career.

With hindsight, the film was a cinematic tour de force – thanks once again to the mastery of director of photography, Robert Richardson – even if perhaps its story's entertainment quotient was less easily judged compared to its predecessors. Indeed, Gavin Smith in *Sight & Sound* pointed to *Nixon* at the time as being Stone's 'most introspective, claustrophobic film'.[44] Nevertheless, thanks to Richardson's cinematic reference points, *Nixon* brilliantly namechecked the visionary genius of Orson Welles, paying homage along the way to *Citizen Kane* (1942) in a comparison of two men's rise and fall in each film that, Phillip Gianos notes, is 'the stuff of classical tragedy'.[45] Could the film have used a more attractive, Capraesque figure as inquisitor and narrator? White House Counsel, John Dean maybe, or First Lady, Pat Nixon? Perhaps, as the film all too readily conveys, it was just not easy to feel empathy, let alone love for the man, despite the feel of a Greek tragedy throughout. *JFK*'s cultural authority had rested on Costner's performance to reinforce a widespread belief among Americans that their government had not been entirely candid with them. Even if the film did not entirely succeed in correcting injustice, it was perceived by many Americans to be aspiring to a wider and nobler truth.

With *Nixon*, there was no wrong to be fixed – or at least there was no easy target. As José Arroyo commented in his review on release: '[In Stone's] other films, the leading characters are just vehicles to examine an issue. In Nixon they *are* the issue.'[46] The Watergate saga from break-in to resignation had been played out on national television, and its effects on the country's psyche were nothing short of cataclysmic. Stone's portrayal of political figures fixated on power called for self-examination from a population that already had feasted on the first Gulf War and the dissolution of the Soviet Union, and who, a full year before the film's release, had signed up to Newt Gingrich's 'Contract with America' in such numbers that the mid-term elections had delivered both Houses of Congress to the Republicans for the first time since 1955. Notwithstanding Democratic President Bill Clinton, the country's politics were sliding to the Right. Hollywood had caught the emerging mood already in films such as the ostensibly nostalgic, but at times perceptibly reactionary, *Forrest Gump* (Robert Zemeckis, 1994). Here was a picture that in a seemingly unintended way, parodied history – and perhaps itself – in its unashamedly pro-American recasting of the Vietnam era.

Gump (Tom Hanks), much like Rambo before him, collapses the war into a one-man rescue mission designed to readjust audiences' perceptions of the conflict and the times. *JFK* had located the moment at which audiences wanted a reaffirmation of American values predicated on the unveiling of new facts, unknown truths and redemptive assertions about America's ability to renew itself. *Forrest Gump* was Hollywood's answer. In the light of that film's overwhelming success, Stone could not easily locate these similar marks with *Nixon*, or with an audience that was losing interest in any kind of national self-examination – a trend confirmed in the success of films such as *Independence Day* (Roland Emmerich, 1996), *Air Force One* (Wolfgang Petersen, 1997) and *Saving Private Ryan* (Stephen Spielberg, 1998), as well as reimaginings of the presidency in *Dave* (Ivan Reitman, 1993) and *The American President* (Rob Reiner, 1995). *Nixon* was praised, even lauded, for its ability to spot the cinematic reference points in history and politics itself during the twentieth century: the looped cultural narration of America's past seen through fragments of iconic imagery and self-conscious recall, to the construction of history paraded in the stopping and starting of the tapes throughout the picture, from which Nixon tries to construct a new narrative contrary to the evidence at hand.[47] All this tempted audiences with far more cerebral fare than other historical movies of the time. Stone took stock, and his answer was to move his politics into a different generic field: documentary.

Documentary as politics

Following the release of *Any Given Sunday*, which premiered in the closing days of 1999, Stone took his first significant break from filmmaking since the production of *Salvador* in 1986. However, the four-year gap that separated *Any Given Sunday* from his next mainstream feature, *Alexander* in November 2004, proved to be less of a break than a redirection of effort. Stone proceeded to produce three documentaries. Two of these, *Comandante* (2003) and *Looking for Fidel* (2004), concerned the Cuban revolutionary leader Fidel Castro, while the third, *Persona Non Grata* (2003), provided an account of the Arab–Israeli conflict.

In *Comandante* (2003), Stone offered a mainly sympathetic view of Cuba's revolutionary leader, in answer to his long-standing perception that Castro had been at best misrepresented, and at worst demonised by the US media. The documentary premiered at the Sundance Film Festival in January 2003, and was scheduled for transmission by HBO in May of the same year. However, in the time in-between, a number of events combined to put Stone's view of Castro into sharper, but alas more isolated, relief. The incidents further induced HBO to take the very unusual step of stopping the transmission of the film, and making an editorial intervention that required Stone to return to Cuba to gather more materials.[48]

All the while, diplomatic tensions between the USA and Cuba worsened throughout spring 2003. A round-up of twenty dissidents on 18 March included several independent reporters who had attended a journalism workshop the previous week at the home of James Cason, the senior US diplomat in Havana.[49] Two plane hijackings on 19 March and 1 April saw Cuban airliners diverted from Cuba to Key West in Florida; while on 12 April 2003, three hijackers who had attempted to take a Cuban ferry to Florida were executed by firing squad. The political temperature in the USA was high in any case following the commencement of military action against Iraq on 20 March 2003, and HBO and parent company Time Warner were anything but oblivious to the negative publicity that a sympathetic reappraisal of Castro might have elicited at this time.

Given these circumstances, it would be easy to see *Comandante* as an ideologically charged piece of hagiography, providing the kind of platform for a left-wing, firebrand revolutionary that would automatically prove inflammatory in America in early 2003. In truth, the tone and the pacing of the film is reflective rather than proselytising. Stone's questioning is respectful, and the response from Castro for the most part is almost meditative – even when the conversation touches on sensitive issues such as Vietnam and the Cuban missile crisis. The documentary, which was filmed in Havana over three days in February 2002, focuses on the recollections of the then seventy-five-year-old president, more than it attempts wholesale historical revisionism. Castro's early political activism is given an airing, before the focus turns to the successful revolutionary war against Cuban President Fulgencio Batista, which concluded in 1959. Archive footage of the removal of a large Texaco sign bears witness to the far-reaching nationalisation of American corporations that took place, and which prompted such a hostile reaction after Castro seized power. The man himself offers reflections on the drug problems in contemporary society and on the environmental challenges facing humanity: a cocktail of subjects that might not have been out of place in a Larry King interview.

Castro's objection to the hypothetical question posed by Stone about locating a McDonald's restaurant in Havana is expressed in terms that defend cultural variety rather than making a case for political ideology. The tell-tale glimpse of a Nike logo on Castro's shoe is not commented on, but seems to underscore some kind of minor movement in economic and commercial terms since that Texaco sign had been pulled down at the dawn of the revolution all those years before.

Stone reminds his audience about the interventionist approach adopted by the Castro regime in the mid-1970s, when it became heavily involved in the civil war in Angola. However, the mood is counterbalanced with a visit to Castro's cinema room, where the president recalls an admiration for several actors including Sophia Loren and Gérard Depardieu. As they drive to the Latin American School of Medicine in Havana, Stone invites Castro to speculate a little on the Kennedy assassination. Castro obliges, but again in understated terms. He ponders the difficulties of making repeated shots using a telescopic sight, and comments that for this reason he never believed the 'lone gunman' theory. All of these scenes grab attention and yet remain rather independent of each other, trapped within their own anecdotal vignette, lacking recall to any significant wider agenda.

In the latter portion of the film, Stone moves Castro towards discussing the Bay of Pigs, as well as the missile crisis and alleged involvement of Cuban military advisors in Vietnam. Castro recalls meeting Nixon in 1959, arguing that this led the then vice-president to recommend an expedition to President Eisenhower that would put an end to the Cuban revolution: the precursor to the Bay of Pigs invasion of April 1961, just three months after Kennedy's arrival in the White House. Castro makes clear that both knowledge of the preparations for the Bay of Pigs that were taking place under CIA guidance in Guatemala, as well as the US embargoes on sugar and oil, drove Cuba towards the Soviet Union, and indicates that Soviet Premier Nikita Khrushchev gave his personal support. Cuba was allowed to purchase armaments, and in due course Khrushchev authorised the installation of nuclear weapons on the island.

It is at this point that one senses a distinct lack of self-knowledge and/or candour for the first time in Castro's responses to Stone's questions. The treatment of US prisoners of war in Hanoi is brought up, and Stone recalls that he had read accounts from about two dozen veterans who had recorded being beaten by Cuban military advisors. Clearly agitated, Castro vehemently denies any Cuban involvement in torture. As Stone moves on to talk about the island's slow progress in dealing with the legality of homosexuality and discrimination more widely, one senses that the good will available to him is drying up.

Despite these pointed remarks, the film was criticised by some for giving Castro an easy ride. In reviewing *Comandante* for the BBC, Jamie Russell suggested that Stone's interviewing technique was insufficiently challenging and thought he was 'painfully embarrassed by the necessity of asking tough questions.'[50] Russell continued:

> Had Stone kept a lid on his hero-worship *Comandante* might have become the definitive warts 'n' all portrait of this great dictator. Instead, *he sacrifices objectivity and candour in favour of kicking back and shooting the breeze with Fidel.* (emphasis in original)

Accepting some of the criticism, Stone acknowledged in the *New York Times* that perhaps the questioning in *Comandante* had not been resolute enough: 'Perhaps I was pandering, perhaps I was softballing him with the questions, as some people say.'[51] In truth, Russell's critique only followed HBO's editorial thinking; the message was that it was not really acceptable to give someone like Castro a sympathetic hearing, and Stone thought the objections reeked of ideological conservatism, even if he himself could have been a tougher inquisitor.

Nevertheless, with whatever goodwill remained, and with renewed enthusiasm from HBO following *Comandante*'s cancellation, Stone returned to Cuba in May 2003 to shoot a more focused documentary about the Castro regime's handling of dissidents. In *Looking for Fidel* (2004), the opening credits of the film make reference both to the arrests of more than seventy-five dissidents in March and April 2003, and to the execution of the three hijackers. In one early sequence, Stone questions Castro about the executions, commenting that he understood that there had been a seven-day trial, and that all three hijackers had been shot on the eighth day. He then adds: 'In the norms of international justice, it's very rare to shoot somebody after a trial so quickly without appeal.' Castro concedes the point, but defends the action in terms of it being virtually a situation of war. Stone pursues the issue, referencing how US justice offers an extended appeals process, with family access possible. Castro counters by asking Stone about the number of family visits that have been made to the nearly 800 prisoners in the 'special prison' at Guantanamo Bay naval base. These initial exchanges give a fair indication of the tone of the rest of the film.

Stone pushes Castro on a number of specific points, and Castro in turn refutes Stone's suggestions, leading the *New York Times* to opine that more often than not the Cuban leader seemed angry during the film. Castro refutes Stone's suggestion that he has been in power for forty-three years, claiming that it is the people who are in power; he rejects use of the word *caudillo* (leader), but accepts that he is a 'type of spiritual leader ... a kind of moral chief'. Again, Stone nudges Castro on his continuing prominent position within the government, asking if there is not someone he can train and trust. Castro tacks back and forth, claiming that he has been training people for fifty years, and that he does not want to give George W. Bush the pleasure of seeing him go. The interview then picks up on one of the key events that supposedly triggered the earlier film's cancellation: the arrest of dissidents including the journalists who had visited Cason. The president claims that all of these were in receipt of funds from the US government and were engaged in counter-revolutionary activities. In repeated exchanges, Stone presses Castro on the imprisonment of prisoners of conscience in Cuba, and on the restrictions to free media access imposed on dissident representatives. Finally, he closes the film with some outdoor footage of Havana and Castro, in more of the reflective mood that infused the bulk of *Comandante*. Castro observes that everything passes, even the empire of the USA. As to whether a deal might be made with the USA, Castro talks about the difficulty of trusting the USA to keep its word. He concludes that: 'The only thing the US accepts is that you sell out.' *Looking for Fidel* certainly produced a more rounded appraisal of Castro, although one that happened by accident or insistence – HBO's somewhat confused position on the subject – rather than design.

Castro finally stood down as president on 24 February 2008, confirming that he was in poor health; however, following some rehabilitation, Castro received Stone at his home in Cuba for a third set of filmed interviews in 2009. Released as *Castro in Winter* (2012), once again the dominant tone is reflective, with the retired leader talking about his life as well as current affairs. This Cuban trilogy was driven by something personal in Stone as much as it was a deliberately conceived political triptych – but what it did signal was a shift in style, agenda and outlook.

In 2010, Stone returned to Latin America with *South of the Border*, a documentary about Venezuelan president Hugo Chávez, who died in March 2013. Stone's film stands as testament to the undoubted shifts in the political and economic prospects for the continent, projected forward beyond the grim reality that

Uruguayan journalist and writer Eduardo Galeano first surveyed in *The Open Veins of Latin America*, originally published in 1971. In the closing lines of an addendum in 1976, Galeano wrote: 'In these lands we are not experiencing the primitive infancy of capitalism but its vicious senility.'[52] That prognosis was some way off. At this point several of South America's leading states including Argentina, Bolivia, Chile, Paraguay and Uruguay were in the grip of a right-wing military repression aided and abetted by a CIA-funded programme known as Operation Condor.[53] However, as Edward Williamson has described, urbanisation and the emergence of a new literary awareness in the 1980s would progressively undermine the hallmark patriarchal power structures of the indigenous and colonial societies.[54]

Stone's documentary reflected the momentous political changes that the continent had experienced since the 1970s. While *South of the Border*'s appraisal initially focused on Chávez, it adopted something of a road movie structure which then solicited opinions on both Chávez and US foreign policy more generally, as well as the influence of the International Monetary Fund (IMF), from seven regional heads of state, including Evo Morales (Bolivia), Luiz Lula da Silva (Brazil), Cristina Kirchner (Argentina), Fernando Lugo (Paraguay), Rafael Correa (Ecuador), and Raúl Castro (Cuba), as well as former Argentinean president Néstor Kirchner. The introductory section of the film records Chávez's rise to power in 1998 and the US-supported military coup in April 2002 that almost toppled his regime. In a remarkable editorial published on 13 April 2002, the *New York Times* described Chávez as a 'ruinous demagogue', and hailed the transfer of power to a 'respected business leader', Pedro Carmona.[55] Three days later the same paper, having absorbed the news that a wave of popular unrest had returned Chávez to power (and perhaps also remembering that it was not, despite appearances, the mouthpiece of the American administration), recanted in these terms:

> In his three years in office, Mr. Chávez has been such a divisive and demagogic leader that his forced departure last week drew applause at home and in Washington. That reaction, which we shared, overlooked the undemocratic manner in which he was removed. Forcibly unseating a democratically elected leader, no matter how badly he has performed, is never something to cheer.[56]

Paul Krugman, Professor of Economic and International Affairs at Princeton University, writing in the *Times* on the same day, lamented the fact that the US administration had appeared content to voice no opposition to the removal of a democratically elected leader.[57] The brief failure of perspective at the *New York Times* highlighted exactly what Stone was airing in *Comandante* and *South of the Border*: the tendency in the mainstream US media to side with the administration and see geopolitical issues solely through the lens of US political and economic interests. The latter film *did* air the role of the local media in Venezuela in fomenting opposition to Chávez before the coup. However, their interpretation of events was the one that the US media picked up and promulgated, only underlining Stone's point still further.

The reception of *South of the Border* in the US mainstream media, especially the *New York Times*, highlighted continuing animosities which harked back to the exchanges between the director and paper over the veracity of *JFK*. However, the nature of the response called attention to Stone's wider role as dramatist and political agitator, and how that role was expanding to encompass documentary film. Stephen Holden noted in the *New York Times* that Stone's 'paranoid tendencies', so much in evidence in *JFK*, were more contained in this 'provocative, if shallow, exaltation of Latin American socialism'. He concluded that the film was 'a valuable, if naïvely idealistic, introductory tutorial on South America's leftward political drift', grudgingly commending Stone's didactic and pedagogic approach.[58] However, writing in the same paper one day later, Larry Rohter offered a pointedly dismissive assessment:

> 'South of the Border' is meant to be a documentary, and therefore to be held to different standards. But it is plagued by the same issues of accuracy that critics have raised about his movies, dating back to 'JFK'.[59]

Stone's response was unequivocal:

> We are dealing with a big picture, and we don't stop to go into a lot of the criticism and details of each country. It's a 101 introduction to a situation in South America that most Americans and Europeans don't know about because of years and years of blighted journalism. I think there has been so much unbalance that we are definitely a counter to that.[60]

Rohter's criticism recalled questions about historical drama and dramatic history in the vein of Robert Brent Toplin's work on Stone's feature presentations.[61] As part of a discussion with historians including Toplin and Robert Rosenstone, Stone had attended a 1997 meeting of the American Historical Association in New York to talk ostensibly about *Nixon* (1995). In a published volume emerging from the gathering, a now-familiar debate was laid out about our understanding of written history, its representation on screen, and the degree of latitude that a filmmaker might reasonably claim in the dramatisation of historical events. In the closing pages, Stone observed that there was not yet a 'marketplace of history' for the Kennedy era, and that *JFK* was a contribution towards a better understanding of what really happened.[62] He also refuted the claim that he was a 'cinematic historian'. He was a dramatist, he insisted, accepting that this meant combining fact and fiction and that, as a consequence, details would be fudged from time to time.

Stone's argument rested on the distinction between illusion and deception. In *JFK*, Costner's star persona gave Garrison a particular individual hue that a different actor might not have achieved. Should we see that as a deception, or as part of the cinematic illusion, he asked. Consequently, should we be suspicious of the entire edifice that a filmmaker like himself can construct on film? As Stone explained in his response to the American Historical Association papers, his approach had always been to use protagonists as a guide to the events being examined. The intention was to 'create an empathetic (if not sympathetic) central character who dominates the foreground and takes us into the background of his or her time'.[63] Rosenstone had been a critic of Stone's stance, but nonetheless argued that for a film to be historical, it must not indulge in 'capricious invention' or ignore findings or assertions that are already known. Instead, it must situate itself 'within the ongoing debate about the meaning of the past' – just as Stone surmised.[64]

While it may seem an obvious point, much the same can be said about documentary cinema, although the history of the genre is populated with examples, such as Leni Riefenstahl and Frank Capra, whose triumph – emerging out of feature film routines, but ultimately making their name with documentary construction – was as much about aesthetics as truth and reality. With his treatments of Castro and Chávez, Stone stripped down his filmmaking to its constituent element: the meaning of the past. Both films followed protagonists around who were reconsidering the world – their world – of contemporary politics. In doing so, Stone was engaging in a very deliberate piece of political advocacy that called the mainstream media to account. In fact, his approach might be called a provocation: a challenge to the kind of establishment-oriented, lazy journalism to which he felt he had been subjected as far back as he could remember.[65]

Stone wrote *South of the Border* with the campaigner, writer and activist Tariq Ali, and their response to criticism of the film's historicism was to call upon a variation of John Stuart Mill's *On Liberty* (1859).[66] Implicitly framing Mill's 'marketplace of ideas' contention within the broader discussion of Chávez, they both assumed the US media to be as guilty of censorship as the US government was in covering up or burying news that it did not want the public to or engage with or hear. Stone's view was that the US government, aided and abetted by the media, was 'ethnocentric', and that reporting amounted to 'an unofficial censorship of the mind arising from the way that our news is presented to us'.[67] Reflecting on the wider implications of this trend in early 2010, Stone went even further:

> [The US is] not really in a people's democracy where the majority control policy. Obama was elected by the people, yet he still has finished up doing what the joint chiefs and the military complex want. Kennedy was the last president to really challenge the system and say this is insanity, and he was killed. We are really in a gridlock like the Soviet Union was, and we can't get out of it. The only possible end was indicated in the 2008 financial crisis – that we would go broke and could not afford to continue with the rigid control of the world that we are seeking.[68]

In the further pursuit of media accountability, Stone later joined a long list of petitioners, including Noam Chomsky and Michael Moore, in May 2013 asking Margaret Sullivan, the public editor at the *New York Times*, to investigate what they saw as disparities in the paper's coverage of Venezuela and Honduras.[69] The petition argued that the reporting of the Hugo Chávez regime in Venezuela had been largely negative, while the reporting on Honduran President Roberto Micheletti and his successor Porfirio Lobo Sosa had been much more neutral. The petition concluded that:

> We urge you to examine this disparity in coverage and language use, particularly as it may appear to your readers to track all too closely the US government's positions regarding the Honduran government (which it supports) and the Venezuelan government (which it opposes).[70]

Stone's wish to be associated with the petition was hardly a surprise, given his previous criticisms of the paper. However, it was a further sign of a filmmaker continuing to broaden his base politically beyond core film drama as an outlet.

Stone's move towards documentary, and more particularly the criticisms from people such as Stephen Holden raised some wider questions about where documentary sat in relation to drama, and the debate about historical veracity. Is documentary different from dramatic history? Can we reasonably say that documentaries deal with facts in a way that historical drama does not? As a number of scholars have noted, the trend in early twenty-first-century documentary-making was to mix information, the presentation of 'facts' with entertainment.[71] From early offerings by the Lumière Brothers to Robert Flaherty, John Grierson and others in the early 1920s and 1930s, documentary filmmakers were regularly staging re-enactments as part of the construction of their films. During the same period, Soviet documentarian Dziga Vertov introduced cinematic techniques such as slow motion as aids to observation.

In due course, a trend in polemical and carefully edited documentaries emerged from Leni Riefenstahl, Pare Lorentz, Frank Capra and others which all highlighted the propaganda power of documentary. Later decades saw the introduction and development of *cinema vérité* styles that shifted towards reality formats and rolling news style portrayals, from D. A. Pennebaker's iconic portrait of Bob Dylan in *Don't Look Back* (1967), to his record of the 1992 presidential election in *The War Room* (1993). By the time this latter film emerged, Michael Moore had shown already how the on-screen personality of the filmmaker could be woven into the mix of information presentation and dramatic action – 'infotainment' – with his memorable interview of General Motors' CEO Roger Smith in *Roger & Me* (1989), followed by *Bowling for Columbine* (2002), *Fahrenheit 9/11* (2004) and *Capitalism: A Love Story* (2009).

Moore brought a particularly distinctive style to his work, and the contrast with Stone has been instructive. While there is some variability in the mix of components, Moore's on-screen presence is noticeably more acerbic than that of Stone. All of the films are anchored by Moore's particular sense of humour. By contrast, Stone's style was more subdued, considering that he was renowned as a director who could outgun anyone aesthetically and photographically. Part of Stone's empathy for Chávez, like Castro, came from his military past, and that it was reciprocated surprised Stone somewhat. At the beginning of *Mi Amigo Hugo* (2014), Stone admitted that he had been unprepared for the particular expression of friendship from Chávez that had been recorded mid-way through *South of the Border*, and the follow-up film was as much a homage to the deceased president as it was a further assault on the mainstream US media. In *Persona non Grata* (2003), made for HBO's *America Undercover* series, Stone's work is immediate, often (apparently) unmediated, and certainly gains access to those of influence and power in the Arab–Israeli dispute. Its mixture of Claude Chalhoub's crossover western–Arabic soundtrack, allied to everyday sounds from the street, and the freewheeling style without voiceover but with Stone much in the picture, make this a much more raw and direct experience than many other filmmakers working on the subject, and prophesises some of the approaches to come later in the decade. Even Benjamin Netanyahu seems surprised at one point, as cameramen roam around him, while Stone asks about Palestinian influences in Jordan and Lebanon – a tactic self-consciously revealed in the film's edit to show the crew periodically in shot.

So the visual style in Stone's documentary work was markedly different from the approach of Moore – the most successful documentary filmmaker of the 1990s and early 2000s – and different too from the glossy palate he established in *JFK* and *Nixon*. The *cinema-vérité* style that framed Castro, Chávez and the Palestinian and Israeli leaders was notably different from the didactic approach employed in the subsequent *Untold History* series, yet both shared a utilitarian approach to structure and presentation that perhaps only Errol Morris has matched. The comparison of *Untold History* with, say, Eugene Jarecki's *Why We Fight* (2005) is interesting too. Jarecki's film found many plaudits and nothing like as much disquiet as Stone's series, although the issues of empire, unbridled corporate influence, the steady enlargement of the military industrial complex and the crucial concept of 'blowback' – retaliatory action against American interests in response to a previous covert action – are explored in similar ways, woven into narratives around 9/11, the initial bombing of Iraq and the influence of the Project for the New American Century. Jarecki's film found its place more easily in the current documentary canon, although its sensibilities also received criticism.[72]

In both drama and documentary, Stone's advocacy of 'counter-myths' carried his arguments beyond the media and into wider concerns about democratic accountability. Owen Fiss draws three important lessons about the concept of accountability in the media that have a crucial bearing on Stone and his work. First, Fiss argues that a free market is not a guarantor of democratic values.[73] In other words, we cannot assume a serendipitous alignment between the commercial self-interest of the entertainment industry and the functioning of a democracy. In interview, Stone too has commented on the deleterious consequences of television news becoming a for-profit undertaking.[74] Second, Fiss observes that cinema plays a key role in the construction of our cultural values. He argues that it is one of the means by which 'the public finds out about the world that lies beyond its immediate experience'.[75] In practice, the way in which cinema contributes to that wider perspective is constrained by the vagaries of corporate profitability and consumer choice. Stone has noted much the same:

> A provocative movie just can't make as much money, because you can't get the broad base for financial success, including the kids and the 'right thinkers'. You can only get the 'free thinkers', and they are in limited numbers in any society.[76]

Finally, Fiss contends that free speech is protected by the American Constitution, not because it is a form of self-expression, but because it is 'essential for collective self-determination'.[77] Stone's developing political agenda, particularly expressed in the Castro and Chávez documentaries, sought to advance all three aspects of Fiss's argument. Stone's experiences, not least with the cancellation of *Comandante*, underscore his commercial concerns for film, as well as the industry coming under pressure from politically motivated censorship. The *Untold History* series advanced this argument still further, with Stone reminding his fellow citizens that they had a responsibility to understand their nation's history, and to act on that understanding.

Conclusion

What to make of Stone's political stance both on-screen and off, and its development since the mid-1990s? That he grew up a Republican conservative in the Eisenhower era believing that the US mission was to fight communism, is not an altogether unique parabolic curve of enlightenment for those scarred by war. His father taught his son to fear the Russians, so he volunteered for Vietnam and found the outside world's complexity in the jungles of South-East Asia. However, he also found a very different *American* social milieu there from the middle-class Manhattan existence into which he had been born. Combat did not radicalise him politically straightaway, but the shock treatment woke him up to institutional duplicity, complacency and deceit.

Stone's radicalisation took its time. However, with the release of the Pentagon Papers and the revelations surrounding Watergate at the beginning of the 1970s, his Republican leanings were fast ebbing away; but it was his exposure to the politics of Central America in the mid-1980s that was formative. It launched a questioning perspective about the decade that saw the roots of American amnesia in *Salvador, Platoon, Wall Street, Talk Radio, Born on the Fourth of July* and *The Doors.* Each was a direct challenge to Ronald Reagan, to his 'morning again in America' mantra, and to the political complacency that such a stance was building in American minds. Even so, the films were more than just an interrogation of Reagan; they were an indictment of a political establishment that had completely lost its way in the era of *JFK* and *Nixon*'s setting.

Relaying and retelling Vietnam was crucial to Stone's political education and thinking. It was easy for him to see Afghanistan and Iraq through the prism of Vietnam, because they were the same war in so many ways. What worried Stone was the institutionalisation of that recurrent feeling of fighting Vietnam over and over. When President Barack Obama decided to open his second term in office with the nomination of two Vietnam veterans – Senators

John Kerry and Chuck Hagel, as (respectively) Secretaries of State and Defense – the irony was not lost on Stone. Politics institutionalised war and vice versa. Stone had never opposed a government response to terrorism, contrary to what some had asserted, although he had argued long and hard for a more intelligence-led engagement.[78] What his position really desired was accountability, and accountability comes from different debates and ideas being shared.

Like other Democrats, the arrival of Barack Obama in the White House in 2009, and his subsequent re-election in 2012, disappointed in its failure to live up to the future president's campaign promises in 2008. Stone voted for Obama, but was concerned from the beginning about the president's commitment to American security, empire and power abroad. Critique of empire was to be a central theme of the *Untold History* series, and in a number of media appearances discussing the project, Stone was critical of both Obama and his first-term Secretary of State, Hillary Clinton. US citizens were not just living in a national security state but a global security state, he mused. Concerned that Obama was constructing a new American exceptionalism, Stone conceived of an extension to the Bush Doctrine of endless war, applying it to the containment of China as well as ongoing issues in the Middle East.

Thus Stone's view of himself as someone who should (and must) make a contribution to the information marketplace has been resilient and unwavering. He has highlighted alternative political and historical perspectives in a way that has helped call the establishment and mainstream media to account.[79] In a *Financial Times* article in July 2013, Stone, writing again with Peter Kuznick, made reference to the revelations from Edward Snowden and his leaking of the details of widespread NSA surveillance of the internet and social media to the *Guardian* and *Washington Post* the previous month. They began thus:

> On the campaign trail, Barack Obama lambasted the policies of George W. Bush that had made the US an international pariah – war and contempt for human rights. For us, part of the senator's attraction as a candidate was that he promised transparency, opposed the Iraq war and repudiated militarism. So it is hard not to feel disappointed.[80]

As well as criticising the misuse of the NSA's capabilities by the Obama administration and those before it, Stone and Kuznick criticised the president for massively increasing the use of drone attacks as conflict alternatives. They could not help but conclude that:

> Mr Obama has become a more amiable and efficient manager of the American empire. And, in the name of national security, he is laying the foundation for a frighteningly dystopian future by combining full-spectrum surveillance with full-spectrum military dominance.

Stone had lost none of his appetite for broad-based critiques of US administrations then – even those he originally supported. In addition, the media's conventional renderings of the American myth have been held up to scrutiny, and the politics of terror, surveillance, security and central empowerment has left Stone bitter but unbowed about the prophecies that he had laid bare in the years before, and since the trauma of 9/11. Stone said that documentary was 'an effort to put pressure where I can best put it, even if it's a reduced impact'.[81] Whatever that impact may have been, politicians, the public and the media know that the man's response and reaction has rarely lessened, nor reduced its scope. In *Persona non Grata*, Stone managed to get an interview with members of Hamas, the Palestinian organisation with a military wing controlling areas of the West Bank and the Gaza Strip. He proceeded to enquire not just about their ideology, tactics or philosophy in the battle to end the 'occupation' of their land as they saw it, but also, pragmatically, how much it would cost to buy a tank. The seemingly odd questioning was actually what still remains prevalent in politics for Stone: it is about power, persuasion and accountability, and those things are still acquired by the same age-old means: influence, connections and money.

Notes

1 Interview with Oliver Stone, Santa Monica, CA, 8 December 2011.

2 Richard Heffner, 'The Open Mind, 'History as an "Act of Faith": Dallas, November 1963' (15 January 1992; emphasis in original. Available at http://www.thirteen.org/openmind-archive/history/history-as-an-act-of-faith-dallas-november-1963/ (accessed 7 December 2015).

3 Rita Kempley, 'JFK', *Washington Post* (20 December 1991). Available at www.washingtonpost.com/wp-srv/style/longterm/movies/videos/jfkrkempley_a0a288.htm (accessed 1 March 2016).
4 Jonathan Rosenbaum, 'JFK', *Chicago Reader* (1 December 1991). Available at http://jonathanrosenbaum.net/1991/12/jfk/ (accessed 7 December 2015).
5 Vincent Canby, 'JFK; When Everything Amounts to Nothing', *New York Times* (20 December 1991). Available at http://nytimes.com/movie/review?res=9D0CE5DC1230F933A15751C1A967958260 (accessed 7 December 2015).
6 David Ansen, 'Celebrate the Unexpected', *Newsweek* (27 January 1992). Available at http://newsweek.com/celebrate-unexpected-197906(accessed 7 December 2015).
7 Fletcher Knebel and Charles W. Bailey, *Seven Days in May* (New York: Harper and Row, 1962).
8 Oliver Stone and Peter Kuznick, *The Untold History of the United States* (New York: Ebury, 2012), p. 322.
9 Pat McGilligan, 'Point Man', in Charles Silet (ed) *Oliver Stone Interviews* (Jackson, MS: University Press of Mississippi, 2001), pp. 14–38.
10 James M. Welsh and Donald M. Whaley, *The Encyclopedia of Oliver Stone* (Lanham, MD: Scarecrow Press, 2013), p. 234.
11 James Riordan, *Stone: The Controversies, Excesses, and Exploits of a Radical Filmmaker* (London: Aurum, 1995), p. 178.
12 McGilligan, 'Point Man', p. 30.
13 James Riordan, *Stone: The Controversies, Excesses and Exploits of a Radical Filmmaker* (New York: Hyperion, 1995), p. 150.
14 Pauline Kael, 'Pig Heaven', *New Yorker* (28 July 1986), pp. 77–9.
15 Tom Wicker, 'Does "J.F.K." conspire against reason?', *New York Times* (15 December 1991). Available at http://nytimes.com/1991/12/15/movies/film-does-jfk-conspire-against-reason.html (accessed 7 December 2015).
16 'Twisted History', *Newsweek* (23 December 1991). Available at http://newsweek.com/twisted-history-201132 (accessed 7 December 2015).
17 Shaw, a New Orleans businessman, founded the International Trade Mart in the city in 1947. Banister, a former FBI agent and police officer, operated as a private investigator in New Orleans. Ferrie, a former pilot with the Civil Air Patrol, shared anti-Communist sentiments with Banister and was involved with Banister in the anti-Castro movement in New Orleans.
18 Jim Marrs, *Crossfire: The Plot that Killed Kennedy* (New York: Basic Books, 1989).
19 George Lardner Jr, 'On the Set: Dallas in Wonderland; How Oliver Stone's Version of the Kennedy Assassination Exploits the Edge of Paranoia', *Washington Post* (19 May 1991). Available at

https://www.washingtonpost.com/archive/opinions/1991/05/19/on-the-set-dallas-in-wonderland/0c958035-3fc2-48a7-a108-da0855c92a94/ (accessed 7 December 2014).

20 Bill Carter, 'Rather Pulls CBS News Back to the Assassination', *New York Times* (4 February 1992). Available at http://nytimes.com/1992/02/04/arts/reporter-s-notebook-rather-pulls-cbs-news-back-to-the-assassination.html (accessed 7 December 2014).

21 *Final Report of the Select Committee on Assassinations*, 95th Congress, 2d session, H.R. 1828 (Washington: GPO, 1979), p. 3.

22 Indeed, by this point Stone was already on the verge of releasing the now famous *JFK: The Book of the Film* which, together with the annotated screenplay, had hundreds of research notes and culled reviews, as well as invited commentaries together from ninety-seven sources to produce one of the most comprehensive addendums to a motion picture ever.

23 Richard Zoglin, 'More Shots in Dealey Plaza', *Time* (10 June 1991). Available at http://content.time.com/time/magazine/article/0,9171,973142,00.html (accessed 7 December 2015).

24 Roger Ebert, 'Oliver Stone Defends "JFK" Against Conspiracy of Dunces', *Chicago Sun-Times* (22 December 1991). Available at www.rogerebert.com/interviews/oliver-stone-defends-jfk-against-conspiracy-of-dunces (accessed 7 December 2015).

25 Congressional Record 102nd Congress (1991–1992) June 25, 1992, H5307-5308. Available at http://thomas.loc.gov/cgi-bin/query/F?r102:1:./temp/~r102u7kLVa:e0 (accessed 1 March 2016).

26 Lawrence Van Gelder, 'Oliver Stone's Quest', *New York Times* (6 March 1992). Available at http://nytimes.com/1992/03/06/movies/at-the-movies.html?module=Search&mabReward=relbias%3As (accessed 7 December 2015).

27 Tim Weiner, 'Kennedy had a Plan for Early Exit from Vietnam', *New York Times* (23 December 1997). Available at http://nytimes.com/1997/12/23/us/kennedy-had-a-plan-for-early-exit-in-vietnam.html?module=Search&mabReward=relbias%3As (accessed 7 December 2015).

28 National Archives and Records Administration, 'Press Release: National Archives Opens JFK Assassination Materials' (20 December 2004). Available at http://archives.gov/press/press-releases/2005/nr05-29.html (accessed 7 December 2015).

29 Todd McCarthy, 'Natural Born Killers', *Variety* (8 August 1994). Available at http://variety.com/1994/film/reviews/natural-born-killers-2-1200438238/ (accessed 7 December 2015).

30 Interview with Bob Daly, Santa Monica, CA, 18 October 2010.

31 Interview with Oliver Stone, Santa Monica, CA, 19 January 2010.

32 Interview with Oliver Stone, Santa Monica, CA, 19 June 2010.

33 *Ibid.*

34 The Beltway – an idiom used to reference the political concerns of the elites in the US capital – takes its name from the road that

encircles Washington, DC: interstate 495, also known as the Beltway.

35 Luc Herman, 'Bestowing Knighthood: The Visual Aspects of Bill Clinton's Camelot Legacy' in Peter C. Rollins and John E. O'Connor (eds) *Hollywood's White House: The American Presidency in Film and History* (Lexington, KY: University Press of Kentucky, 2003), p. 310.

36 Herman, 'Bestowing Knighthood', p. 311.

37 Terry Christensen and Peter J. Haas, *Projecting Politics: Political Messages in American Films* (Armonk, NY and London: M. E. Sharpe, 2005), p. 151.

38 Richard Maltby, *Hollywood Cinema* (Malden, MA and Oxford: Blackwell, 2nd edn, 2003), p. 289.

39 Richard D. Heffner, *Oral History: Reminiscences of Richard D. Heffner*, Volume 2, Session 4, 15 October, 1997, p. 180. Available at Columbia Oral History Archives, Rare Book & Manuscript Library, Columbia University, New York City.

40 Geoff King, *New Hollywood Cinema: An Introduction* (London and New York: I. B. Tauris, 2007), pp. 14–24.

41 Oliver Stone, 'On Nixon and JFK' in Robert Brent Toplin (ed), *Oliver Stone's U.S.A.: Film, History and Controversy* (Lawrence, KS: University of Kansas Press, 2000), p. 277.

42 Stone, 'On Nixon and JFK', p. 277.

43 Roger Ebert, 'Nixon', *Chicago Sun-Times* (20 December 1995). Available at http://rogerebert.com/reviews/nixon-1995 (accessed 7 December 2015).

44 Gavin Smith, 'The Dark Side', *Sight & Sound*, 6, 3, 1996, p. 6.

45 Phillip Gianos, *Politics and Politicians in American Film* (Westport, CT: Praeger, 1998), p. 185.

46 José Arroyo, 'Nixon', *Sight & Sound*, 6, 3, 1996, p. 48; emphasis in original.

47 Smith, 'The Dark Side', p. 7.

48 Alessandra Stanley, 'A Noted Filmmaker in a Tense Land', *New York Times* (5 June 2003). Available at http://nytimes.com/2003/06/05/movies/television-review-a-noted-filmmaker-in-a-tense-land.html (accessed 7 December 2015).

49 David Gonzalez, 'Cuba Arrests a Score of Dissidents linked to a U.S. Diplomat', *New York Times* (20 March 2003). Available at www.nytimes.com/2003/03/20/international/americas/20CUBA.html (accessed 7 December 2015).

50 Jamie Russell, 'Comandante', *BBC* (30 September 2003). Available at www.bbc.co.uk/films/2003/09/29/comandante_2003_review.shtml (accessed 7 December 2015).

51 Elvis Mitchell, 'On Second Thought: A Castro Follow-Up', *New York Times* (11 April 2004). Available at http://events.nytimes.com/2004/04/11/movies/11MITC.html?pagewanted=print&position=&_r=0 (accessed 7 December 2015).

52 Eduardo Galeano, *The Open Veins of Latin America: Five Centuries of the Pillage of a Continent* (New York: Monthly Review Press, 1997; orig. pub. 1971), p. 285.

53 Alexei Barrionuevo, 'Italy Follows Trail of Secret South American Abductions', *New York Times* (22 February 2008). Available at http://nytimes.com/2008/02/22/world/americas/22condor.html?pagewanted=all&gwh=9777F483EBCD8B2742AC554E226DB358&gwt=pay (accessed 7 December 2015).

54 Edward Williamson, *The Penguin History of Latin America* (London: Penguin, 1992), pp. 375–7, 558–66.

55 Editorial, 'Hugo Chávez Departs', *New York Times* (3 April 2002). Available at http://nytimes.com/2002/04/13/opinion/hugo-chavez-departs.html (accessed 1 March 2016).

56 'Editorial: Venezuela's Political Turbulence', *New York Times* (16 April 2002). Available at http://nytimes.com/2002/04/16/opinion/venezuela-s-political-turbulence.html (accessed 7 December 2015).

57 Paul Krugman, 'Losing Latin America', *New York Times* (16 April 2002). Available at http://nytimes.com/2002/04/16/opinion/losing-latin-america.html (accessed 1 March 2016).

58 Stephen Holden, 'Oliver Stone, Tour Guide', *New York Times* (24 June 2010). Available at http://nytimes.com/2010/06/25/movies/25south.html (accessed 7 December 2015).

59 Larry Rohter, 'Oliver Stone's Latin America', *New York Times* (25 June 2010). Available at http://nytimes.com/2010/06/26/movies/26stone.html (accessed 7 December 2015).

60 Rohter, 'Oliver Stone's Latin America'.

61 Brent Toplin (ed), *Oliver Stone's U.S.A.*

62 Stone, 'On Nixon and JFK', p. 293.

63 Oliver Stone, "Stone on Stone's Image' in Brent Toplin (ed), *Oliver Stone's USA*, p. 46.

64 Robert A. Rosenstone, 'Oliver Stone as Historian' in Brent Toplin (cd), *Oliver Stone's USA*, p. 34.

65 Lardner Jr, 'On the Set: Dallas in Wonderland'.

66 John Stuart Mill, *On Liberty* (London: Penguin, 1974; orig. pub. 1859), p. 108.

67 Interview with Oliver Stone, Santa Monica, CA, 19 January 2010.

68 *Ibid.*

69 Roy Greenslade, 'New York Times Accused of Treating Latin Political Leaders Differently', *Guardian* (22 May 2013). Available at http://theguardian.com/media/greenslade/2013/may/22/new-york-times-venezuela (accessed 7 December 2015).

70 'Urge NYT Public Editor to Investigate Biased Reporting on Honduras and Venezuela', *NYTimes eXaminer* (14 May 2013). Available at https://nytexaminer.com/2013/05/petition-on-venezuela-honduras/ (accessed 1 March 2016).

71 Christensen and Haas, *Projecting Politics*, p. 233.
72 Manohla Dargis, 'Casting a Harshly Critical Eye on the Business of Warfare in America', *New York Times* (20 January 2006). Available at http://nytimes.com/2006/01/20/movies/20figh.html (accessed 7 December 2015); Roger Ebert, 'Why We Fight', *Chicago Sun-Times* (16 February 2006). Available at http://rogerebert.com/reviews/why-we-fight-2006 (accessed 7 December 2015).
73 Owen M. Fiss, *The Irony of Free Speech* (Cambridge, MA: Harvard University Press, 1998), p. 56.
74 Interview with Oliver Stone, Santa Monica, CA, 19 January 2010.
75 Fiss, *Free Speech*, p. 53.
76 Interview with Stone, 19 January 2010.
77 Fiss, *Free Speech*, p. 3.
78 Interview with Oliver Stone, Santa Monica, CA, 8 December 2011.
79 *Ibid.*
80 Oliver Stone and Peter Kuznick, 'Obama Is Laying the Foundations of a Dystopian Future', *Financial Times* (10 July 2013). Available at https://next.ft.com/content/de81a466-e40d-11e2-91a3-00144feabdc0 (accessed 7 December 2015).
81 Interview with Oliver Stone, Santa Monica, CA, 8 December 2011.

3
Money

Introduction

> In *Wall Street: Money Never Sleeps*, the banks have taken over Gekko's job. I was shocked when I went back to this in 2010. In *Wall Street*, Gekko had been the outsider, the inside trader guy, the thief, the blackmailer – and that's what the banks do now. In the old days the banks would never have done that, it was considered immoral, but by 2010 the whole thing had shifted because of deregulation.[1]

By the time *Wall Street: Money Never Sleeps* hit cinemas in September 2010, banking, the financial markets and capitalism in general had all changed in rather complicated ways. Not only had they changed since the time of Oliver Stone's original *Wall Street* in 1987, but they had renegotiated their relationship with institutions and the public in a dramatically short space of time: over the previous two-and-a-half years. Therefore, Stone's updating of arch protagonist Gordon Gekko's exploits for the financially strapped twenty-first century was a prescient cautionary tale and a morality fable of sorts; but it was also a vignette about Hollywood as an industry, as it gravitated increasingly towards box office viability and away from the creatively free hand offered to auteurs in the 1970s. By 2010, as Stone discovered, even auteurs with final cut in their contracts needed to push back against executive encroachment on the directing process.

More than that, Stone's world view surmised that the financial meltdown and philosophy of money that he had identified as

America's talismanic totem for so long through his career, had further social and cultural ramifications for the era in which America now found itself. For in his follow-up movie of 2012, *Savages*, Stone proceeded to excoriate the capitalist psyche of the USA, not always in coherent ways, but with as bilious and flaming a passion as any of his classic films from the 1980s and 1990s had displayed.

The corrupting effect of money has long been an established theme in Stone's work. In their various ways, his early writing projects such as *Midnight Express* (Alan Parker, 1978) and *Scarface* (Brian De Palma, 1983) as well as *Wall Street* (1987), *Talk Radio* (1988), *Natural Born Killers* (1994), *U Turn* (1997) and *Any Given Sunday* (1999) all had something to say about personal ambition, greed and a belief that there was somehow a shortcut to material wealth. In some of these narratives the pursuit of money is sufficient to induce individual moral implosion, while in others – for example, *Talk Radio* and *Natural Born Killers* – the mechanism is more complex, mediated by corporate money and ego.

In *Wall Street: Money Never Sleeps* and *Savages*, Stone pursued the theme of monetary corruption by taking narrative swipes at two of the most lucrative forms of American late capitalism: connected, as it turned out, not just at the point of consumption, but as collaborating business ventures. In July 2012, caught between the releases of both features, British-based financial powerhouse HSBC admitted to the US Department of Justice – as part of a 'deferred prosecution' agreement – to money-laundering for a Mexican drug cartel, among other illegal activities.[2] To say, as the bank's then Head of Compliance, David Bagley, did in front of a Senate Committee, that HSBC had fallen short of its own expectations, hardly did justice to the bank's active engagement in a process which had been bringing chaos, disruption and loss of life to Mexico for at least a decade; the whole thing adorned with a seemingly limitless supply of gratuitous violence.[3] HSBC was not alone. By January 2013, ING Bank, American Express Bank International, Wachovia, Union Bank of California, Lloyds, Credit Suisse, Barclays, ABN Amro and Standard Chartered had all signed similar deferred prosecution agreements with the US Department of Justice, acknowledging their part in various money-laundering operations.[4]

On the face of it, then, Oliver Stone's fabled ability to condition the zeitgeist to his own storytelling ends might be seen to have borne fruit, with such tales straight out of the newspaper front page headlines. Just as the original *Wall Street*, and just like its literary companion of the time, Tom Wolfe's caustic novel, *The Bonfire of the Vanities* (1987),[5] had parodied the hubris and greed of the Reagan era, so *Wall Street: Money Never Sleeps* and *Savages* appeared to be lambasting the vacuity and hollow moral leanings of the contemporary age. Yet both films ended up receiving criticism for failing to deliver an even greater indictment of the busted bankers and degenerate drug cartels. Certainly, *Wall Street: Money Never Sleeps* offered a tale of betrayal, vengeance and redemption in the wake of the 2008 financial crash; but it barely scratched the surface of the minutiae of short-selling and mortgage-backed securities any more than the original *Wall Street* had got to grips with insider trading. So while the public continued to nurse grievances about the 2008 financial meltdown and the beggaring of government resources to fix the problem, *Wall Street: Money Never Sleeps* was held culpable by some for *not* providing that moment of catharsis. Roger Ebert, in the *Chicago Sun-Times*, reflected the tone that some others saw in the film, when he commented that Stone's narrative seemed 'more fascinated than angry'.[6] Indeed, as this chapter will go on to outline, other pictures of both documentary and feature film form were paraded as stronger condemnations of the modern Wall Street mentality, not least *Inside Job* (Charles Ferguson, 2010), and *Margin Call* (J. C. Chandor, 2011).

While cultivating a moral tale of betrayal, vengeance and redemption inside the drug wars, *Savages* did not delve that far into the politics of the problem either – not that Stone did not have such intent. He sought to draw attention not just to the violence south of the border and the consequences of the US policy on drugs, but to the relative absence of US media commentary on the complex set of economic and foreign policy dicta that were fuelling the violence: a position he expounded on in interviews promoting *Savages*. However, on-screen his dramatic instincts produced a less visceral indictment than of old, prompting critic Peter Bradshaw to comment in the *Guardian* that the film lacked any of the 'docu-realist fervour of Steven Soderbergh's *Traffic* [2001]'.[7] If *Savages* was short of some of the disruptive energy that had distinguished *Natural Born Killers* (1994), or a little of the realist immediacy of *Traffic*, that change had as much to say about the entertainment industry's steady commodification of violence, and society's tolerance of it, as it did of Stone's commitment to his aesthetic: the very issue – reality/fantasy, twenty years later, the real/virtual world – that Stone was raising in *Natural Born Killers*. What seems clear is that the desire to criticise the establishment was not dissipating so much as it was finding new channels to express itself – documentaries, media appearances, protests – leaving the dramatic work not bereft of critique, but less obviously infused with it.

Whatever the critical reservations, both *Wall Street: Money Never Sleeps* and *Savages* were about the desire for making money, the power and influence that money incites and buys, and the extent to which moral frameworks may be stretched to accommodate those desires. Money figures in the narratives of both films as a measure of wealth. However, the role of money as an indicator of personal, institutional and even establishment excesses are not always understood, even by economists.[8] Classical economic theory rests on the building blocks of rational behaviour, transparent markets, supply and demand and liquidity; while the business of banks and the role of money in the twenty-first century are all tested to destruction in a world where any activity – even money-laundering – can be accommodated, and where the language of bridge or poker – 'overcalls', 'pre-emptive bids', 'bluffs' – seems to capture more accurately the nature of day-to-day business.

This chapter pursues the argument that both *Wall Street: Money Never Sleeps* and *Savages* have rather more to say about money and capitalism as it is practised than much of the commentaries on the films acknowledged in the first instance. Indeed, they speak to the enduring theme of finance that Stone has pursued as much, if not more, than in any of his previous pictures. These films articulate a particular kind of moral collapse that is different from the moral implosions that drove Bud Fox, Barry Champlain and Wayne Gale. In their various ways, the productions of the late 1980s and early 1990s were all a response to the changes in individual and corporate psyches that had just been ushered in by Ronald Reagan's deregulatory fervour. Money was a marker for a range of ideological commentaries about individual responsibility, and even personal honour.

These themes can be seen in *Wall Street: Money Never Sleeps* and *Savages*, but what is noteworthy is the way in which retribution is foregrounded in the narratives: a retribution that almost revisits the traditional notions of frontier ethos and Darwinian laws of nature. The result was two films which signposted very important questions about the American Dream. What are the moral boundaries to the pursuit of wealth in a fully globalised corporate economy? Stone's answer suggested that there are no limits. Taken together, *Wall Street: Money Never Sleeps* and *Savages* invite us to question a set of assumptions about market economics and the meaning of the American Dream that, in the wake of almost half a century of neo-liberal political and economic dominance, have come to appear as immutable facts rather than ideological preferences.[9]

Wall Street

In summer 1987, the US stock market was experiencing a boom that was coming close to eclipsing the previous record of the century, achieved in the five years preceding the crash of 1929. Just a few months earlier, in January 1987, the economist John Kenneth Galbraith had written what proved to be a prophetic warning about the direction that the market was taking. In particular, Galbraith detected a real danger signalled by the reoccurrence in 1987 of four aspects of the booming market of 1929.[10] First, a similarity concerned the 'dynamics of speculation'. This referred to a process whereby a boom would self-perpetuate by drawing more and more people into a rising market, on the unsustainable premise that all can prosper. Second, there was a re-emergence of esoteric financial structures. One of the most lethal in 1929 proved to be the pyramid holding company: a layered structure of ownership built on borrowings and sale of stock in the intermediate floors of the structure. This allowed control to be retained with a relatively small stock holding, while profits accrued from rising stock prices.

In the mid-1980s a series of corporate takeovers had been financed by borrowing and based on assumptions about the rising stock market which, Galbraith argued, created a common link between these acquisitions and the pyramids of the 1920s. The link was debt, and that eventually it would prove as unsustainable as it had been in 1929. Third, another characteristic parallel identified by Galbraith was that some of the greatest exponents of the boom would be seen to take the biggest falls. At the time, investment banker Dennis Levine had been charged with insider trading, and Ivan Boesky was cooperating with a Securities and Exchange Commission investigation for the same reason. More were soon to follow, including junk bond trader Michael Milken. The final strand of Galbraith's warning was that in the 1980s, as in the 1920s, funds that otherwise might have flowed into new capital expansion were flowing into the new investment structures. Galbraith summed up the situation in short shrift:

> The controlling fact is not the tendency to brilliant invention; the controlling fact is the shortness of the public memory, especially when it contends with a euphoric desire to forget.[11]

Galbraith's prediction came true on 19 October 1987. Following falls on foreign markets the previous Friday, the US markets crashed when dealing commenced the following week. Just three months before, Oliver Stone had completed shooting on *Wall Street*, having worked on the screenplay and filmed incessantly since the Academy Awards that March: an event that saw *Platoon* being awarded four of the eight Oscar nominations it had received, including Best Director. Working with Stanley Weiser, Stone had the script for *Wall Street* more or less finished by the commencement of shooting in May 1987. In what subsequently became one of the film's defining moments, Gordon Gekko (Michael Douglas), talks positively about the 'greed is good' mentality in almost biblical overtones, echoing something that Boesky had said at an address at Berkeley on 12 September 1985: 'Everybody should be a little bit greedy ... You shouln't feel guilty.'[12] In so many respects, then, the film seemed to be bending real life to the will of its cautionary narrative.

So it was that when *Wall Street* was finally released on 11 December 1987, Gekko and his philosophic mantra became part of the fabric of the national debate about the economy. Alongside works such as Caryl Churchill's play *Serious Money* (1987)[13] and Wolfe's *Bonfire of the Vanities* (1987), Stone's morality tale served both as catharsis and warning.[14] It was also a marker for the transition then underway in the film and entertainment industry.

Still flush from the first wave of regenerative profits flowing from a raft of Lucas–Spielberg productions, and aided by the easing of regulatory constraints, Hollywood was resetting its scope and ambitions after the slow wind-down at the end of the studio era. Wall Street money was finding its way into exhibition deals and buyouts – not least Rupert Murdoch's acquisition of Fox in 1984, the studio that would go on to produce *Wall Street*. In addition to the takeover at Fox, the 1980s also saw a series of amalgamations and deals involving Columbia, United Artists (UA), Disney and MGM. Significant as these developments were, they were a prologue for the deal of the decade: the announcement in September 1989 of a merger between Time Inc. and Warner Communications Inc. The new Time Warner corporation had emerged following a hostile bid for Time by Paramount Communications Inc. (PCI). Time Warner's holdings at the point of the merger – estimated to be worth $25 billion, – included film, television, cable, music recording, theme park and book and magazine publishing interests. Among the most bankable assets were *Superman* and *Batman*. The other protagonist in the takeover battle, PCI, had a similar profile of cross-media and distribution holdings.[15] In addition, deregulatory politics were assisting the new studios. US Department of Justice anti-trust efforts to prevent local cinema chains from agreeing schedules to avoid showing the same film at the same time – a practice known as 'splitting' – pushed many of these businesses into financial difficulty. The new studios were able to acquire these exhibitors, unchallenged by the Department: a move that essentially undid the strictures of divorcement contained in the 1948 *Paramount* Supreme Court ruling, which had forced the studios to divest themselves of their exhibition arms.[16]

Operating then as an avatar both for the changing movie industry and the excesses of the financiers, *Wall Street* did well on its initial release, taking some $42 million at the US box office on a budget of $15 million. However, it was the slow maturation of its cultural capital that proved more striking, with the film slowly transforming into a touchstone for many of the patterns and excesses that defined the 1980s – and not just economically. So permeable had the boundary between fiction and history become at this juncture, that Gekko and his quotable dictates became a sine qua non for Wall Street malfeasance – even to the point of being listed alongside 'real' perpetrators.[17] Raymond Arsenault argues that *Wall Street* was the only 'serious cinematic effort [of the time] to dissect the economic mania of the Reagan years'.[18] It is not too much of a stretch, then, to assert that Stone's film and its lead character became *the* cultural signifier for the 1980s, every bit as much as F. Scott Fitzgerald's *The Great Gatsby* and its eponymous subject, Jay Gatsby, had become for the 1920s.

More than twenty years later, Stone returned to the scene of the financial crime (Figure 5). Gekko's re-emergence in *Wall Street: Money Never Sleeps* begins with his release from prison. The story that develops concerns the efforts of a trader, Jake Moore (Shia LaBeouf), to settle a score with a rival, Bretton James (Josh Brolin). Moore blames James for the death of his mentor, Louis Zabel (Frank Langella). Moore's engagement to Gekko's daughter, Winnie (Carey Mulligan), allows Gekko to propose a deal whereby Moore helps Gekko with his desire to reconcile with his daughter in return for assistance in a scheme intended to ruin James. Gekko, it turns out, has an ulterior motive. He persuades Moore to involve Winnie in a scheme to repatriate $100 million secured in a trust fund for her, to use in a renewable energy project that Jake has been promoting. The money is released to Gekko as intermediary, but he uses it to establish his own trading company. Winnie, who is pregnant, is distraught at her partner's betrayal. As the story concludes, Moore lets Gekko know that he will soon be a grandfather. The denouement sees the young couple reconciled. Gekko, having reflected on his daughter's pregnancy and having redirected $100 million to the energy project, also finds happiness in the new family arrangement. The acquisition of money is a central motivation for all of the key characters, but it manifests itself in subtly different and indeed sometimes irrational ways. For Gekko it has always been about power: being a player. For Moore and indeed Winnie, it is not explicitly about being rich, but the trappings of money: they are both clearly comfortable in their existence as young professionals in Manhattan. For Moore's mother (Susan Sarandon), her property investments seem akin to compulsive gambling. Bretton James's share dealing has a similar motivation, although his role is akin to institutional gambling. These characters' motivations mark a departure from the original film, where some moral clarity about right and wrong always existed.

Figure 5 Michael Douglas and Oliver Stone on the set of *Wall Street: Money Never Sleeps* (2010)

By 2010, Stone's shading of the characters in draft scripts underlined how blurred the lines between right and wrong had become. Despite the 'Occupy Wall Street' protests, this approach accurately reflected the evident reticence on the part of the business and political community to take more decisive action in the wake of the crash, as well as an absence of sufficient public pressure for such action.

In contrast with the original 1987 screenplay, the new story sought to shift the focus from the trading floors of Wall Street to the Federal Reserve Building, where many of the key meetings involving the chiefs of the major banks had taken place in the midst of the unfolding crisis in mid-September 2008.[19] However, the story also emphasises a key structural adjustment in the financial markets since the making of the original *Wall Street*. While Gordon Gekko's crime in the 1987 film was insider trading, it is revealed that James has been involved in short-selling his own company. In following this tack, the new screenplay sought to highlight a subtle but critical recent development on Wall Street: the emergence of publically quoted investment banks that had become overly dependent on their own trading operations as a source of capital. Zabel laments the changes, and is positioned in the narrative as a moral reference point for Moore and the audience. Acquisition appears to be a key driver for James, Gekko and even Moore: they are all acquiring their material share of the American Dream. Tellingly, Moore's decision to go after James is all about retribution rather than justice. Moore embodies a version of the American Dream, but one which exhibits a self-serving morality – allowing him to break the law to deliver his own judgement on James' guilt.

While Gekko's revival was made manifest and prescient in the wake of the October 2008 market crash, discussions about a film sequel pre-dated the economic upheavals, and were by no means straightforward. Public confirmation of a deal between producer Edward Pressman – who had first encountered Stone during the writing of *Conan the Barbarian* (1982) – and 20th Century Fox emerged in the *New York Times* in May 2007.[20] In September, *Fortune* magazine, which had secured a place as a prop in the original film, reported news of two storylines in development and confirmed earlier reports that Stone had been approached to direct the sequel, but had declined.[21] In fact, Stone was less lukewarm about the story than he was about working with Pressman again. A year earlier, in a 5 May 2006 letter, he wrote to his former collaborator explaining that there had been 'too many mishaps over the years' to chance another partnership, and thus he was passing on *Wall Street 2*.[22] A few days earlier, Stone had written to Michael Douglas explaining his position, as a courtesy to the star who had been keen to reprise the role. Stone openly shared his misgivings about working with Pressman again, but commented too that neither he nor Stanley Weiser could come up with a satisfactory treatment for a follow-up story.

Following this decision to pass, Stone initially progressed with discussions about a biopic of Hugh Hefner. However, by February 2007 he was writing to the *Playboy* founder to explain that he did not feel that the project could continue after three aborted script drafts. It was at this point that Stone vigorously pursued the *Pinkville* project concerning the 1968 Mỹ Lai massacre at the height of Vietnam.[23] As economic events unfolded in spring and summer 2008, it started to look like Pressman and Fox's deal from two years earlier was being provided with a ready-made scenario direct off the newsstands. In March, the US government had provided $29 billion to finance a rescue of the Bear Stearns investment bank; while in early September, $200 billion had been pledged to rescue the Federal National Mortgage Association ('Fannie Mae') and Federal Home Loan Mortgage Corporation ('Freddie Mac'). Days later, Lehman Brothers collapsed.

During the latter half of 2008, with inspiration and impetus around them, not one but two versions of the *Wall Street 2* story were refined. One, entitled *Money Never Sleeps* dated 22 July 2008, was prepared by Stephen Schiff. By 30 January 2009 a second screenplay titled *Partners* was beginning to take shape under the pen of Allan Loeb, brought in the previous autumn to give the story another direction (Figure 6).

Meanwhile, Stone had had his interest in the story rekindled by the almost surreal occurrences of 2008. Putting aside his previous differences with Edward Pressman, and keen to explore the economic turn of events in the story, he jumped back into the project in spring 2009. As work progressed, Stone's focus was on teasing out the character motivations and finding a balance between character credibility and dramatic effect.[24] Between March and May 2009, Stone met with Loeb on eleven occasions, totalling twenty-five hours of discussion. This was followed by a further seventeen

Figure 6 Shia LaBeouf, Oliver Stone and Michael Douglas on the set of *Wall Street: Money Never Sleeps* (2010)

days in June that Stone devoted solely to reworking the screenplay. However, he remained concerned about the story and, characteristically, used rehearsals to further refine the detail as the film went into production. Josh Brolin had worked with Stone on *W.* (2008), and felt confident enough in their working relationship to express reservations in the 1 June script about the reconciliation between Winnie, her father and Jake, fearing that it seemed obvious and soft. The ending remained in the final version of the film, and was latched onto by several critics, largely for the reasons that Brolin cited.[25] Even after approval of the script from Fox CEO Tom Rothman in mid-July 2009, Stone continued to harbour worries about character development, and urged Loeb at one point to think 'out of the box' in tackling the issue of Jake's character in the second and third acts.[26]

As the screenplay took shape, Stone found that his business dealings with Fox studios began to underscore some of the film's messages about deals, money and corporations. In the original *Wall Street*, Stone had referenced Robert Wise's 1954 film *Executive Suite*, and had sought to explore both what Wall Street as an institution could deliver for the USA both in terms of investment and growth, and its increasing penchant by that time for esoteric investment vehicles and fast-turnaround, casino-style deals. As a large corporation, Fox offered Stone all the advantages of a well funded studio machine, including production benefits such as the provision of Fox Business News facilities, and newsreaders as production props that aided authenticity. However, the involvement of a big studio inevitably brought big-studio predilections and concerns. The communications in July 2009 between Alex Young, co-president of production at Fox, and Stone appeared to reflect a number of studio preoccupations that, in truth, are not unique to Fox but increasingly endemic across Hollywood: namely, a desire on the part of producers and executives to comment on and rewrite screenplays and even recut finished films, based on the belief they know best what will sell. While debates about the script continued, Young was looking to the marketing effort and slated 23 April 2010 release date. He was concerned whether the film would appeal to a wide-enough audience. On 1 July, Young wrote to Stone asking for a simplification of the technical jargon in the script, and added that 'the draft reads like a hard R because of the language. Let's remove the "fucks" '.[27] In other words, Stone was still preoccupied with establishing the credibility of the characters and language, while Young was thinking about Fox's promotion and revenue even before a cut of the film had appeared.

Stone confided to his agent Bryan Lourd in early August 2009 about another problem. He was unhappy with Fox's Business Affairs unit and its decision not to fund a location shoot in London. He was concerned also both about the fee being offered to Josh Brolin for the role of Bretton James, and the scale fee that had been suggested for Charlie Sheen for his proposed cameo appearance. Stone certainly formed the view that the issue was not just one of tight budget management, but of a corporate culture that was fearful of its leader, Rupert Murdoch.[28] In the case of the scale fee being proposed for Sheen, Stone wrote to Alex Young on 7 August, arguing for an increase, saying that Fox should be grateful that a major television star would come and work for such a relatively low sum. What Stone had not counted on was Sheen's own idiosyncratic perspective on the role. Having agreed a fee with Sheen, Stone discovered in mid-September that Sheen and/or his management were now asking for more money and perks, including a jet to bring Sheen from Los Angeles to New York for the filming.

A few days later on 23 September, producer Ed Pressman called in a favour from a fellow producer Ryan Kavanaugh. In an email, Pressman explained that Sheen would only do the cameo with the private jet guarantee to New York and back, but that Fox had indicated they could not fund this. Pressman asked Kavanaugh if he would bring Sheen to New York in his jet, offering a walk-on role in the same scene as acknowledgement of the favour. Kavanaugh agreed. In parallel, Stone wrote to Alex Young finalising a renegotiation of Sheen's fee, now revised to $100,000. Stone's decision to use Sheen offered a sanguine and prescient moment of reflection. The actor's career trajectory at that moment was as much of a downward spiral as Wall Street's fortunes. Both embodiments of the American Dream, but both at this moment at least, seemingly headed for self-destruction.[29]

Stone's disagreement with Fox over Sheen's fee formed only one part of a wider contest of wills between studio and director. Less than two weeks before the resolution of the Sheen crisis, on 9 September, Stone had written a long memo to Young essentially asking him to back off, stop questioning Stone's every choice and allow him to work in the best way that he could. The sentiment echoed an earlier note from Stone to Young dated 10 July 2009.[30] In that correspondence, Stone was responding to a proposal from Young, only twenty-four hours earlier, to remix the first forty pages of the screenplay. Stone's irritation with the attempted interference is evident in his response:

> First of all, the 7/7 script is not 'MUCH better' than the 6/17 draft. It is truly an outgrowth of our reading with the actors, our talking about it in New York ... it is no longer a film about the machinations of Bud Fox circa 1987 ... I am not interested in making a film about that same person trying to score 23 years later. But there is something about this generation that I know is different from what I saw in the 1980s. I have to respect that, and as a filmmaker represent that to the best of my knowledge and my heart. Perhaps at Fox you have not worked with directors like me, I'm not sure, but without being immodest, I think, in that vision, lies the success of this movie. And the good directors carry that through – a vision, not a settlement.[31]

Stone's closing comment to Young on 10 July about the delivery of a vision rather than a settlement provided not just a succinct working definition of an auteur, but the prism through which Stone's working and artistic style had been forged over many years. His interventions in script development and in pre-production planning ensured that *Wall Street: Money Never Sleeps* was being shaped by two key personal considerations: a sense of what would work dramatically, and a reticence to fall in line with an emerging affectation in cinema – the need to be pessimistic.[32] Like the Fox executives, Stone hoped for a lucrative sequel but commercial success had to follow the vision, rather than set it. Despite Stone's acknowledgement of the importance of industry patrons, his commitment to *Wall Street: Money Never Sleeps* remained with his vision for the film, rather than acceding to the opinions of Fox executives. Ultimately, the film was more important to him than the relationship.

Wall Street: Money Never Sleeps was shot on a fifty-five-day schedule between 9 September and 25 November 2009. Commencement of photography had followed two final rounds of rehearsals during the third week in August and the first week in September. Stone continued to work on the details of the script during the shoot. Indeed, as late as 12 November, Stone was still working with Michael Douglas on the final reconciliation scene. Despite the pressure from Fox for an April 2010 release, Stone resisted, and worked on editing the film throughout the spring. It was eventually released on 24 September 2010 to generally positive reviews.

The performance of *Wall Street: Money Never Sleeps* at the box office was respectable rather than outstanding, taking a total of $52.5 million at the US box office and a further $82 million overseas. Total below-the-line production costs came to just over $30 million, a sum that included editing and music costs. Above-the-line fees added a further $37.5 million of costs. A comparison with the original *Wall Street* is instructive. Above-the-line costs in the original film, covering acting and director's fees, came to just over $3.5 million, with production costs adding a further $14.2 million, bringing the total budget to $17.7 million. Thus while the production costs of *Wall Street: Money Never Sleeps* were double the 1987 original, the above-the-line costs increased tenfold; a result further magnified by an increased reliance on television advertising, which similarly had seen dramatic increases in costs since the 1980s. The figures supported Stone's contention about the 'out-of-control' nature of above-the-line costs in comparison to below-the-line ones, and what that had done to the industry over twenty-five years.[33]

The events surrounding the transcontinental favour that delivered Sheen to New York for filming provided but a glimmer of the world of wealth and below-the-radar political influence that Stone was interested in portraying as part of the film. However, this was not entirely an exposé – that other world was happy to participate. Schmoozing before shooting of the film provided important background materials that assisted the preparation of the lead actors. These preparations included a visit by Stone and Shia LaBeouf to the home of financier George Soros in early September 2009. The cast list for the charity ball scene at the Metropolitan Museum of Art, which was shot in the former Cunard building in lower Manhattan, was a roll call for the money and privilege that the scene sought to capture. The spectacle of rich and famous people playing rich and famous people certainly provided authenticity, but also a whiff of the conceit embedded in those same lives. At the end of October 2009, Ed Pressman was informed by publicist Peggy Siegal that David Koch, co-owner of Koch Industries, was interested in being in the film. Heiress and fashion icon Daphne Guinness also was reported to be interested, but only if she could have a line. While neither made an appearance, Koch's wife Julia did, along with billionaire businessman Warren Buffett, *Vanity Fair* editor Graydon Carter and economist Nouriel Roubini. A scene involving entertainment magnate and future presidential contender Donald Trump was shot but removed during editing.

The clamour among some of New York's most rich and famous residents to appear in the film also provided an important perspective on its social intent and cultural cachet. Here was a film directed by Hollywood's most outspoken political critic about the biggest financial and economic catastrophe since the Great Depression, funded by a major Hollywood operator with its unique Murdoch-infused business culture, and whose production tapped into the divergent political interests that sit behind names such as George Soros and David Koch; the former, a source of significant funds for the Democratic Party, the latter, a bastion of financial support for a range of libertarian causes and institutions, including the Tea Party movement.[34]

Despite's Stone's position on the national stage as an establishment critic, the social elite in New York across the political divide were hardly troubled by that detail; content to rub alongside a kind of celebrity that they understood only too well. Moreover, this select group was drawn from corporate and moneyed interests that were not so very distant from the film's supposed target. What did this mix tell us about Stone, the movie colony and the country? It unequivocally told us that *Wall Street: Money Never Sleeps* was first and foremost dramatic entertainment. The film called attention to the egregious behaviour of Wall Street, but it did not offer comprehensive analysis and indictment. The studio's interest was firmly located in revenue-earning entertainment, and it made every effort to steer its auteur director towards those goals – albeit with minimal success. In any case, Stone's polemical interest was elsewhere, engaged on *South of the Border* (2010) and the *Untold History* series (2012). So while the film seemed to promise comfort to those observers who wanted someone to shout at Wall Street on their behalf – and many did – both the director and the studio were attending to other priorities.

Ends and means

Notwithstanding the absence of outright condemnation, the *Wall Street* sequel did seem to be asking a crucial ethical question: do the ends justify the means? There are several narrative threads in *Wall Street: Money Never Sleeps* that highlight not just the size and reach of the money markets at the time of the 2008 crash, but the ethics of what was happening. In a reflection of the scene in the original film where Gekko talked about greed being good for America, the new film included a four-minute sequence where he is talking to students, drawing on his new book *Is Greed Good? Why Wall Street Has Finally Gone Too Far.* Gekko begins by explaining to the students that they are 'the ninja generation' – no income, no jobs, no assets – and adds with irony that they have a lot to look forward to – if greed had been good in 1987, he suggests, it now seemed to be legal. The sequence is rather longer than the corresponding expository scene in the original film, and for those seeking a critique of the 2008 crisis, this portion does deliver its ode as affectively as other corresponding films of the time, such as *Inside Job* and *Margin Call*.

Gekko begins by explaining that greed was not just the preserve of Wall Street traders, but also it was practised by ordinary people who remortgaged their houses, aided by the government which cut interest rates to 1 per cent after 9/11, so that everybody could 'go shopping again'. In 1987, a clear moral high ground was outlined by Bud Fox when he challenged Gekko by asking him, 'How much is enough?' Gekko, of course, stepped around the question by alluding to it all as a 'game'. However, the audience was left in no doubt about the force of Fox's question. By 2010, as Gekko explains during the pitch for his book, what had changed was that *everyone* now saw it as a game. Bud Fox's question was no longer relevant.

Gekko's thesis of a malaise beyond *Wall Street* was finding its way into expert assessments of the period too. Bethany McLean and Joe Nocera's 2010 treatise, *All the Devils Are Here,* described how existing homeowners took advantage of low interest rates by refinancing their mortgages and withdrawing cash on the assumption of increased capital value.[35] However, the real deals were still being done by Wall Street traders, busy refining mortgage-backed securities into complex financial instruments, aided by the rating agencies that gave these instruments a seal of approval. Initially the securities seemed to be serving the best interests of the consumer, building the American Dream from the bottom-up. Loans for low-risk borrowers were providing Americans with homes, while the fees were making traders rich. However, the move to Collateralised Debt Obligations (CDOs) – the repackaging of higher-risk mortgage loans known as 'sub-prime' loans alongside low-risk loans into instruments whose ratings were massaged to triple A status – proved to be the ultimate Ponzi scheme.[36] This packaging of good and bad debt that was then sliced, diced and repackaged ensured that few, if any, market analysts had any idea what really was being traded. The further insurance of these instruments using Credit Default Swaps (CDS) – a mechanism that allowed institutions to bet on the failure of CDOs – added a final layer of risk and potential instability. Exemplifying J. K. Galbraith's warning about short memories, traders, sub-prime borrowers and the major financial institutions were all equally happy to live in the moment and gamble in a casino that had no house limit.

Back in 1987, Stone had offered a defence of capitalism in *Wall Street* while capturing the hyper-materialism of the era. That defence, anchored in the character of Lou Mannheim (Hal Holbrook), was rooted in a blend of capital endeavour and social responsibility that Stone saw in his father's generation. Lou Stone had been a trader on Wall Street, immersed in a world shaped by the New Deal and the Second World War. Themes aired by the Founding Fathers, including Alexander Hamilton's defence of commerce as an aid to government vitality, and James Madison's call for justice and the public good, had been given a new relevance during the Great Depression.[37] In his inaugural address in 1933, President Franklin D. Roosevelt had castigated the money changers and their failings, adding that happiness lay 'not in the mere possession of money' but 'in the joy of achievement and the thrill of creative effort'.[38] That sense of wider purpose and responsibility is clearly present in *Wall Street* in the discussions about Blue Star Airlines. Gekko's motivations included money and power, and his rivalry with Sir Larry Wildman (Terence Stamp) involved retribution and a desire to bring down the most ruthless shark of all. However, crucially, personal animus was secondary in the diegesis to the primacy of institutional justice.

As was the case with the original, *Wall Street: Money Never Sleeps* is not so much an economic treatise on the difficulties produced by mortgage-backed securities or deregulation, as it is a classic tale about the loss and rediscovery of some form of morality. However, the nature of that reacquisition is very different from the original film, and the evidence of any moral compass in this new world is hazy at best. It is a tale of retribution that sat comfortably in a post-9/11 era where justice at home and abroad was hard to find.

The film's moral fulcrum turns on Moore's intent to damage Bretton James as retribution for Louis Zabel's 'forced' suicide, following the collapse of his firm KZI. Moore assigns guilt and determines the punishment, then shields himself from that truth as he sets out to right a wrong: the end justifying the means. His response certainly foregrounds a self-righteousness that is, in many ways, a cornerstone of American (frontier) ideology; however, it necessarily clouds an appreciation of the wider moral failure within the marketplace by replicating that failure. James and the Churchill Schwartz bank had a hand in crushing KZI, but KZI was betting using CDSs along with the rest of the market. Moore's perspective is similarly blinkered when it comes to financing his fusion energy investment, and he is content to defraud the US Internal Revenue Service as part of the plan to repatriate Winnie's trust fund to support the project. Even Gekko's conversion at the end of the film, where he reclaims and assumes some responsibility for his new extended family and makes a long-term investment in the energy research project, is the result of a piece of emotional arm-twisting by Moore. In the original film, Bud Fox searches his soul and, with guidance from his father, finds atonement through judicial closure. In this second outing, James is arrested, but Moore neither seeks nor finds such closure, despite his reconciliation with Gekko's daughter: his actions are all self-serving. As for Gekko's denouement transformation, this seems so far out of character that we might almost suppose this change signals a direct 'heads up' plea from the director to his audience: reminding them just how far off track the USA has gone, and calling for a fundamental rethink about social worth, the accumulation of wealth and their place in the American Dream.

Of course, the downplaying of institutional justice in *Wall Street: Money Never Sleeps* was a fair representation of the aftermath of the crash. Individual offenders such as Bernie Madoff finished up behind bars, but there was no systemic redress for the egregious behaviour on the part of the institutions that precipitated the financial crisis.[39] Martin Scorsese, Stone's old New York University professor, made the same point in *The Wolf of Wall Street* (2013). Scorsese's celebration of Jordan Belfort's misdemeanours, his prosecution and conversion to state witness and his subsequent reinvention as a sales expert, concludes with an essential truth about the crisis. The film's final shot is of the faces of a group of sales trainees at a Jordan Belfort training seminar: Scorsese's point of view indicating that the raw material for the next crash – and every crash – was already out there, waiting to be activated.

The Wolf of Wall Street was one of several Hollywood treatises providing a perspective on the financial world in the aftermath of 2008's calamity. Both Michael Moore's *Capitalism: A Love Story* (2009) and Ferguson's *Inside Job* provided highly watchable documentary critiques of banking behaviour. While Moore combined his own inimitable comedic delivery with personal drama and key archive footage, including a sequence showing President Roosevelt's 1944 call for a second Bill of Rights, neither Roger Ebert nor *New York Times* reviewer Manohla Dargis were entirely convinced that a clear message emerged.[40] Moore was explicit enough about widespread evidence of exploitation, but what the solution might be was harder to discern.

By contrast, *Inside Job* offered a more forensic analysis of the crisis. Ferguson was in no doubt that an ongoing systemic corruption of the USA was being perpetrated by the financial services industry.[41] However, the film's US box office takings of $4.3 million, compared to Moore's $14 million, told their own story about how entertainment weighs in the balance against detailed indictment. Alongside John Wells' *The Company Men* (2010) and Nicholas Jarecki's *Arbitrage* (2012), Chandor's *Margin Call* provided a dramatic accompaniment to *Inside Job* that offered a tightly focused dramatic exposé of the efforts of an investment bank to dump its bad debt on its customers, right at the cusp of the meltdown. The film's construction built on appreciation of the tensions faced by the fictitious firm (with echoes of Lehman Brothers), although its conscious lack of character development, which served to derail audience empathy, also diluted the moral outrage. As A. O. Scott argued in the *New York Times*, the film sidestepped any pronounced moral commentary, but rather used the microdrama to convey a sense of tragedy, conceit and waste.[42] Therefore, in its efforts to draw lessons, *Wall Street: Money Never Sleeps* sat somewhere between *Margin Call* and *The Wolf of Wall Street*. Although less of a thriller than Chandor's movie, *Wall Street: Money Never Sleeps'* rounded characterisations allowed Stone to explore some of the endemically corrupt motivations at the heart of *Margin Call*'s conclusion. Equally, *Wall Street: Money Never Sleeps* disavowed the cacophonous entertainment proffered by Scorsese's picture. Stone's melodrama steered a middle and arguably more complicated course – it offered perspectives on morality and the evident limitations of judicial redress – but was this a combination that critics and audiences sought, or of which they were in need?

To an extent, Stone's lack of catharsis or outrage did leave him out of step with other Hollywood portrayals in 2010. His concerns chimed with values that had been downgraded in a world of prevailing post-9/11 mores, rooted as they were in the experiences of his parents' generation: the tenets of the New Deal and the nation's role in defending freedom in the Second World War. This version of the American Dream embraced prosperity, good governance and family values in equal measure. Stone's father's adherence to orthodoxies of anti-communism and the primacy of the market were balanced by his mother's more liberal European instincts. In the original *Wall Street*, this tension was harnessed within the narrative and culminated in an affirmation of family, government and justice, as Carl Fox (Martin Sheen) watches his son Bud walk up the steps of the courthouse for his trial. In *Wall Street: Money Never Sleeps* there is some legal redress, but it is much less pronounced than in the original, and less central to the conclusion. This narrative choice within *Wall Street: Money Never Sleeps* did not rob the film of a wider reading that gave a nod to structural failure, but it did explain the criticism from observers such as Ebert, who concluded that the film had not really hit its target hard enough. Despite failing to deliver the cathartic release sought by many liberals, the film's focus on retribution as a motivator was perfectly in tune with the new political zeitgeist, and anchored it in both post 9/11 national predispositions as well as an earlier mythic time of frontier justice that embraced retribution, together with redemption through reinvention. In doing so, it underscored how far Stone, Hollywood and the country had travelled since the late 1980s: a time when a very different political sensibility remained a vivid memory. Crucially, despite the optimism expressed in the ending of *Wall Street: Money Never Sleeps*, the conclusion is pessimistic and uncertain about the potential realignment and recovery of moral purpose driven by government action. All that was left was acquisition, and a return to the morals of the frontier.

Savages

In 1845 John Louis O'Sullivan wrote of the frontier, famously stating that the nation's 'manifest destiny is to overspread the continent allotted by Providence for the free development of our yearly multiplying millions'.[43] Specifically, he was addressing the proposed annexation of Texas from Mexico that took place later that year and preceded a two-year conflict only halted by the Treaty of Guadalupe Hidalgo signed in February 1848. The USA took control of lands that eventually would make up the states of California, Nevada, Utah and New Mexico, as well as much of the territory that is now in Arizona and Colorado. Of all these territories, California was the one that would go on to symbolise the most distinctive expression of manifest destiny, charted through its history by the likes of writers Frank Norris, Nathanael West, Raymond Chandler, John Steinbeck and, more recently, Joan Didion and Hunter S. Thompson. In varying ways these writers sought to shine a light on manifest destiny made real in the West, and on the American Dream which, despite its status as ideological totem, always has eaten away at the soft underbelly of California.

Don Winslow's *Savages*, a bestselling novel first published in 2010, took many of those themes as its mantra, and played them out amid the gratuitous violence of drug cartels. *Savages* alludes to something more than the story of two southern California-based dope producers and their fight with a Mexican drug cartel to recover their kidnapped friend, although the pared down writing style leaves little space for expository detail. While the bulk of the book is primarily about power struggle and kidnapping, Winslow offers a single page near the end that meditates on the Californian obsessions of water and beauty, what the spiritual condition of southern California really is, and an assessment of where the region's real place is in the national ideology. Southern California is, was and always has been a region of narcissism, observes Winslow: a culture that venerates wealth and health, that celebrates everything from film studios to amusement parks and megachurches, a culture that worships only itself. Revealingly, Stone chose to omit this broader cultural critique from his treatment. As with *Wall Street: Money Never Sleeps,* his focus was on an unfolding personal drama which signposted a wider social and political debate, rather than the other way round (Figure 7).

In the book and film, the story's point of departure traces how turf wars among the drug cartels in Mexico are pushing one group north – led by Elena (Salma Hayek) – to take a business interest in two independent marijuana producers working in the southland: Ben (Aaron Taylor-Johnson) and Chon (Taylor Kirsch). When Ben and Chon show reluctance to align their boutique business

Figure 7 Benicio Del Toro and Oliver Stone on the set of *Savages* (2012)

with the cartel, their southern California girlfriend O (Blake Lively) is kidnapped by cartel enforcer Lado (Benicio Del Toro). With help from Dennis (John Travolta) a Drug Enforcement Administration (DEA) officer on their payroll, Ben and Chon kidnap Elena's daughter Magda (Sandra Echeverría) and organise a hostage swap.

Given its enduring themes and prescient focus on border relations and illegal trafficking of many kinds, the attraction of the story to Stone was obvious; but adapting Winslow's book was a slow and fraught business at times. In a 1 September 2010 version of the screenplay written by Winslow himself, the final hostage-exchange shootout is at a pier in Laguna Beach. Chon is killed and Ben and O escape. In a plain cover version produced in November 2010, Stone moved the action to a shopping mall, with O killed and Ben and Chon escaping. This version ends with Ben and Chon in Java, scattering O's ashes. A voiceover from O repeats lines from Winslow's commentary on southern California. In three further versions of the screenplay prepared in January and February 2011, two by Stone, and one jointly by Winslow and his friend and collaborator, Shane Salerno, details are tweaked, although the southern California voiceover remains in all of them. However, behind the various iterations lay a broader disagreement: one that resulted in Winslow, Salerno, Stone and producer Moritz Borman agreeing not to air their criticisms of each other in public.

Stone had the impression that Winslow was slow in producing the screenplay, while Winslow thought that it was difficult to get Stone to focus. There was probably truth in both perspectives. Winslow was already an established author, but he had no track record in screenwriting. Stone's schedule required that he progress his *Untold History* documentary series, launch *Wall Street: Money Never Sleeps* and work on this new screenplay at the same time. Beyond concerns about pace, Stone was also increasingly worried about the sparse character profiles in Winslow's screenplay, and how these would translate to the screen without Stone's increasing involvement in the writing.[44] He had another pressing issue to contend with in spring 2011: the loss of his lead actress, Jennifer Lawrence. She had been the preferred choice for O, but opted to sign a contract for Gary Ross's adaptation of *The Hunger Games* (2012). Stone reflected later that 'when [Jennifer] left to do *Hunger Games*, yeah, it hurt'.[45]

The loss of Lawrence was more than a matter of inconvenience for the production schedule. Stone's reliance on readings and rehearsals to refine the screenplay has always had the effect of utilising the emotional and discursive contributions made by the actors. A late change of actor altered the whole dynamic, and required another reworking of the screenplay. However, the task of finding a replacement for O was concluded quickly at the end of March, by bringing in Blake Lively. Intense preparation brought the screenplay revisions to completion by 1 May 2011.

The final version included two significant deviations from the book and earlier screenplays. From early on in the writing process, Stone had some concerns about the double suicide ending in the book, and indeed Winslow also had concerns about using the suicide ending in the screenplay. For Stone, the suicide ending was a romantic twist that alluded to *Butch Cassidy and the Sundance Kid* (George Roy Hill, 1969), but he was not convinced that it worked dramatically. As he heard the output from actor readings, he became convinced that while the characters of O and Chon might grieve for Ben, the relationships were too shallow to invoke a double suicide. Moreover, this playing out of the negotiation in the film convinced him that the DEA agent should not commit suicide, as he does in the book. Stone reconstructed him as a much smarter character, a wheeler-dealer who was taking money both from Lado and from Ben and Chon, and who would always come out on top.

Both thoughts took Stone towards the idea of using a double ending: the first depicting the suicide scene as a projection by O, followed by a rewind and replay in which Dennis gatecrashes the hostage swap with hordes of law enforcement officers in a bloodless intervention. The inclusion of the second ending led Stone to eliminate the voiceover reference to Winslow's observations of southern California that had featured briefly in the book. He reasoned that this ending seemed to blame the young people in some way for what had happened, and he wanted to conclude on a more hopeful note.

This process, and the proposed changes, demonstrate more than the inside story of a film's production process: they reveal Stone's own filmmaking evolution. Always a dramatist with something to say, what shifted over the years was the range of channels – film, documentary, publications, talk-show appearances – available for

Stone to discuss his work. The result was a distinct shift in emphasis within his dramatic output. The decision to move to documentary work was a response to Stone's own assessment, that it was more difficult to make polemical drama in the post 9/11 era. This line of thinking appeared to accelerate Stone's shift from a realist aesthetic into more distinct melodrama phase of filmmaking: something that first had been signalled with *U Turn* in 1997. Thus, the pursuit of documentary was pragmatic in terms of Stone's political commentary, but it brought forth new styles of drama where social and political observations were less foregrounded. As was the case with *Wall Street: Money Never Sleeps*, Stone did see important social and cultural messages in *Savages* which he was happy to comment on subsequently in interview, but both the style of drama and the purposes that Stone needed it to serve had shifted.

On the surface, the film is a lushly shot kidnap caper set against the backdrop of the drug trade. However, its setting in Laguna Beach rather than Mexico, and the critical switch from the book – the transformation of Dennis – allowed Stone to offer an albeit oblique perspective on a range of American cultural predispositions. Violence and the drug trade are certainly in this mix, but there are also pointers here to exceptionalism, US popular conceptions of Mexico, as well as the acquisition of wealth and the American Dream.

Chon's background as a soldier in Afghanistan brought the psychological strain of violence with it that was familiar to Stone, and seen in previous films. The returning veteran, repatriated into a country he no longer recognises, gave Chon's character a wider perspective that posited connections between Abu Ghraib, Al Qaeda and the cartels. Thus violence and cruelty is brought home, not just in the guise of Chon and his former service buddies, but in the suggestion that military experience gained in Iraq and Afghanistan is percolating into cartel operations. For example, reports in the wider news indicated that members of the Zetas cartel – formerly Mexican army commandos – had received training from US Special Forces while they were still serving military personnel.[46] The polemicist in Stone took up the wider subtext:

> It is about our war on drugs. The drug thing is so ugly because it creates such a false bureaucracy. We have a 'War on Drugs', a 'War

> on Poverty', a war on this, a war on that, a 'War on Terror'. Now we have so many wars we can't keep track any more.[47]

Despite these concerns, Stone's focus within the narrative was on the morality that underpinned the violence. In the film, it is Elena's traditional values of parenthood – her love for her daughter – which is her undoing. Stone sees the cartels as having moved away from more traditional crime organisations built around families with codes of honour, to a purer and more ruthless pursuit of money in which cruelty is not only an operational necessity, but a refined form of publicity and entertainment.[48] The shift from expedient violence to cruelty-as-spectacle has become a calling card for the contemporary cartels themselves, amplified in the Mexican tabloids' coverage of the carnage. The foregrounding of violence parallels a commodification of force within entertainment media more generally, notably within an emerging sub-genre of 'narco cinema' in particular: low-budget, violent portrayals of Mexico's drug violence which have found a market among Hispanic immigrant communities close to the US border.[49] The animated video decapitation of the captured O within the narrative references the media-savvy actions of the cartels in publicising their violence and, by inference, the extent of their control of their own media coverage.[50]

Negotiation to facilitate a trade is the central theme of *Savages*. The key problem for Elena's cartel, as well as Ben and Chon, is in finding the common currency with which they are both willing to work. The cartel's initial offer of a revenue share deal for the marijuana business is declined; instead, Ben offers to give them the business but without his participation, in a desperate attempt to escape the confines of this dangerous occupation in which he finds them all. Wanting to move into environmental work, he later agrees to collaboration as a ruse to buy time to allow himself, Chon and O to disappear. The cartel's enforcer Lado suspects the move, and the cartel kidnaps O, using her as leverage to force Ben and Chon to cooperate in a first transaction with the cartel. The full deal requires that Ben and Chon work for three years, and that in return O will be released after one year. However, Ben reasons that the cartel's interest is in money, and proposes a straight purchase of O and subsequent fulfilment of the remainder of the deal. He agrees a price with Elena, but does not have all the cash. He and Chon then hit on the idea of stealing cartel money to use in the purchase of O. This works to a degree, but Ben must pay a crucial price. In order to allay suspicion, Ben's associates create a fabricated financial history for the cartel lawyer Alex (Demián Bishir) that eventually leads to the lawyer's torture and confession. Ben is witness to this brutality, and Elena instructs him to set fire to the gasoline that has been poured over the beaten and trussed but still alive Alex. During the torture sequence, Ben has learned that Elena's daughter Magda (Sandra Echeverría) is living in southern California, and persuades Dennis to provide details of her whereabouts. Dennis complies, and the pair kidnap the girl, setting up the final hostage exchange sequence. Each barter relentlessly underscores the fundamental truth of a 'business' that trades in lives, and lives are only adjudged according to money. All involved, as the film periodically reminds us, have become nothing more than savages.

In Winslow's version of the story, this swap reaches a bloody conclusion with almost everyone present left dead or dying. Ben is fatally wounded, and O and then Chon opt for suicide. In the film's rewind-and-replay double ending, Ben and Chon are eventually freed with help from Dennis, and together with O they quietly remove themselves from the California scene to some undisclosed paradise in Indonesia. Elena is arrested. Lado, who also has business dealings with Dennis, takes charge of the cartel's California interests, but now works for a new cartel boss.

The completed version of *Savages* with its dual closure revealed much about Stone. As with *Wall Street: Money Never Sleeps*, a strain of personal optimism resistant to a perceived cynicism in contemporary culture abounded.[51] This version also survived mixed feedback at two pre-release screenings and an invitation from the studio to consider changes to the ending, based on feedback from a third screening.[52] While Universal put no undue pressure on Stone for the changes, it did ask him to consider the ending and the feedback collected: this he did. Some additional edits were made, but Stone was not persuaded of the need for wholesale change. He later confessed that the audience response after release was less positive than that observed in the pre-release screenings. However, there was clear resistance to the double ending from pre-release audiences.

Nevertheless, Stone stayed true to his best dramatic instincts, and the senior executives at Universal confirmed that they were happy to proceed. Indeed, they were sufficiently pleased that the proposed autumn launch date was brought forward to the 4 July weekend. However, from Stone's perspective this rescheduling almost certainly depressed the box office takings, pushing *Savages* into direct competition with blockbusters such as *The Amazing Spider-Man* (Marc Webb, 2012) as well two other summer hits, *Ted* (Seth MacFarlane, 2012) and *Magic Mike* (Steven Soderbergh, 2012). *Savages* eventually took just over $47 million at the US box office, and a further $33 million overseas. Some critics, such as the *Guardian*'s Peter Bradshaw and the *Washington Post*'s Ann Hornaday were a little underwhelmed. Hornaday concluded that the film offered 'a strong, if immediately forgettable buzz'.[53] Others saw something more. Roger Ebert in the *Chicago Sun-Times* saw it as a return to form, while A. O. Scott in the *New York Times* detected a film that successfully combined pulp elements with 'gritty geopolitical and economic themes'.[54]

Self-delusion

How then did Stone see those geopolitical and economic themes? *Savages* used money as a device to explore not just the pursuit of wealth, or the brutality of the drug wars, but the pervading awareness of 'otherness' projected from north to south at the border. In the film Mexico has something of the monstrous about it, but as with Mary Shelley's depiction in *Frankenstein* (1818), this monster is the product of its creator and, crucially, of a creator in denial.[55] In its use of the imagery of violence and death, its reflections on the American Dream, its treatise on business ethics, and indeed its explicit and implicit commentary on the drugs industry, *Savages* tapped into Mexico's emergence as monstrous 'other' for the USA: a place to project homegrown fears about the changing American character and the threat to it. Mexico was a place where bad things happen and where people die slowly; for Stone, it was an ideal place to test and expose the American psyche about its neighbours.

Near the beginning of the film, Chon and O watch a video recording from the cartel in which the decapitated bodies of cartel victims are displayed by a figure wearing a Santa Muerte death mask. The mask, or its wearer, does not appear in Winslow's description of the same sequence; it is something that Stone added. The mask certainly references Mexico's *Día de Muertos* (Day of the Dead), and a similar image – *La Calavera Catrina* – which has been used as a satirical commentary on Mexico's obsequy for European culture, not least by Diego Rivera. However, in this context it is a more specific reference to Santa Muerte, a folk saint with origins in pre-colonial Mexico. The veneration of Santa Muerte has acquired a prominence in recent decades as a cult both in Mexico and within Mexican immigrant communities in the USA.[56] It also has acquired a particular association with criminality and the cartels, and a sub-cult has become especially linked with personal gain at the expense of the pain of others.[57] Therefore, the cartel video in *Savages* projects not simply violence, but spectacle and fear, allied to media management as a form of intimidation.[58]

The images of Santa Muerte in *Savages* allude not just to the pursuit of wealth, but also to a pointed lack of self-awareness north of the border. For some US-based observers, this nightmare of accumulation and violence seems the antithesis of the American Dream – the historic 'other' at the border, threatening a way of life – yet it is a construction that does not seem so very far from O'Sullivan's paean to the American Dream. After all, what Providence had given to the multiplying millions, it first had taken of necessity with its own brand of violence from the indigenous tribes.[59] The infusion of Mexican cartel culture with Santa Muerte – self-serving violence bathed in religion – suggests an ambition and method that echoes, rather than refutes, the American Dream.

Indeed, through its presentation of the cartel and Mexico as the outsider, the film sets up more reflections about the American Dream. As Stephen Brooks has noted, the Dream has acquired several patinas: freedom from persecution, the love of open space; but it is the acquisition of material wealth that is at its bedrock – or rather, the possibility of that acquisition.[60] Mexico poses a challenge to that dream on several levels, and these are all signposted in *Savages*. Mexicans represent the largest immigrant groups in the two largest states, California and Texas, yet as a group they are distinguished by their poor economic progress towards the national income mean.[61] Their presence in the USA as a largely unskilled group has been driven in no small part by the effects of the *maquiladora* (manufacturing) economy within Mexico. US-owned and funded corporations have exploited labour pay differentials systematically through the operation of the North American Free Trade Agreement, and specifically through the placing of production facilities just south of the USA–Mexico border.[62] The general effects of *maquiladora* development – low-skilled work and declining opportunities, as US corporations found even cheaper labour rates in China – are part of the employment context for the country reflected in *Savages*. Lado's day job as a gardener in Laguna provides easy cover for his criminal activities *and* dreams of a better life, and it is employment with which many immigrant communities in southern California are all too familiar. Mexicans coming north to seek work and a stable future is intrinsic to the film's pursuit of the Dream. What *Savages* further signposts is the way in which the cartel – an alien threat from beyond the border – has become a symbol for something that is, in truth, embedded in US culture. Ben and Chon's pursuit of the American Dream has no firmer moral basis than Lado's – and if, as we might reasonably suppose, they both banked with HSBC or a raft of other US financial institutions, the reciprocity of amorality could not be strengthened further.

While the Santa Muerte imagery and Lado's gardening business in *Savages* offer some tentative insights into the ways in which the desire for money and pursuit of the American Dream are being played out across the USA–Mexico border, it is business ethics and attitudes to drug consumption where the film exposes the contradictions inherent in the 'War on Drugs' and media constructions of the cartels as monsters.

A moral turning point in the film arrives when Ben conspires to frame cartel member Alex, to deflect attention from his and Chon's theft from the cartel. Chon later justifies the resulting torture and killing by saying that Alex had done similar to others, but Ben remains unconvinced. The deeper moral dilemma here is the conceit that the US drugs business is somehow immune from criticism about its own contribution to the social hardships that accrue from distribution and use. Drugs can be understood as a rational response to an irrational world, the screenplay posits – citing the use of marijuana as a general relief from pain, in the case of Dennis's dying wife. Ben and

Chon's outlook assumes an alter ego as the benefactor for needy African villagers: a contorted kind of American exceptionalism that valorises the same behaviour that Dennis will later condemn (Figure 8).

Therefore, *Savages* projects a more complicated vision of cartel violence, drug culture and establishment largesse. Ethical business practice, prohibition verses regulation and the protagonists' self-serving moral universe are all brought forth as interrelated cogs in an unethical environment. Ben and Chon's profits are primarily out of state, and out of mind. Ben's genius, we are told, is in taking 99 per cent of the paranoia and violence out of the business. The remaining 1 per cent is justified retaliation by Chon, where people do not pay up. In this moral universe there are good American dope dealers entitled – indeed, imbued with a manifest destiny – to make money doing worthy deeds, and nasty Mexican cartel people who trade in death: the thoughtful, small entrepreneurial business, and the single-minded, behemoth cartel. Even institutional representative Dennis is in on the act. After Elena's arrest on a Native American reservation, he gives a press conference remarking that:

Figure 8 John Travolta, Taylor Kitsch and Oliver Stone on the set of *Savages* (2012)

> Today we have made great strides to further protect our children and our freedoms by dismantling the leadership of the Baja cartel and the curse of illicit drugs in our country. It is on an Indian reservation. It is technically not our country but as we know – it is![63]

Of course, Dennis is lying about all of the essential issues here, save for the comment about the reservation. He knows that he has not dismantled the cartel; he is part of the operation. He knows that far from winning the 'War on Drugs', the money will continue and the battle will rage. We know from his earlier confession to his wife what he thinks of the people with influence in the USA: '[A] nation of whores; Wall Street, Washington.' He knows he is no better, but he also knows he is no worse. The lack of a firm moral purchase is a crucial aspect of the wider US narrative on drugs that Stone is calling attention to in *Savages*, and Dennis's remarks point to the hypocrisy that envelops the US government's perpetual mishandling of the so-called 'drug wars'.

As for the acquisition of wealth, all of the key players in the film are motivated by the accumulation of money, and all are compromised by it. The same motivations drove those involved in bringing alcohol across the border during the prohibition era, and they endure in HSBC's participation in money-laundering, an act not simply achieved by the malfeasance of a few executives. HSBC's US entity HBUS rated Mexico as low risk for money-laundering between 2000 and 2009, despite extensive US government reports of malpractice dating back to 2002. Inexplicably, HSBC Group only revised its rating from the lowest risk level in 2012.[64] None of this activity resulted in any criminal proceedings against anyone employed at the company. Also in 2012 the US Department of State estimated that the total annual haul of laundered cash across all involved Mexican and US financial institutions was $39 billion.[65] Large numbers of Mexicans living in California might not be living the Dream, but the drug war has helped ensure that cartel bosses and senior bank executives have all had more than their share of it.

Savages continued to point towards the ongoing crisis of illegal immigrants crossing into Texas and California, as well as the corrupting effects of large fortunes being fought over in turf wars, well beyond its release. A reported $15 billion was spent by the DEA in 2013 in efforts outside the USA to disrupt supply.[66] Both in interviews at the time of release and subsequently, Stone used the film to lend his name to those calling for an end to the 'War on Drugs'. For him, the widespread denial within the USA about the futility of the 'War on Drugs' was the real monster within. With the worst of the violence still south of the border, the possibility was in believing that the problem was external. The Santa Muerte mask may have looked Mexican, countered Stone, but the face behind it was very much American.

Conclusion

In both *Wall Street: Money Never Sleeps* and *Savages*, Stone put his own distinctive spin on the pursuit of wealth in twenty-first-century America. Both films celebrate aspects of the American Dream – the possibilities and freedoms that wealth can offer – but the narratives also highlight the presence of a distorted sense of entitlement, and share an emerging realisation of the limitations for redress that are available through institutional justice: as crucial a development for Stone as it has been for the country as a whole. Stone's narratives anchored themselves not in late-twentieth and early twenty-first-century liberalism, with its concomitant praxis of government-driven social justice, but in an earlier and more problematic version of the American Dream that put its faith in individual action. However, such morality always has been fraught with contradiction and problems in the contested space where American exceptionalism sits. Jake, Ben and Chon all inhabit a world that is very different to the one in which Bud Fox lived. Stone's philosophy returned again to Henry Luce's vision of the 'American Century'. Assertions of exceptionalism can veer off all too easily into a corrupted, self-serving morality. Despite the optimistic denouements in both *Wall Street: Money Never Sleeps* and *Savages*, an underlying pessimism still reared up concerning broader national mores, recovery and reassessment.

In all of this, the shift in Stone the filmmaker and the corresponding shift within Hollywood the industry is all-too apparent. In the intervening years since the 1980s, camerawork, editing and pure visceral depictions that were the hallmarks of Hollywood's own *enfant terrible* have passed over into more conventional plotting and framing. Stone nurtured a strain of melodrama that became freer of polemics. His commitment to this emerging style of drama also said something about his own perspective on money. Stone chases projects that he believes in, rather than simply signing his skills over to a studio. This may have limited his budgets on occasion, but as noted in the Introduction, he always has managed to maintain a steady audience and respectable income by any Hollywood standards. Therefore, money was never the end, but a means to an end. The decision to work on the *Untold History* series for five years – a series that Stone himself acknowledged as a kind of *pro bono* project – reinforced an artist chasing something beyond the commercial bottom-line.

Yet, as businessman, auteur and commentator, Stone remains very much *in* the movie colony rather than *outside* it. He is a critic of the establishment of which he is also a part, and as such his prognoses often appear to be about reform more than revolution. Not a denunciation of capitalism per se, rather it is more the articulation of a particular version of the American Dream; one that draws on his personal history and reflects a belief in the importance of individual decisions and personal responsibility supported by a broader societal consensus about the pre-eminence of social values over profit. *Wall Street: Money Never Sleeps* left the question of retribution open, and thus wondered about the broader consensus at large: a public surety that suffused the closing sequence of the original *Wall Street* that had gone lame by the relentless pursuit of reward. By contrast, *Savages* was in many ways a more complex and nuanced film, using Mexico as a mirror and highlighting questions about business ethics and broader societal self-awareness.

Stone's liberalism has been always individual as well as civically minded, and his interest in ethics with regard to money is not so much theoretical as it is a spur to action. His treatise on money in *Wall Street: Money Never Sleeps* and *Savages* was more praxis than analysis, in the Marxist sense: less of a public call to action, than a necessary personal preparatory step for his own assertions as an advocate for change.[67] The films were imbued with Stone's concerns about the US embrace of an increasingly blurred moral purchase, but ultimately they were not the primary means of expression of those concerns. This caused some worries for Stone's supporters, but his choices were part of a wider exploration of new aesthetic possibilities that were already establishing themselves in his drama, most obviously in the increasing prominence given to a theme not often noted in his films: the subject of love.

Notes

1 Interview with Oliver Stone, Santa Monica, CA, 19 August 2013.
2 Nathaniel Popper, 'In Testimony, HSBC Official Resigns Amid Bank Apology', *New York Times* (17 July 2012). Available at http://dealbook.nytimes.com/2012/07/17/hsbc-says-official-will-step-down-as-bank-vows-to-fix-scandal/ (accessed 7 December 2015).
3 By the time of the Senate hearings, activities causally related to HSBC's actions had already claimed an estimated 55,000 fatalities in Mexico. See Eduardo Porter, 'Numbers Tell of Failure in Drug War', *New York Times* (3 July 2012). Available at http://nytimes.com/2012/07/04/business/in-rethinking-the-war-on-drugs-start-with-the-numbers.html?adxnnl=1&adxnnlx=1383577287-6GF8FoeWWwoMVczwlDfHtg (accessed 7 December 2015).
4 Robert Mazur, 'How to Halt the Terrorist Money Train', *New York Times* (2 January 2013). Available at http://nytimes.com/2013/01/03/opinion/how-bankers-help-drug-traffickers-and-terrorists.html (accessed 7 December 2015).
5 Tom Wolfe, *The Bonfire of the Vanities* (London: Vintage Books, 2010; orig. pub. 1987).
6 Roger Ebert, 'Wall Street: Money Never Sleeps', *Chicago Sun-Times* (22 September 2010). Available at http://rogerebert.com/reviews/wall-street-money-never-sleeps-2010 (accessed 7 December 2015).
7 Peter Bradshaw, '*Savages* – review', *Guardian* (20 September 2012). Available at http://theguardian.com/film/2012/sep/20/savages-review (accessed on 7 December 2015).
8 Milica Z. Bookman and Aleksandra S. Bookman, *Economics in Film and Fiction* (London and New York: Rowman and Littlefield Education, 2009), pp. 77–9.
9 Ralph Gomory and Richard Sylla, 'The American Corporation', *Daedalus*, 142, 2, 2013, pp. 102–18.
10 John Kenneth Galbraith, 'The 1929 Parallel', *The Atlantic*, 259, 1, 1987, pp. 62–6.
11 Galbraith, 'The 1929 Parallel', p. 66.
12 Haynes Johnson, *Sleepwalking Through History* (New York and London: W.W. Norton & Co., 2003), p. 215.
13 Caryl Churchill, *Serious Money* (London: Methuen, 2010; orig. pub. 1987).
14 Leonard Silk, 'Is Wall Street as Bad as It's Painted', *New York Times* (3 January 1988). Available at http://nytimes.com/1988/01/03/arts/is-wall-street-as-bad-as-it-s-paintedhtml?pagewanted=all&src=pm (accessed 7 December 2015).
15 Jon Lewis, *Hollywood v Hard Core: How the Struggle Over Censorship Created the Modern Film Industry* (New York: New York University Press, 2000), pp.75–81.

16 Lewis, *Hollywood v Hard Core*, pp. 69–72. *U.S.* v. *Paramount Pictures Inc.*, 334 US 131 (1948). Available at: http://caselaw.findlaw.com/us-supreme-court/334/131.html (accessed 1 March 2016).
17 Jennifer Steinhauer, 'After Scandals, New Legal Stars Rise on Wall St.', *New York Times* (20 May 2005). Available at http://nytimes.com/2005/05/20/business/20comply.html?ex=1274241600&en=2bc557b2c38b3391&ei=5090&partner=rssuserland&emc=rss&_r=0 (accessed 7 December 2015).
18 Raymond Arsenault, 'Stoned on *Wall Street* (1987): The Stockbroker's Son and the Decade of Greed', *Film & History*, 28,1–2, 1998, p. 20.
19 John Cassidy, 'Anatomy of a Meltdown: Ben Bernanke interprets the crisis', *New Yorker* (1 December 2008), pp. 48–63. James B. Stewart, 'Eight Days: Behind the scenes of the financial crisis', *New Yorker* (21 September 2009), pp. 58–81. John Cassidy, 'What Good is Wall Street? The financial sector tries to justify itself'. *New Yorker* (29 November 2010), pp. 48–57.
20 Michael Cieply, 'Film's Wall Street Predator to Make a Comeback', *New York Times* (5 May 2007). Available at http://nytimes.com/2007/05/05/movies/05movi.html?_r=1&oref=slogin (accessed 7 December 2015).
21 Telis Demos, 'Where's Gekko? 'Wall Street' turns 20', *Fortune* (21 September 2007). Available at http://money.cnn.com/magazines/fortune/fortune_archive/2007/10/01/100400996/index.htm (accessed 7 December 2015).
22 *Wall Street 2*, Screenplay 3 June 09 file, Box WS2 Script, Ixtlan Production Files (hereafter I-PF), Los Angeles, CA.
23 *Pinkville*, Script file, Box Pinkville, I-PF.
24 *Wall Street 2*, Script file, Box WS2 Script, I-PF.
25 See for example, David Edelstein, 'Old Greed, New Greed', *New York Magazine* (19 September 2010). Available at http://nymag.com/movies/reviews/68372/ (accessed 7 December 2015).
26 *Wall Street 2*, Screenplay 3: June 09 file, Box WS2 Script, I-PF.
27 *Wall Street 2*, *Casting 3/08* file, Box WS2 Production Casting, I-PF.
28 *Wall Street 2*, *Casting 2 7/09 file*, Box WS2 Production Casting, I-PF.
29 *Wall Street 2*, Screenplay WS2 file, Box WS2 Script, I-PF.
30 *Ibid.*
31 *Wall Street 2*, Screenplay 3: June 09 file, Box WS2 Script, I-PF.
32 Interview with Oliver Stone, Santa Monica, CA, 8 December 2011.
33 Interview with Oliver Stone, Los Angeles, CA, 19 January 2010.
34 Jane Mayer, 'Covert Operations', *New Yorker* (30 August 2010), pp. 45–55.
35 Bethany McLean and Joe Nocera, *All The Devils Are Here* (London: Portfolio Penguin, 2010), p. 126.
36 McLean and Nocera, *All The Devils Are Here*, pp. 119–22.

37 James Madison, Alexander Hamilton and John Jay, *The Federalist Papers* (London: Penguin, 1987), pp. 134–8, 122–8.

38 Franklin D. Roosevelt, 'First Inaugural Address, 1933' in Richard D. Heffner, *A Documentary History of the United States* (New York and Harmondsworth: Penguin/Mentor, 6th edn, 1999), p. 324.

39 Diana B. Henriques, 'Madoff Is Sentenced to 150 years for Ponzi Scheme', *New York Times* (29 June 2009). Available at http://nytimes.com/2009/06/30/business/30madoff.html?pagewanted=all&_r=0(accessed 7 December 2015).

40 Roger Ebert, 'Capitalism: A Love Story', *Chicago Sun-Times* (30 September 2009). Available at www.rogerebert.com/reviews/capitalism-a-love-story-2009 (accessed 7 December 2015). Manohla Dargis, 'Greed Is Good? He Begs to Differ', *New York Times* (22 September 2009). Available at http://nytimes.com/2009/09/23/movies/23capitalism.html?_r=0 (accessed 1 March 2016).

41 A. O. Scott, 'Who Maimed the Economy, and How', *New York Times* (7 October 2010). Available at http://nytimes.com/2010/10/08/movies/08inside.html (accessed 7 December 2014).

42 A. O. Scott, 'Number Crunching at the Apocalypse', *New York Times* (20 October 2011). Available at http://nytimes.com/2011/10/21/movies/margin-call-with-zachary-quinto-review.html?_r=0 (accessed 7 December 2015).

43 John O'Sullivan, 'Annexation', *United States Magazine and Democratic Review*, 17, 1 1845, pp. 5–10.

44 *Savages*, Production and Distribution file, Box-Savages I-PF.

45 Interview with Oliver Stone, 19 August 2013, Santa Monica, CA.

46 George W. Grayson, 'Los Zetas: The Ruthless Army Spawned by a Mexican Drug Cartel', *Foreign Policy Research Institute*, May 2008. Available at http://fpri.org/article/2012/07/los-zetas-the-ruthless-army-spawned-by-a-mexican-drug-cartel/(accessed 1 March 2016).

47 Interview with Stone, 19 August 2013.

48 Ed Vulliamy, 'Oliver Stone tackles the drugs war in America's backyard', *Observer* (23 September 2012). Available at: http://theguardian.com/film/2012/sep/23/oliver-stone-interview-savages-vulliamy (accessed 1 March 2016).

49 Julián Aguilar, 'Guns, Sex, Drug Cartels, Narco Cinema!', *International New York Times* (28 March 2013). Available at http://nytimes.com/2013/03/29/us/narco-cinema-tales-of-mexican-drug-cartels.html?_r=0 (accessed 7 December 2015).

50 Jo Tuckman, 'Journalists on Front Line of Mexico Drug War: "Fear Is Terrible and Well Founded"', *Guardian* (9 April 2013). Available at http://theguardian.com/world/2013/apr/09/mexico-drug-war-journalists-fear (accessed 7 December 2015).

51 Interview with Oliver Stone, 8 December 2011, Santa Monica, CA.

52 *Savages*, Production and Distribution file, Box-Savages I-PF.

53 Ann Hornaday, 'Savages: Stone's Sign of the High Times', *Washington Post* (6 July 2012). Available at http://washingtonpost.com/gog/movies/savages,1145341.html (accessed 7 December 2015).

54 Roger Ebert, 'Savages', *Chicago Sun-Times* (4 July 2012). Available at www.rogerebert.com/reviews/savages-2012 (accessed 30 January 2014). A.O. Scott, 'Stone and His Stoners Face the Weed Killers', *New York Times* (5 July 2012). Available at http://nytimes.com/2012/07/06/movies/review-savages-oliver-stones-adaptation-of-don-winslows-novel.html?pagewanted=1 (accessed 7 December 2015).

55 Marina Warner, *Managing Monsters: Six Myths of Our Time* (London: Vintage, 1994), p. 20.

56 Steven Gray, 'Santa Muerte: The New God in Town', *Time* (16 October 2007). Available at http://content.time.com/time/nation/article/0,8599,1671984,00.html (acceded 7 December 2015).

57 Robert J. Bunker, 'Santa Muerte: Inspired and Ritualistic Killings: Part 1', *FBI Law Enforcement Bulletin* (February 2013). Available at https://leb.fbi.gov/2013/february/santa-muerte-inspired-and-ritualistic-killings-part-1 (accessed 7 December 2015).

58 Mónica Medel, 'Journalism in Times of Threats, Censorship and Violence', Report from the Seminar "Cross-border Coverage of U.S.–Mexico Drug Trafficking", conducted March 26–27, 2010 at the Knight Center for Journalism in the Americas at the University of Texas at Austin. Available at https://knightcenter.utexas.edu/SRI2010_en.pdf (accessed 7 December 2015).

59 O'Sullivan, 'Annexation', pp. 5–10.

60 Stephen Brooks, *American Exceptionalism in the Age of Obama* (New York and London: Routledge, 2013), p. 103.

61 Brooks, *American Exceptionalism*, p. 115.

62 Graciela Bensusan, 'Norms, Practices and Perceptions: Labor Enforcement in Mexico's Garment Industry' (21 November 2008). Summary available at http://en.archive.maquilasolidarity.org/node/820 (accessed 7 December 2015).

63 *Savages* (2012).

64 United States Senate Permanent Subcommittee on Investigations, 'US Vulnerabilities to Money Laundering, Drugs and Terrorist Financing: HSBC Case Study' S Hrg. 112 Congress, July 17, 2012, p. 38. Available at www.hsgac.senate.gov/download/report-us-vulnerabilities-to-money-laundering-drugs-and-terrorist-financing-hsbc-case-history (accessed 1 March 2016).

65 *Ibid.*, p. 40.

66 Mattathias Schwartz, 'A Mission Gone Wrong. Why Are We Still Fighting The Drug War?', *New Yorker* (6 January 2014), pp. 44–55.
67 Karl Marx, 'A Contribution to the Critique of Hegel's Philosophy of Right: Introduction', in *Karl Marx: Early Writings* (Harmondsworth: Penguin, 1980), p. 251.

4
Love

Introduction

> I liked *Heaven and Earth* and *Alexander* for their tenderness. I dedicated both to my mother for that reason.[1]
>
> With the exception of *U Turn*, all of my films have an aura of optimism about them. In *World Trade Center* it is feelings of family that help pull the people out of the hole. In *W.* Laura Bush is a binding force. In *Wall Street* love is also important. *U Turn* demonstrates the problem of isolation.[2]

In the opening scenes of *Salvador* (1986), Richard Boyle (James Woods) is arrested for multiple traffic offences and then bailed by his friend Doctor Rock (James Belushi), whereupon Rock asks Boyle to drive him to the dog pound to release the his pooch, Bagel. During the drive, the pair get into a discussion about women:

> ROCK: Oh man, everything's turned to shit. Miriam's thrown me out, man. You know she says I'm too old to be a rock 'n' roll disc jockey any more. She wants me to sell computers in Silicon Valley – can you believe that?
>
> BOYLE: You know, you know I can't take these yuppie women. You know, with the Walkmans and the running shoes and the, the ... they'd rather go to the aerobics jazz class than fuck. Forget about it!
>
> ROCK: Yeah, yeah, they got those pussy exercises too.

BOYLE: You see Latin women? Now, they're totally different. They're kind, they're understanding. Take Claudia – she's the greatest, man. I mean, she doesn't give a shit what I do.

ROCK: The best thing about Latin women is they don't speak English.

The scene closes with a riff from Jackson Browne's 'Running on Empty', a signification not only of a cultural deficit in relation to the protagonists' views of women, but a wider national malaise concerning the government's malfeasance in Central America, where much of the rest of the film resides. Although the tone of the film and the characters' attitudes towards women changes after the pair find their way to El Salvador, this initial exchange is emblematic of critical perceptions towards gender and sex that Stone epitomised for some, particularly in his emergent phase as a writer and filmmaker. *Salvador* offers more evidence too. Boyle's girlfriend Maria (Elpidia Carrillo) is a central motivation for his character to evolve, and she is in considerable danger as the narrative progresses. Yet the screenplay gives her little to say of significance, and Stone's off-screen reputation around Hollywood for indulging in drugs and women at this time probably did as much – if not more – to feed the negative assessments of his narrative.[3] While the historical image of Stone as a womaniser presented in, for example, Jane Hamsher's *Killer Instinct* (1987) and Eric Hamburg's *JFK, Nixon, Oliver Stone and Me* (2002), may have dissipated over the years, his escape from this straitjacketed personality trait has been harder to achieve. An interview in the *Observer* in 2010, for example, continued to contemplate an 'almost hyper-masculinity to Stone's oeuvre'.[4]

One consequence of this reportage has been to cloud Stone's views on gender and the representation of women more generally in his films. It also has clouded our assessment of the centrality of love as a theme in many of Stone's pictures. In the case of *Salvador*, Boyle goes to extraordinary efforts later in the film to obtain the *cédula de identidad* (identity card) for his girlfriend Maria that will allow her safe exit from El Salvador. The ultimate reversal and failure of that scheme at the very end of the film, with Maria removed from a bus, allowed Stone to use the pathos experienced by the lovers to speak to the audience of the personal as well as national tragedy that the US government was party to in that strife-ridden country.

The particular focus of this chapter is on the dramatic constructions that Stone has used to explore themes of love in his more recent films, taking their cue from earlier explorations such as those above in *Salvador*. Pathos and parental love became important components in films such as *Wall Street* (1987), *Born on the Fourth of July* (1989) and, perhaps most particularly, *Heaven and Earth* (1993). In these films the parent–child relationship is a nurturing one. In *U Turn* (1997), *Alexander* (2004 and various cuts of the film thereafter) and *W.* (2008), the parent–child relationship becomes disruptive. In both *U Turn* and *Alexander*, parental love is infused with the more troubling prospect of incest. In *W.* the suggestion of emotional distance between father and son is played out alongside warm and close emotional bonds between George W. Bush and his wife Laura. Indeed, the prominence and conventionality of the portrayal of Laura (Elizabeth Banks) poses its own challenges to established caricatures of Bush that are used elsewhere in the film. At the same time, all three films adopt a distinctly melodramatic tinge, both in the performances and in some of the cinematic flourishes and realisation of scenes. A more nurturing parent–child dynamic is once again in evidence in *Wall Street: Money Never Sleeps* (2010) and *Savages* (2012), providing insights into Stone's changing personal perspective on the subject through the 2000s.

This chapter will explore these interwoven developments – familial as well as personal love – in Stone's filmmaking, highlighting the importance of a transition that began in the mid-to-late 1990s with *U Turn*: a film generally regarded as one of Stone's darkest and most problematic. The argument here posits that this film in particular represents a marker in Stone's career, not because of the loss of aesthetic vitality that had been integral to earlier films, as some critics observed, but precisely because the film marks the emergence of a distinctive melodramatic shift in Stone's work, and a shift towards the darker aspects of parental love in particular. The contention here is that in the rush to classify *U Turn* as a noir thriller, critics and observers of Stone not only pre-emptively closed the door on any recognition of the film's overt melodrama, but also in later reappraisals continued to miss a bigger opportunity to find a key interpretive clue to Stone's personal as well as cinematic development. Then, the significance of a melodramatic filter for viewing Stone's later films is used to assess *Alexander* and *W.*, before investigating the way in which relationships and emotional love are worked into both these films and then *Wall Street: Money Never Sleeps* and *Savages*.

Stone's later cinematic output has been faulted on several occasions by a range of critics for a loss of dramatic urgency and controversy that he displayed so explicitly in earlier years. What supposedly did change? One key shift was in a revived representation of women. From the rather minor role afforded to Maria in *Salvador*, Stone shaped a series of increasingly important roles for his female protagonists as the years passed. Starting with Hiep Thi Le as Le Ly Hayslip in 1993, and Joan Allen's portrayal of Pat Nixon in 1995, strong female roles became integral to the plot and gender discourse. Beyond that, there was a noticeable shift towards a different aesthetic – one less wedded to the realist and hyperrealist style that Stone made his own in the late 1980s – that was more interested in situation-driven moral dilemmas.

Integrating love and melodrama into his pictures more deliberately, Stone shifted registers. Less urgent perhaps, but engaging gender in a different way allowed him to foreground questions of love that, if they were present in earlier films, nevertheless were confined and conditioned by other concerns. The shift was aesthetic, but inevitably it was also personal. Stone's settled marriage as well as his embrace of Buddhism redirected his more visceral creative energies into the task of marshalling a broader critique of sex, relationships and love. However, even this task was still infused with a love of country – politics, capitalism and community – as an expression of the American myth belatedly grounded in family and partnerships. For example, as Chapters 2 and 3 of this book on politics and money amplify, Stone's exploration of love is grounded ultimately in personal passion that stretches beyond the confines of human relationships. Within his screenplays, Stone always has had one eye on a broader set of questions about what love means in the context of American culture: questions that are couched not as some intellectualised consideration of culture, but as a very personal expression of love for a particular vision of what it means to be an American. The expression of that love enabled the melodramatic counterpoints of personal love considered here to flourish, as Stone's career progressed.

Love and melodrama

Love, pathos and visceral emotion were important elements in Stone's early work. In particular, familial love emerges more than once. Stone's Oscar-winning screenplay for Alan Parker's *Midnight Express* (1978) privileges love and forgiveness expressed for Billy Hayes (Brad Davis) by his father (Mike Kellin) in the early moving prison scenes. In fact, the film displays two archetypes of familiar love in these moments. In comparison to Hayes, the somewhat racially prejudicial relationship between the prison warden Hamidou (Paul L. Smith) and his two cowed sons bears witness to their father's sadistic tendencies. The racism is undoubtedly gratuitous, but it offsets the essential message about deep commitment and loyalty between Hayes and his father that Stone was trying to get at. More controversial still was the film's brief allusion to homoerotica, in a dream-like sequence involving Hayes and another inmate exercising and bathing. The author Billy Hayes later commented that while his book, on which Parker's film was based, largely refuted the sanitised scene, its filming gave an almost romantic gesture to these moments that somewhat affected Hayes. 'I'm happy that someone from the Midwest who is freaked out by the idea of homosexuality can look at the scene and feel the delicacy of it. The line from my book expresses it best – "It's only love"'.[5] Stone also engaged in another cinematic prop that helped propel emotion and feelings through the narrative; the protagonist's voiceover. Here, as later in *Platoon* (1986), hopes and fears are rhetorically unveiled, conveying deep affect and love together with the hope for an alternative future.

In *Scarface* (1983), Stone's script for Brian De Palma used love to dilute the violence by bestowing a complex set of emotions on the protagonist Tony Montana (Al Pacino). Montana's struggles with the sexual independence of his sister Gina (Mary Elizabeth Mastrantonio), and his evident frustrations at the lack of love in his own life and marriage, certainly suggest a macho conservative conventionality. However, a scene where Montana decides to abort a car bomb assassination, prompted by some inner moral reserve because of the presence of the diplomat's family in the car, suggests something more in Montana's psyche than simple paternalism. His search for the American Dream succeeds in material terms, but the absence of any love that might nourish his better moral instincts leads inexorably to a slow hollowing out of his entire being, resulting in a death surrounded by materiality but little value.

More optimistically, in *Wall Street*, Stone returned to the father–son dynamic, and a crucial hospital scene where the bond between father and son Carl and Bud Fox (played by father and son, Martin and Charlie Sheen) provides the impetus to help Bud seek a higher moral course of action. Parental love is perhaps even more apparent in *Born on the Fourth of July*, where the combination of conservative restraint and pathos felt by Ron Kovic's father (Raymond J. Barry) for his wounded veteran son (Tom Cruise) becomes the device that allows the audience to grasp the personal tragedy of returning veterans.

In one of Stone's most contentious and criticised films, *Natural Born Killers* (1994), the central unifying thread is that Mickey and Mallory, for all their misguided rage, are in love. Mickey (Woody Harrelson) even acknowledges that love is 'the only thing that kills the demon.' Indeed, Stone's own assessment was that the film connected so well with young audiences precisely because of its love story; a coda to earlier relationships played out in similarly violent circumstances, not least the bond established by the protagonists in Arthur Penn's *Bonnie and Clyde* (1967).[6]

However, perhaps love is explicated most carefully in *Heaven and Earth* (1993), Stone's final chapter in his Vietnam trilogy. Based on the personal experiences of Le Ly Hayslip growing up in the 1950s, the film charts a succession of disasters that befall Le Ly and her village of Ky La. Destroyed by the French in 1953, the village is ravaged by a succession of interlopers, from the Viet Cong, to the South Vietnamese army and US military, as Vietnam collapses into war and the turmoil of the 1960s. Le Ly's father (Haing S. Ngor) later explains to his daughter how the Vietnamese had previously fought against the Chinese and Japanese, and emphasises to her that: 'Freedom is never a gift ... it must be won and won again.' Le Ly endures torture by the South Vietnamese army, is suspected by the Viet Cong who capture and rape her, and all the while the bond with her village is broken. This symbolic withdrawal of love precipitates an asymmetry where Le Ly struggles to find an enduring and shared love. Moving to Saigon, she becomes a source of sexual gratification for the businessman she works for, and later is induced into prostitution by and for US army personnel. Le Ly manages to return to her village to see her dying father and, in reconciliation, he tells her that she must return to the son and other life she now has, rather than stay. In leaving her home for the last time, the absorption of strength and forgiveness from her father is something she later draws on, when her subsequent relationship with another US serviceman Steve Butler (Tommy Lee Jones) eventually ends in tragedy. Given this overview, it was surprising for Stone to claim in a 1994 interview with *Entertainment Weekly* that the film was not in any sense feminist in outlook. Even if true, retrospectively it is far easier to see how Le Ly's story became more foundational for Stone's appreciation of female roles in his films, and, following this, the performances from Joan Allen, Jennifer Lopez and Cameron Diaz in later pictures confirmed the understanding.[7]

From *Midnight Express* to *Heaven and Earth*, Stone's use of deep pathos was a thread winding its way through his canon. After the mid-1990s, changes ensued. A new mode of filmmaking emerged that was less hyperrealist – blending messages about history with kaleidoscopic flourishes of colour and composition – to one that was stripped back to a concentrated examination of personal and moral choices. *Wall Street: Money Never Sleeps* and *Savages* were less concerned with their historical and cultural contexts than with foregrounding the moral choices facing their protagonists. Alongside these moral choices emerged melodramatic tendencies in new guises, visible in different forms in *U Turn* and *Alexander*, and later in *World Trade Center* (2006) and *W.* In other words, love and melodrama were distinct elements that were less staging posts for institutional and historical assessment, than driving forces for more self-conscious storytelling. Melodramatic devices in turn contributed to a shift in the way that female roles contributed to the narratives, resulting in a much richer examination of gender than in the early films.

In *Any Given Sunday* (1999), Christina Pagniacci (Cameron Diaz) assumes a strong role that is not in any way propped up by her sexuality. She is playfully undaunted by the sight of naked football players in the changing rooms, while asserting her own corporate power throughout. Acknowledged as business-savvy and tough, there is a grudging recognition of her abilities as owner of the team in an overbearingly patriarchal environment. In *World Trade Center*, the familial love expressed by Donna McLoughlin (Maria Bello) and Allison Jimeno (Maggie Gyllenhaal) anchor the film, and provide a counterpoint to the ordeal of the Port Authority officers buried in the rubble of the towers. Stone seeks to portray and understand the small-scale, human aspects of the story rather than be consumed by the geopolitical dimensions – a deliberate ploy that drew criticism from some observers, but which rewarded viewers with an emotional depth rarely seen in Stone's movies previously. The cumulative result from *U Turn* onwards was a remix of character approaches that flew in the face of accepted wisdom about Stone, his 'hyper-masculinity' and his (perceived previous) failure to position important female characters within his stories.[8]

Therefore, familial relations, a degree of pathos and female empowerment added up to a more expressive use of melodramatic markers for Stone that circled themselves around concepts and concerns about love. However, critics such as Barry Langford have not been slow to note the pejorative associations of 'melodrama'.[9] The historicisation of melodrama through genre, suggests Langford, impedes our ability to acknowledge these markers – not as a failure of cinema's realist instincts, but as a distinct, deliberate and coexistent form of cinema. One-dimensional characterisations and obvious narrative contrivances may not necessarily point to a failure of psychological expression as a way to impart meaning for the viewer. Instead, different means of expression locates meaning, to use Langford's terms, 'not as a process but as a *situation*, fixed and externalised in a binary oppositional structure (good/bad, desire/frustration, happiness/misery, and so on)'.[10] Indeed, as Langford and others have suggested, melodramatic markers can be present in all of the predominant genre categories of film used by critics and scholars alike.

This complication is crucial here to our reading of *U Turn* and its significance as a signal of change in Stone's filmmaking. The film was read by many critics, including Janet Maslin at the *New York Times*, as simply classic noir reheated. Others, such as Roger Ebert, went further and thought it was actually derivative noir.[11] These elements – the femme fatale, the hint of the dark city and the seeming presence of transgressive sexual desire – all ascribe to the noir label, as homage or pastiche.[12] *U Turn* has a lead female, Grace, who is engaged in sexual exploitation and has some femme fatale qualities. However, it is the film's tension between sexual ascendancy and emotional pathos that gives us pause for thought, and which re-emerges in a similar binary between sexual predator and victim in the framing of Olympias, (Angelina Jolie) Alexander's mother in *Alexander*. In both instances sexual dynamics are strong, but sexuality does not drive each character. Rather, passion is displaced as pathos anchors their motivations. In the rush to pigeonhole *U Turn* as some kind of overacted, noir-esque holiday from serious filmmaking for Stone, and in the later film to lambast Jolie for her accent and overacting, crucial new trends were eschewed. Stone was doing something different, to be sure; but it was not by making a poor job of a new genre or losing control of his actors. Rather, it was by foregrounding devices which represented a distinct alternative to his previously realist, hyper-driven cinema.

U Turn

Isolation and incest

In *U Turn*, Stone employed a melodramatic overlay to explore two essentially counter-hegemonic aspects of love: isolation and incest. If the first theme was a magnification of something that perhaps could be inferred from the text on which the film drew – John Ridley's *Stray Dogs* (1997)[13] – the second was pure Stone: a development that emerged during his preparation of the screenplay.

Stone's personal assessment of Ridley's book was that there was a good basic plot, but that the story did not go far enough in exploring its characters' psyches. Nonetheless, the film does follow the basic outline of the book in telling the story of a small-time gambler, Bobby Cooper (Sean Penn), who is waylaid on a trip to Las Vegas to pay off a gambling debt. The failure of the radiator hose on Billy's 64½ Mustang diverts him to the small Arizona town of Superior, where he soon encounters Darrell (Billy Bob Thornton), a mechanic at Harlin's garage. Despite his reservations, Bobby leaves his treasured automobile in Darrell's care and heads towards town in search of a bar to await the completion of the repair. During a brief casual conversation with a blind Native American beggar (Jon Voight), Bobby's attention – and, as it turns out, the direction of his life – is diverted when he sees a young woman in a red dress further down the street. He introduces himself to Grace McKenna (Jennifer Lopez) and helps her carry some shopping. Grace flirts with Bobby, and he quickly finds himself invited to her home. However Bobby's tête-à-tête with Grace is interrupted by the return home of her jealous husband, Jake (Nick Nolte): a development that quickly leads to Bobby's unceremonious expulsion from the McKenna home.

Despite the brief fracas at the McKenna residence, Bobby and Jake have a conversation soon afterwards during which Jake confesses the depth of his jealousy arising from the behaviour of his younger wife, and indicates to Bobby that he would be willing to pay to have Grace killed. Bobby declines, and instead prepares to wait for the repair to his car. However, following the loss of his gambling stash in a grocery store robbery, he relents. He needs the money, not least to pay for the repair of his car, and he accepts the deal. Having entered into this contract with Jake, Bobby conspires to take Grace to a local beauty spot and overlook where he plans to push her to her death. However, when the moment comes he draws back, driven in part by lust for Grace, but also some residual sense of morality. Despite not consummating their love, the couple enter into a new pact. Bobby and Grace formulate a plan to kill Jake, and steal the money that Jake has kept hidden at the couple's house.

By the film's midpoint, fairly conventional noir elements do arise. Playing on something of a revival during the 1990s in the genre which had seen critical and commercial success for films such as *Basic Instinct* (Paul Verhoeven, 1992), *Red Rock West* (John Dahl, 1993), *The Last Seduction* (John Dahl, 1994) and *L.A. Confidential* (Curtis Hanson, 1997), a number of aspects of Stone's story still disrupt its categorisation as any shade of noir.[14] The film's western elements provide a useful starting point for investigating a reworking of Ridley's novel and, by extension, the starting point for rereading *U Turn* as a modern neo-noir. The integration of extensive scenic and emotional topography, stock characters and moral dilemmas with a hegemonic maleness are important elements of the western that underpin the narrative in *U Turn*. While Ridley's book devotes a chapter to the noir world of Las Vegas spiced with misogyny and gambling, Stone gave this aspect of the story little more than a passing reference, involving a brief flashback to help explain how Bobby parted company with two fingers of his left hand.

By contrast, Stone gives full vent to the western elements – the gambler, a land baron and his Native American wife – in a narrative where the construction of maleness is more dystopic than misogynistic. The desert landscape was the base material for this configuration, and Stone went to considerable lengths to find the appropriate location for the shoot in the desert of the southwestern United States. In the introduction to the published script for *U Turn*, Stone opined that 'it speaks to me of America far more than any other single region of the nation, and reflects my own innermost cultural totems about this country'.[15] The location of Superior, Arizona exemplified for him the physical exhaustion and emotional attenuation that much of the West had endured as waves of settlers arrived, displacing the native population and consuming the resources only to depart elsewhere (usually California), leaving a hollowed-out spirituality whose scar tissue was the physical disfigurement of the landscape caused by the spoils from now-abandoned mines.

While *U Turn's* literary inheritance may have promised a low key noir–western hybrid, the film's on-screen reworking by Stone foregrounded the physical threat of the desert heat and its deleterious impact on the psychology of a remote community. The result, to appropriate Langford once more, was a film that represented a situation rather than a process, exploring two particular aspects of life and love in this fragmented American outback.

For one, the theme of isolation permeates all of the characters. People are stark and overblown in their delivery: a melodramatic affectation that confers a one-dimensionality accentuating their disengagement from each other, if not life. Darrell fills the hours between car repairs with pornography. Jenny (Claire Danes) and Toby Tucker (Joaquin Phoenix) are shut away from the excitements of a different life at which their bickering vaguely hints. Bobby's inability to engage fully with Darrell and Grace says as much about his own social dysfunctionality and isolation, as it does about the town of Superior and its people. The brief flashbacks to his life playing professional tennis highlight that the loss of control in his life began before he arrived in Superior. Bobby's isolation, as manifested in his dealings with Darrell and Grace, invites us to see the town not just as the passive recipient of his distain, but as a victim in its own right that requires more careful analysis. Stone's use of brief *cinema vérité*-style shots of local inhabitants unconnected with the rest of the story suggests a direction for this analysis, underlining the distance and lack of mutual understanding between urban and rural communities in their historical as well as contemporary sense, as well as highlighting the decay and interiority of rural America.

The visual possibilities offered by the remote south-western town clearly help develop the theme of isolation, although Stone is not building a simple duality between socially and economically impoverished hinterland and the metropolitan antithesis. Instead he allows Bobby's arrogance to project a more nuanced perspective on the mutual lack of empathy and respect offered by either world to the other. Bobby's initial dealings with Darrell reflect his contempt for the man and the place he lives in, but Bobby's hostility and prejudice speaks to a lack of self-worth too. When Darrell slams the hood of his car shut, Bobby objects:

DARRELL: It's just a car.

BOBBY: No, it's not just a car. It's a 64½ Mustang Convertible. That's the difference between you and me. That's why you're living here, and I'm just passing through.

The deadpan comedy inherent in Darrell's initial interactions with Bobby suggests that he understands rather more about his own situation than Bobby is prepared to give him credit for. More importantly, his response to Darrell convinces the audience of the nature of Bobby's arrogance: it is both personal and metropolitan in its failure of perspective.

Bobby's pursuit of Grace reflects a similar high-handed attitude, seeing her as no more than a sexual diversion that he can indulge in without consequence. However, Grace highlights his arrogance during their initial encounter at her home. When Grace rebuffs Bobby's overtures, he accuses her of playing games, to which she replies: 'And what game you want to play? You carry my boxes for me and then I fall into bed with you?' Grace's initial encounters with Bobby also suggest a boredom that flows from the isolation of the town, but her unfolding story embodies not just isolation but the other key theme in the film: incest. It is the nature of the presentation of Grace's story that provides the film's depth. Her listless flirtation with Bobby is not the key to the narrative trajectory of the film; rather it is the key to her own persecution. While Bobby's encounters with Darrell, Grace, Jake, the Native American beggar and Toby and Jenny all contain a sense of a simple narrative manipulation, and while Jake's nascent plot to dispose of his wife has a similar feel – albeit with some growing sense of moral disturbance on his part – our sense of Grace is completely different. Even in her encounter with Bobby at her home, we start to see not just a bored, flirtatious young woman, but a woman who immediately recognises when she is being used.

The depiction of sexuality in the screenplay differs significantly from Ridley's book, with the crucial element of incest missing from the latter; but it is also missing from early drafts of the shooting script. Grace's backstory is also largely absent in the book, apart from a brief indication that she had grown up on a reservation, and later sought out an older man with money as a way of improving her circumstances. Stone's initial rewrite still did not introduce the controversy, although elements of sexual abuse were apparent. A 30 October 1996 rehearsal note cited Grace's father as having been killed in a mine, after which she and her mother were taken in by Jake.[16] However, Grace was being raped by him: a situation that drove her mother first to alcoholism, and then death in an apparent suicide. Despite this, Grace's account to Bobby indicated that she took some pleasure from the situation with Jake: 'I liked it … I liked being controlled by Jake. It was a relief. The truth was as far out and crazy as he got. I wanted more.' In the same scene, Grace goes on to explain how it was the sight of her dead mother that made her vow revenge.

Stone's subsequent reworking of the script to include incest had two key effects on the story. First, the eroticisation of abuse which is apparent in the 30 October rehearsal was deftly turned on its head, resulting in a dark and disturbing bedroom scene involving Grace and her husband. Second, Grace's character is given more strength. Her motivation for seeking Jake's death is redirected and made clearer, as is the reason for her ultimate failure to trust in Bobby.

Stone's decision to add the additional layer of incest, and to recast Grace as Jake's actual, rather than adopted, daughter, arose out his incessant use of readings, rehearsals and discussions with actors and the circumstances of the shoot to refine and develop his scripts. Indeed, Stone and his friend, chief scout and co-producer Richard Rutowski, continued to tinker with the screenplay after shooting had started. Incest is revealed only slowly, as though they were unsure of its presence here and what it meant. An early scene has Jake discussing his jealousy with Bobby, although the Nolte's delivery ensures that the film's early lighter mood is not completely disrupted. The juxtaposition of comedic and dark elements almost places the audience in an uncomfortable emotional space, as Jake's persona becomes clearer. He explains almost in exasperation:

> I hate loving her. I hate having to tolerate the little games she plays, like fucking half this town behind my back and laughing at me. The bitch! You know, she wants me to hit her, and then when I hit her she likes it. She just likes to fuckin' torture me, goddam it. But … she's my family, she's my little girl, my baby.

The devastating and jumbled emotional turmoil of the rant underscores Grace's situation. She is trapped and in search of any way out. Abused by her husband/father and used by Sheriff Potter (Powers Boothe), she falters even as she tries to believe in Bobby. He is flaky and self-centred, and there is no evidence that she sees him as anything more than her ride out of town – but she is unable to sustain the trust that would be required for him to make good, even on this limited commitment. Through the construction of Grace's story and her response to the men around her, Stone sets her apart from their one-dimensional motives and characterisations. Ultimately, her story is one of love betrayed. That she is unable to trust in Bobby is tragic in one sense, but it also preserves her integrity. She is neither 'action babe' nor helpless female waiting to be rescued. That she does not get away in the end is not Hollywood conventionality putting an end to her aspirations for freedom. Two of the three men in her life who have wronged her have had their fates sealed by her. Jake is lying dead beside her in the ravine, and the sheriff is lying dead on the highway. Bobby gets the better of her momentarily, but she is still alive and close enough to hear the intervention of fate as Darrell's repair to the Mustang's radiator hose expires. With it, Bobby will expire too. Grace may be dying, but she knows how the story ends.

From early in his career, Stone established a recurring reputation for shooting on a tight timetable and looking for extremely high levels of commitment and engagement from those around him. These factors no doubt contributed to some on-set tensions during *U Turn*. However, of more significance was the discomfort that arose as a consequence of how Stone had chosen to depict love and relations through sex: in particular, the scenes involving Jake and Grace on the evening of his murder. These scenes were, Stone recalls, an issue for his long-term cinematographer, Robert Richardson. While critics would show up Richardson's ability to reference and utilise classic cinematographic technique – Chris Salewicz likened his camerawork here to Godard on *À Bout de Souffle* (*Breathless*, 1960) – *U Turn* would prove to be his last film for Stone.[17] The relationship reputedly ended because Richardson felt these concluding confrontations between Jake and Grace were unnecessarily extreme, even perverse, in their nature. Stone argued that the editing brought attention to Grace's unacceptable abuse and Jake's underlying moral corruption. Richardson walked away anyway.

Stone's parting from his cinematographer was a personal loss as much as a diminution of his cinema's aesthetic bravura. In interview, he stated that relations with Richardson had been uneasy dating back to *Natural Born Killers*, but confessed to missing him and his presence on the next few films, *Any Given Sunday* and *Alexander*.[18] That said, Stone had only good things to say of cinematographer Salvatore Totino's dynamic realisation of gridiron in *Any Given Sunday*, and he concluded that the difficulties in *Alexander* were not with Rodrigo Prieto's cinematography, but with the editing process deployed for the film.[19] In subsequent pictures, Stone worked with first-rate cinematographers; no doubt the loss of Richardson was not just about ability, but cumulative vision built up over years which had produced a singular approach inherent in so many other classic Hollywood partnerships.

U Turn was to be premiered at the Cannes Film Festival in May 1997. However, at a press conference in Paris on 22 April 1997, the Festival chair, Gilles Jacob, indicated that his committee had seen the film: far from intimating that it had many things to say about relationships, loyalty and sacrifice, Jacob said it was just too violent.[20] Rebuffed, the film eventually made a festival appearance at Telluride at the end of August, and opened in the USA on Friday 3 October 1997, although not before some changes had been made to the version prepared in the spring. In an internal memo from Phoenix Pictures to Stone dated 12 June 1997, enthusiasm for the film was tempered with some concern about the final half-hour. The memo commented that 'we seem to lose all the engaging energy surprises and good will of the story and find ourselves in a deeply disturbing place – almost another movie'.[21] A total of eleven tweaks were then proposed, all of which were directed at toning down the sexual content of the film. Interestingly, considering all that had gone on with the script that would precipitate Richardson's exodus, Stone adopted all the proposals.

On release, critical response was divided. In *Variety*, Todd McCarthy described Stone as 'displaying ... stylistic urgency and restlessness, without the slightest speck of Hollywood complacency in evidence'.[22] Janet Maslin's *New York Times* review understood the film to be 'a showcase for the filmmaker's terrific arsenal of visual mannerisms and free-association imagery'.[23] However, Roger Ebert's assessment turned out to be closer to the majority audience reaction. He accused the film of being 'a repetitive, pointless exercise in genre filmmaking – the kind of movie where you distract yourself by making a list of the sources'.[24] *U Turn* had a disappointing opening weekend at the box office, taking only $2.7 million from more than 1,200 screens; Columbia TriStar immediately scaled back the release and the film quickly disappeared from cinemas. Its domestic gross was only $6.6 million. Eric Bryant Rhodes later argued that the film had not received its just recognition because it aroused hostility in those who find Stone's portrayal of the USA as increasingly anti-American, and that it disappointed fans looking for a clearer political statement from the director.[25] Unwittingly this time, the film's concerns were part of a growing national debate.

The issue of abuse and incest had been prominent in the American media during the mid-1990s – not least as a result of the abduction, rape and murder in 1994 of seven-year-old Megan Kanka in Hamilton Township, New Jersey by Jesse Timmendequas. The trial that brought her assailant to justice concluded in June 1997, in the wake of extended press coverage not just about the murder, but about the family history of the murderer.[26] The progressive introduction of community notification laws since 1994 ensured that the issue remained prominent in public debate. These taboo subjects also had further cultural interest. In April 1996, media mogul Ted Turner was reported to have intervened to have a production of *Bastard Out of Carolina* – Anjelica Huston's directorial debut – dropped by Turner Network Television (TNT).[27] At issue were scenes of molestation and child abuse, including a particularly vivid rape scene involving a twelve-year-old girl. In the following year, and just a week before *U Turn* was released, a remake of *Lolita* directed by Adrian Lyne struggled to find a US distributor, prompting Anthony Lane to comment in *The New Yorker* that a febrile national climate was informing the debate about the film.[28] *Lolita* eventually aired on Showtime.[29]

With some justification, then, Stone concluded that *U Turn*'s focus on incest was a topic that American audiences did not want to hear about. Producer Mike Medavoy had warned that the film might be too brutal, and cinemagoers clearly agreed.[30] Yet here was evidence of Stone moving in a new direction subject-wise and cinematically. The early sequences of the film with their stock characterisation, overlays of comedy and situational contrivances signalled something *entirely* new in Stone's oeuvre. Within this aesthetic wrapping, he set about the corruption of familial love and the loss of hope, invoking a deep pathos and a dark message of despair. It was a denouement like no other Stone had constructed to this point.

From his own account of the circumstances leading up to the making of *U Turn*, it is clear that Stone was suffering from a sense of professional and personal isolation. In the two years before shooting he had faced widespread media criticism following the release of *Natural Born Killers*. Further shocked by the disappointing critical and public response to *Nixon* (1995), he also had ended up in divorce proceedings. As recompense, Stone returned to finish his semi-autobiographical book, *A Child's Night Dream* (1997). Completion of the manuscript brought back a complex mix of emotions and memories about his childhood, his relationship with his father and mother, his experiences in Vietnam, and later in the Merchant Marine Corps. Although some of the original manuscript was missing – Stone had thrown half of it in the East River in New York in 1967 – he was able, with the help of editor Robert Weil, to reconstruct a shorter version of the book which was published in October 1997, at the same time as *U Turn*, mostly to favourable reviews.[31]

U Turn was designed as a low-key, low-budget exercise without the burden of political messages. 'It was good for me to make [something] that was fun,' Stone was reported as saying – although he also acknowledged the depth of the piece and perhaps, inevitably, that it did have something to say.[32]

Some observers saw *U Turn* as a kind of misfit production, but it nevertheless carried important clues to an evolving mentality in Stone's handling of 'love', his portrayal of women, and his application of a melodramatic signature related to these developments. In *Alexander*, Stone returned to some of the film's key elements, such as an exploration of disruptive love within a melodramatic narrative enclosure. Love and pathos remained key to the historical figure of Olympias in the later film and, far from being insular and closed off, *Alexander*'s grand patina attempted to bring love and emotion into a giant epic about power, history and antiquity.

Alexander

Alexander (2004) offered Stone the kind of challenge he always relished. A life story that was incomplete both in its execution and in the contemporary record, Stone's aim was to recreate some of the grandeur of the legend of this larger-than-life figure. To do that, he wanted large scale battles of the old Hollywood school, including the pivotal clash with the Persian King Darius III at Gaugamela in 331 BCE. However, Stone also wanted to convey something of Alexander's relationships with his father King Philip (Val Kilmer) and his mother Olympias (Angelina Jolie), as well offer some insight into Greek cultural and sexual mores. Therefore, issues of structure, time and sexuality would all prove to be central elements in the film's production, editing and reception.

Stone's own production archives indicate an interest in making a film about Alexander the Great as far back as 1989. Seven years of negotiation followed, but after a deal collapsed involving German producer Thomas Schühly and Cinergi Pictures in 1996, the project lay in abeyance until 2001 when Moritz Borman and Stone agreed to a production commitment.[33]

The journey to the finished screenplay was long, as was the filming that followed. The final shooting schedule was set at 103 days, with locations in Morocco, Thailand and at Pinewood Studio and Shepperton Studio in England. It was the longest of Stone's career (Figure 9). Preceding this timetable, in August 2003, was horse training for the principal actors and a boot camp for weapons training. Dale Dye, who had first worked for Stone on actor training for *Platoon*, supervised these activities as part of his role as second unit director. Dye's contributions were complemented by the meticulous planning of the battle scenes. Preparations for the recreation of the battle of Gaugamela ran to 73 pages of storyboards. However, even here the intuitive side of Stone's filmmaking played a part. Confronted with a sandstorm in the midst of shooting the battle, Stone opted to incorporate the ensuing chaos rather than abandon filming and the time and money that it would cost. While time pressures remained an issue in post-production, it was the treatment of love, familial relations and sexuality that were defining issues for the film's release and reception, rather than its epic military confrontations.

The multiplicity of difficulties presented by attempting to impose some kind of narrative structure on an open-ended piece of history, coupled with an overlay of explicit sexuality, had been apparent before production began. Joanna Paul records in her essay, published in *Responses to Oliver Stone's Alexander*, how pre-production press speculation about how the film might deal with suggestions of Alexander's bisexuality drew predictable criticisms from more socially conservative commentators in the south of the USA, as well as a less expected intervention by the Greek culture minister, Evangelos Venizelos, who described the proposed film as a slur on Greece.[34]

In differing ways, these responses highlighted the presence of a highly combustible mix in the making of *Alexander*. There was the presence of an icon from antiquity, whose cultural capital had stock in the contemporary world, plus a director whose stock-in-trade was the questioning and validity of such capital. For many Americans, the heart of the 'War on Terror' moment in 2004, complicated by Stone's portrayal of an allegedly homosexual general,

Figure 9 Colin Farrell and Oliver Stone on the set of *Alexander* (2004)

provoked a predictable backlash. Indifferent reviews were met with low US box office receipts for the initial theatrical release of the film. Conservative political commentator and film critic Michael Medved summed up the prevailing attitude:

> There's a certain audience out there that just loves war movies, battle movies – 'Braveheart,' 'Saving Private Ryan,' 'We Were Soldiers'. There are probably a bunch of people who will go to see 'Alexander' looking for a he-man, a superwarrior. When they find out he's playing for the other team, that will probably create a certain indignation in some of the audience.[35]

Distributing and marketing the film, Warner Bros. executives were alert to Medved's prediction. Moritz Borman received a seven-page memo from the studio in September 2004 detailing a series of proposed changes and cuts to the version of the film they had seen two days earlier. The changes were intended to reduce the running time, as well as deal with 'difficulties' surrounding the representation of violence and homosexuality. The screenplay referenced Alexander's love for his friend Hephaestion, as well as his attachment to a young male eunuch, Bagoas. Several suggestions for saving additional time also coincidentally reduced the emphasis on the homoerotic aspects of the dialogue.

Behind the concerns about running time lay a further timing constraint. Shooting had finished in early February 2004, with release scheduled for November of the same year. In response to a proposal by Warner Bros. that editing be concluded in August, Stone had answered combatively that 'you must really be on drugs, if you're not crazy'.[36] He was worried, though. The film needed a considerable post-production effort, and the space was not there. Later reflecting on the time constraint, he commented: 'I wish to God I'd had the courage to tell Warner Brothers that I needed more time, but it would have been a scandal.'[37]

The structural problems and range of criticism directed at the film gnawed away at Stone. The criticism and poor box office for *Nixon* had riled too, but Stone had been content that he had delivered the film as intended. However, in having to accept the timetable for the original *Alexander* release, and in acquiescing to studio requests to tone down some of the homoerotic aspects of the film, Stone felt compromised. In the event, he took it upon himself to commence what was a labour of love: an arduous effort to undo and overcome some of the blemishes he felt responsible for in the original film. In the end, *Alexander* was cut into four versions over the space of a decade. Following the original theatrical version released in the USA in November 2004, a second version of the film arrived in August 2005. It was an effort to improve on the overall structure, but in the process some more controversial material was removed. While the first film had accumulated plaudits from gay and lesbian advocacy groups, the director's cut was criticised by the same community for seemingly bowing to convention and removing a key scene between Alexander and Hephaestion.[38]

Despite the alterations made to the first two versions of the film, structural problems remained relating to, for example, the portrayal of Alexander's youth and the build-up to the Battle of Gaugamela. Therefore, to then have the opportunity to cut a third version of the film was unusual. 'The next reworking was for me, and thank God I had one ally with Warners Home Entertainment who gave me a shot; they gave the chance to put out my version on Blu-ray,' Stone said.[39] The eventual appearance of *Alexander Revisited* (2007), with a running time of 214 minutes, was not only a remarkable statement of persistence but, in an important way, an act of contrition. Stone commented again in 2011 that:

> The [original] script actually resembled the third version [*Alexander Revisited*, 2007] more than the first two. Warners were upset with me. I promised them a sanitised film. I saw a list of their cuts and we went back and forth. There was no way I was going to make all of those cuts. They wanted all the homosexuality out. They hated Bagoas. There was also huge problems with blood.[40]

Despite his assessment that *Revisited* was his best effort, Stone nevertheless went on to undertake a fourth cut of the film. This highly unusual development came as a result of an invitation from Warner Bros., who had been pleased with the commercial response to the 2007 version. Stone had watched this version three or four times at festivals, and had become convinced that he could improve on the editing. *Ultimate Cut* is eight minutes shorter than the *Revisited* version, and takes a slightly quicker route still to the Battle of Gaugamela. *The Ultimate Cut* premiered the Karlovy Vary International Film Festival in July 2013, and released on Blu-ray and DVD in June 2014. With as much certainty as he could muster in the circumstances, Stone declared in interview in August 2013: 'I am now signed off on it! I'm finished! I can't do more.'[41]

Inevitably, Stone's efforts to address the difficulties that he perceived within the early versions of the film were limited by the available footage. In the third version he was able to reintroduce some of the homoerotic aspects of the story that had been previously cut or toned down. There was also some scope to work with the structure, both in the third and fourth versions; however, there were issues that reached beyond the constraint arising from available footage. Joanna Paul notes a complication related to the dramatic imbalance injected by (truthfully) ending the main action in the film with Alexander's premature death, rather than, for example, ending the cinematic action more conventionally with the climactic battle in India, thereby gifting the film a more conventional hero/quest narrative and ending. Paul's proposed solution, drawn from Aristotle's *Poetics*, was the suggestion that the ideal epic narrative should be constructed around a single action – in this case, the murder of Philip – rather than a single hero.[42] Langford's observation about melodrama is crucial here. In drawing the distinction between a process and a situation, Langford was making the point that whereas realism might rely on the use of an individual character to guide the audience through a complex narrative, melodrama relies on the moral embodiment of a situation.[43] Stone responded that:

> Dr Paul, in pointing to Aristotle's 'single action,' has opened my eyes to what I missed at the time. It was there certainly in my subconscious from the beginning, struggling to be heard, but its implications frightened me. The theme, the main action of this piece, was always murder – the murder of Philip – and whether Alexander was involved or not.[44]

Following Paul's line of reasoning, the film contained at its heart a not-fully realised melodramatic component. There were two possible resolutions: either the minimisation of this aspect – for example, by using a different and more conventional hero/quest ending; or its full embrace by a structural foregrounding of the murder of Philip as the centrepiece of the film. With neither option fully realised, the consequence appeared to be the presence of a subtle but significant incongruity in the structure. In the same article, Stone speculated in hindsight that his unwillingness to foreground Philip's murder may well have been driven by a desire to avoid any commercial damage to the film, as a result of his conspiracy theorist reputation being reheated by an unsympathetic press.

This concern to minimise any commercial backlash certainly figured in discussions about the film's sexual content. Stone acknowledged that an early scene involving Bagoas at the harem was cut from the original film because of the 'tremendous amount of hostility the eunuch received at the early screenings we held for Warner Bros. personnel'.[45] Indeed, a contradiction at the heart of the US reception to *Alexander* was that while media coverage about the film's bisexual content did appear to damage its US box office takings, the presentation of sex was remarkably conventional. The most explicit sex scene is a heterosexual one involving Alexander (Colin Farrell) and his wife Roxane (Rosario Dawson). References to Alexander's relationships with Hephaestion (Jared Leto) and Bagoas (Francisco Bosch) are essentially confined to knowing looks and supporting dialogue.

Complicating all these speculations on structure – the absence of a conventional hero/quest story, the not-fully realised component of Philip's death, and the presentation of sexuality – is the fact that the relatively low box office was not replicated in non-US markets. While the film took some $30 million in America (a small but not-insignificant sum), the takings for the rest of the world actually added a further $130 million and made the movie something of an international success. The lack of conventional narrative used in the likes of *Gladiator* (Ridley Scott, 2000) and the homoerotic dimension may have put off US-based audiences, but that was not the effect everywhere.

Conservative ideology at home also shaped national consciousness at this time. Just two weeks before the US release of *Alexander*, voters in Arkansas, Georgia, Kentucky, Michigan, Mississippi, Montana, North Dakota, Ohio, Oklahoma, Oregon and Utah had all approved anti-same-sex marriage amendments by double-digit margins.[46] In July 2004, President George W. Bush indicated that he supported Congressional moves to amend the Constitution to ban same-sex marriage.[47] That initiative failed, but the position of the eleven states made political, cultural and social projections about homosexuality a bedrock of conservative reactionary thought in the 2000s. Stone's film no doubt felt some of the effects of that reaction, as its publicity took a hold.

Alexander also reflected on the invasion of Iraq. WMDs had failed to materialise, and insurgency followed initial military successes as the more difficult 'rebuilding' of Iraq commenced and quickly stalled. By May 2004 the *New York Times* was questioning its earlier supportive coverage of the administration and belief in assertions about the presence of WMDs, although the paper remained cautious about returning to these stories and putting the record straight.[48] Amid a polarised media discourse, the parable of military overreach and the limits of empire offered by *Alexander* gave the film a measure of contemporary perspective, ensuring that it remained aloof from the 'patriotic war experience' category of movies described by Carl Boggs and Tom Pollard, which might have produced a different commercial result for the picture.[49] By July 2005, during preparations for the recut DVD release of *Alexander*, Stone acknowledged publically some of the difficulties in the *New York Post*:

> You cannot associate homosexuality with the military in this country. Audiences want their war films straight. From the day we opened, we did not do business in the South.[50]

The structure and commercial sensitivities were questioned further in the light of something Stone had rarely confronted in his career. Whatever the merits of his films, even his harshest critics were loath to criticise the performance of his players. However, Colin Farrell, Rosario Dawson and most notably Angelina Jolie were perceived as every bit the film's problem, not its saving grace. In *USA Today*, critic Mike Clark saw the performances of all three actors as camp, while Nathan Lee in the *New York Sun* saw Jolie as poised somewhere between camp and conviction.[51] Elsewhere, concerns were voiced about Farrell's hairstyle and the accents used by some actors, as well as a more general sense that the performances were all somehow overblown. Nonetheless, most of this distain was reserved for Jolie, and that word 'camp', as well as 'overacting', kept re-emerging.

In an early scene, Olympias warns her then 18-year-old son about the dangers inherent in Philip installing Eurydice (Marie Meyer) as his new wife and having a new heir. There is a distinct sense of sexual tension between mother and son throughout the scene. She suggests that 'a mother loves too much', and then pulls her son's head into her lap. The closeness in age between the two actors, and indeed Jolie's media persona garnered through her appearances as *Lara Croft* highlighted, from an audience perspective, the countercultural innuendo of incestuous love in the relationship between mother and son, even as the dialogue drew attention to the relationship between Alexander and Hephaestion. The scene is infused with Olympias' hatred of her husband, and her fear that her son will lose everything if he leaves for Asia without an heir in place. Jolie mixes these passions with the delivery of a temptress in a way that ensures that hatred, fear and love are all set out of balance and against type. In this imbalance we may begin to sense the significance of the use of 'camp' as a descriptor of her performance.

In her 'Notes on "Camp"' originally published in 1964, Susan Sontag wrote that camp was a mode of aestheticism that emphasised style at the expense of content. In addition, Sontag suggested that a camp sensibility could be found in the androgyne – 'going against the grain of one's sex' – and in a relish for the exaggeration of sexual characteristics and personality mannerisms.[52] In the context of *Alexander*, two connected points seem to follow from this line of reasoning. First, in view of the particular sexual subject matter that Stone was working with – Olympias' love for her son and Alexander's love for Hephaestion – a camp aesthetic seemed consistent with such an 'against the grain' representation of sexuality. Second, the accompanying presence of exaggeration and externalised emotionality were quintessentially melodramatic elements that sat uneasily within a conventional biopic narrative structure. This mismatch troubled both critics and audiences, leading many to misread the tone of the performances as simple excess, when the explanation had much more to do with a mix of aesthetic and narrative choices.

Alexander was undoubtedly an obsession of sorts for Stone; an effort to tell a very complex story without recourse to familiar, audience-friendly tropes of heroic narrative which, for example, had carried *Troy* (Wolfgang Petersen, 2004) to US box office earnings of $133 million earlier the same year. Instead, Stone sought to stay closer to the historical record, with its vagaries and essential inconclusiveness about Alexander's life. The film's construction comprised four layers: a not-fully realised melodramatic core tied to Philip's murder; a more realist biopic structure; a camp performance aesthetic; and a post-production effort to conventionalise the presentation of sexuality and, to some extent, the narrative structure – the last, Stone acknowledged, somewhat working *against* the first three elements.

At several levels the film aggravated the preoccupations of American critics and audiences in a way that depressed its value. From a realist perspective, there were just too many aesthetic clashes which, when mixed with the discomfort evoked about homosexuality, masculinity and the 'War on Terror', limited the film's audience significantly. While some observers *did* read *Alexander* as a commentary on President Bush, Stone was less interested in the allegory, although he accepted the confluence with events taking place in Iraq.[53] *Alexander* was a truly enormous undertaking, and in its various guises bears witness to Stone's evolving aesthetic, as well as a studied patience in reaching a conclusive on-screen rendering of the story with which he was finally satisfied.

The melodramatic flourishes visible in *U Turn* had been revealed not as a one-off piece of cinematic distraction, but as a distinct aesthetic trend. Stone's interest in this style of representation, and the ways in which it might amplify aspects of the subject of love, was evidenced not only in the persistence with *Alexander*, but in varying degrees in the films that followed. *World Trade Center*, *W.*, *Wall Street: Money Never Sleeps* and *Savages* all had things to say about love and relationships. In addition, the presence of strong female roles first established in *Heaven and Earth* was worked with in varying ways within these narratives.

However, it is with *W.* that Stone brought the aesthetic innovations first seen in *U Turn* back to his core subjects of politics, history and power. Reducing the scale of the melodrama, but re-engaging with the state of the nation, the dynamics of love played out in the Bush family dynasty found further inflections in this, Stone's third presidential biopic, essentially confirming his predilections and interest in the human and familial – the universal in us all.

W.

In important ways, *W.* followed a similar narrative trajectory to *Alexander*. Here was another story with crucial off-screen action impinging on the narrative, and with contextual history influencing people and decisions in ways that logic and rationality cannot always comprehend. The unseen forces that precipitated Philip's murder in *Alexander* are marshalled by Alexander, as he uses the murder to galvanise support for the war against Persia. In *W.* the first Gulf War, the failure to topple Saddam Hussein in 1991, and the defeat of his father, George Bush Sr, in the 1992 presidential election, are all seen as staging posts in the politicisation of George W. Bush and shapers in his prosecution of the 'War on Terror'.

Picking up the story, co-written with Stanley Weiser, of Bush (Josh Brolin) in 2002, Stone used a conventional biographical structure employing a series of flashbacks to move between the Bush administration's preparations for the Iraq War, and his more formative years at Yale University, his aborted careers and later his conversion to aspiring politician and evangelical Christian. These flashbacks allow the audience to piece together the critical influences on Bush's life and the ways in which they affected his approach to the presidency. In particular, Weiser and Stone kept coming back to this theme of a task left undone: a quest left hanging by the father for the son. Less conventional was the way in which the flashbacks and Oval Office scenes were used to intuit a personality, rather than build a detailed history either of Bush's formative years or his time in the White House. The conceptualisation of Bush lent itself to an externalised emotionality – one that Josh Brolin's performance made manifest – in that its trademark buffoonery and awkwardness, the use of figurative scenes, lent the film a distinctly melodramatic hue at times. A figure almost half-realised, half-created, almost built and filled in by media and populace alike. A figure, like Alexander, almost so mythical as to be not quite real, we might suspect.

Two parallel narratives depict Bush's progress. One is his struggle to establish himself and win approval from his father (James Cromwell), and the second is his romance and marriage to Laura Bush (Elizabeth Banks), depicted with almost no gratuitous sentiment. Once again parental love is problematised, as Stone explored the way in which a seemingly distant love expressed by the father for his son had a crucial effect on the psychology of the future president. Bush's struggle in *W.* is about recognition as much as it is about achievement. Through the portrayals of wife Laura and George's mother, Barbara Bush (Ellen Burstyn), the audience is given a window into the psyches of both father and son. Laura's unconditional love is the counterweight to her husband's search for his father's approval. Here, as elsewhere in the film, Stone's refusal to engage in a straightforward vilification of Bush Jr leaves space for a more measured pathos. Several scenes focus on the relationship between George W. and Laura, including the family barbeque where they met, the Texas congressional election debate with Kent Hance, and the preparations for the governor's speech.

In these scenes Stone fused together two very different perspectives which attempted to unlock some prevailing stereotypes of Bush. The White House incumbent is a caricature of malapropisms and instinctive, untutored thinking. In notable exchanges with vice-president Dick Cheney (Richard Dreyfuss) during lunch, and in the cabinet discussion about going to war, Stone parodies Bush's visceral mode of decision-making. Yet Laura, this attractive, intelligent and sincere woman, loves him. Why does she do that? In forcing us to recalibrate our sense of Bush, we are gradually taken away from the simple desire to laugh or ridicule towards a more uncomfortable place, captured in the atmosphere of the final press conference scene. Stone is perhaps evoking pity, but the portrayal points to the wider implication that we still need to understand, and perhaps even forgive, our fellow human beings – whether they are leaders and powerful figures or not. The film's narrative is indeed anchored in the notion of redemption and Bush's rebirth as a born-again Christian. Therefore, the deeper message carries a universal note about love: an acceptance of imperfection in someone who has made mistakes on a truly global scale.

Brolin's performance in this regard is very well judged and was well received by critics, some of whom were not otherwise as enthusiastic about the film. From Bush's punctilious eating habits and his need to remind Cheney that he is 'the decider', to his near-tantrum as the search for WMDs draws a blank, the back-and-forth emotional vent in Brolin allows Stone to reinforce his central point: that this man does not quite belong here. The mystical and mythical flourishes in the film try to pin him down too: the son not quite fitted to the role, the history not quite read and understood as it should be. In a scene towards the close, father and son circle an Oval Office stripped back to its bare walls, as Bush's deepest personal fears transpire about Iraq, and his presidency begins to shift on the axis of approval and history. He is still a disappointment to his father, and history is conspiring to make him a failure. His incomprehension at all this is manifest in the closing scene as Bush looks skywards, waiting in the outfield for a baseball which never returns to earth. The final moments frame his quizzical expression and ready susceptibility to all that has failed.

Stone filmed and rejected other similarly figurative scenes. He also discussed with producer Eric Kopeloff a possible scene depicting Bush in an orange jumpsuit, conflating his persona and decisions with the symbolic imagery inherent in the meaning of Guantanamo Bay. Eventually, the scene was rejected for appearing overly judgemental in the circumstances, given that Stone was trying to present the evidence and ask the audience to make up their own minds.[54] Taking a very different approach compared to previous political and historical outings, Stone commented:

> We did talk about a possible end-scene with Bush in an orange jumpsuit at the Hague – that's funny! – but I don't think it was in the script. Everyone was attacking Bush and I felt we shouldn't

> hammer him ... It's a lighter movie but it's made about a man who is a lighter man. He is a two-dimensional man. He's Peter Sellers in *Being There* – he just doesn't belong.[55]

If Stone thought the neutrality of the film's position was brave, some critics were less sure of what he was attempting to do. Helen O'Hara in *Empire* magazine felt that too much of importance had been overlooked: the power grab in 2000, 9/11 itself, the partnership with Laura, and the working relationship with political advisor, Karl Rove.[56] O'Hara suspected that the real problem with the film was that Stone was sitting on the fence. Manohla Dargis concurred in the *New York Times*, concluding that the film was neither send-up nor takedown.[57] Inevitably, there were also scholarly complaints about the mix of history and drama. Kingsley Marshall, for example, concluded that Stone had missed several opportunities in the film to mount a serious and sustained critique of the decision-making process that took the US military into Iraq.[58] Marshall thought the decision to psychologise Bush produced a film that was neither history nor drama. These points were not without merit. Concluding in late 2004, but with Bush all too aware of the strategy collapsing around him, the plot exonerated the president in some areas both past and yet to come that really were an indictment of his 'little boy lost' mentality in the White House. The job was too big for him for sure, but he had made critical decisions too that needed to be accounted for – and for some critics, the film did not do that nearly enough.

Nonetheless, this was not a documentary for Stone, not even docudrama, let alone a conventional biopic. It was instead a melodrama, pure and simple: an examination of, if not expression of empathy for, a man who was loved and loathed in his own way like so many of us, but who also happened to be out of his depth in ways that had grievous consequences.

In both *Wall Street: Money Never Sleeps* and *Savages* Stone had continued to explore aspects of love in the screenplays, but without the melodramatic flourishes of these earlier films. Indeed, the lush photography and construction of *Savages* in particular seemed to suggest a return to the imagery more often associated with films such as *The Doors* (1991) and *Natural Born Killers*. In *Wall Street: Money Never Sleeps*, Stone persisted with the theme of familial love. He had provided a figurative father figure in the form of Lou Mannheim (Hal Holbrook) in the original film. In this second outing, the benign patriarch is configured through the character of Louis Zabel (Frank Langella) who, we learn, has provided a loving and guiding hand to a young protégé, Jake Moore (Shia LaBeouf). Indeed, it is Zabel's suicide that provides one of the principal narrative drivers, as Jake sets out to avenge Zabel's death.

Stone also uses 'love' as a redemptive device at the close of the film. As previously mentioned in Chapter 3, the behaviour of the resurgent Gordon Gekko (Michael Douglas) throughout suggests that little has changed after his spell in prison. He is even prepared to engage in duplicity to access the trust fund set up for his daughter, Winnie (Carey Mulligan). However, Winnie's pregnancy finally causes Gekko to relent (even to repent), and instead put his family before his business ambitions. The 'happy ending' did not please all who reviewed the film, but it was a very deliberate statement from Stone about the importance of love and the possibilities for positive change.

In *Savages*, the theme of love is a motivational tool woven into the screenplay at various junctures. Most straightforwardly, love seals the fate of Elena (Salma Hayek) as she is drawn across the Mexican–USA border to be with her daughter; a move that eventually leads to her capture by the DEA. Love also informs the conventional narrative decisions taken by Ben (Aaron Taylor-Johnson) and Chon (Taylor Kitsch) as they strive to free O (Blake Lively) from the drug cartel. However, the film then works with several further manifestations of love, including Dennis's (John Travolta) devotion to his wife, and Elena's *in loco parentis* relationship with the captured O. The choice taken by Lado (Benicio Del Toro) to be north of the border is, we learn, at least partly motivated by his desire to give a better life to his children. The effect of these manifestations of love develops character and reasoning as an emotional concoction. Dennis's testament of his love to his wife and his confession to her about the immorality inherent in his work is deeply affecting. O's playfulness in the presence of Elena makes manifest her need to be mothered: an antidote to a hedonistic lifestyle that has not worked out the way she thought it might.

Stone confessed that his more positive outlook on love and life prompted him to rewrite the ending in the film, taking away Don

Winslow's denouement where the protagonists were all killed, to be replaced with one where hope and a second chance were on offer. It was a flourish that reflected Stone's mood and his unwillingness to ape what he saw as an emerging cultural propensity towards cynicism in an age that, he felt, needed hope more than ever. A similar optimism infused the *Untold History* documentary series of the same period. This was optimism not borne out of some whimsical recollection of the nation's past, but a firm belief that, despite missed opportunities, the possibilities for change were always there, waiting to be grasped. In *Savages*, Stone reinforced that view, a message that nevertheless had its roots nearly twenty years before, in *Natural Born Killers.*

Conclusion

Pathos and love have been components of Stone's filmmaking from the outset. Parental love has been a perennial theme, and in *Heaven and Earth* Stone signalled a willingness in the 1990s to depart from Hollywood trends and tell a story of grief, endurance and love from a woman's perspective. It was a choice that did him no favours critically or commercially, as the film disappointed critics and isolated audiences who were perhaps unwilling to empathise with a Vietnamese point of view. *U Turn*, and several productions that followed, applied a different aesthetic to their storytelling and imagery. Stone's increasing use of melodrama left the films vulnerable to charges of whimsy and overacting. However, the shift in style allowed for a more pronounced portrayal of moral dilemmas, notable throughout *U Turn, Alexander* and *W.* Moreover, the personal and optimistic infuses so much that was at the heart of *Wall Street: Money Never Sleeps* and *Savages*, although these changes came with a cost. In the latter two projects, Stone stuck to his instincts in a way that perhaps he had failed to with the original release of *Alexander*, and he spent a decade wrestling with the challenge of bringing that film back towards his own vision. This effort was its own labour of love, and in it lay a persistence and single-mindedness that was moving Stone away from the self-examination alluded to in James Riordan's earlier biography of the director, towards a concerted world gaze more embracing and other-directed.[59]

While Stone has been criticised by several observers for the limited and limiting female roles as well as stereotypical machismo in scenes and dialogue, the accumulated evidence points to a more subtle rendering of gender, love and sexuality than has been often appreciated. Hiep Thi Le's portrayal of Le Ly in *Heaven and Earth* was steeped in pathos, Juliette Lewis's explosive performance in *Natural Born Killers* was lauded by critics, and Joan Allen's portrayal of the president's wife in *Nixon* was a strongly captivating performance on screen, evidenced by Allen's nomination for Best Supporting Actress both at the Oscars and BAFTA awards of 1996. What was in evidence in these earlier films, and again in *U Turn*, became progressively more constant as the 2000s went along. Female roles acquired increased diegetic agency, while Stone's longstanding preoccupation with parental love rather than relationships just based on sexuality and/or power were a key ingredient. Familial relationships became recurrent plot components, while the presentation of sexualised female roles was sparser. In fact, sexualised roles were never an abiding preoccupation for Stone, and more often than not, the presence of sex on screen has signified tension rather than passion. In *Salvador*, *The Doors*, *U Turn* and *Alexander* the sex scenes are never straightforward, providing instead subtexts that push at the boundaries of convention.

In her 1995 assessment of Stone's first-half career, Susan Mackey-Kallis noted how *Heaven and Earth* was as significant for what it said about the director's ability to tell a story from a woman's perspective, as it was as a piece of counter-hegemonic storytelling about Vietnam.[60] As the concluding part of the trilogy, *Heaven and Earth* extended Stone's philosophy first constructed in *Platoon* and *Born on the Fourth of July* about what the effects of war are for those living through it. While *Heaven and Earth* was constructed within the same realist aesthetic as its earlier companion pieces, the focus on familial love was becoming a trend already in Stone's writing. The female protagonist marks it as a precursor to the raft of later films that would continue with the theme of parental love framed within melodramatic moral choices, and making use of a more expressive melodramatic aesthetic and a greater range of female personification.

None of Stone's later films gave a female protagonist as much prominence as *Heaven and Earth* did, but they are distinguished by a number of leading and supporting roles where the contributions are not incidental but central to the narrative, philosophy and motivations. Stone was becoming progressively more interested in the intricacies of love, and the ways in which it moves our lives. It became an unexpected legacy of his art from a man whose outlook and past found so many of these themes hard to reconcile in his life. In *Natural Born Killers*, love 'is the only thing that kills the demon' is the mantra, and Stone's second-half career played on that register time and again – and not just in the dramas. As he moved into documentary work, Stone was mapping out an understanding of the analogy that linked the personal and the political. The individual condition was tied immutably to the condition of the country. As Stone discovered, the quest for happiness and the universal themes of love that were traced in the melodramas were mirrored in his abiding preoccupations about the condition of the USA. In Stone's eyes, love and happiness – conventionally understood as being rooted in the very personal – were wrapped up increasingly in the reified corporate establishment that now drove every aspect of American life, as the final chapter explains.

Notes

1 Interview with Oliver Stone, Santa Monica, CA, 19 August 2013.
2 Interview with Oliver Stone, Santa Monica, CA, 19 January 2010.
3 James Riordan, *Stone: The Controversies, Excesses and Exploits of a Radical Filmmaker* (New York: Hyperion, 1995), p. 113.
4 Carole Cadwalladr, 'Oliver Stone and the politics of film-making', *Observer* (18 July 2010). Available at www.theguardian.com/film/2010/jul/18/oliver-stone-chavez-wall-street (accessed 1 March 2016).
5 Quoted in Norman Kagan, *The Cinema of Oliver Stone* (Oxford: Roundhouse, 1995), p. 32.
6 Interview with Stone, 19 January 2010.
7 Greg Kilday, 'Oliver Stoned' in Charles L. P. Silet (ed), *Oliver Stone Interviews* (Jackson, MS: University of Mississippi Press, 2001), pp. 114–21.
8 Kagan, *The Cinema of Oliver Stone*, pp. 255–6.
9 Barry Langford, *Film Genre: Hollywood and Beyond* (Edinburgh: Edinburgh University Press, 2005), p. 34.
10 Langford, *Film Genre*, p. 38; emphasis in original.
11 Roger Ebert, 'U Turn', *Chicago Sun-Times* (3 October 1997). Available at http://rogerebert.com/reviews/u-turn-1997 (accessed 7 December 2015).

12 Janet Maslin, 'U Turn (1997) A Darker Shade of Noir, From Oliver Stone', *New York Times* (3 October 1997). Available at http://nytimes.com/movie/review?res=9C0DEFDA173DF930A35753C1A961958260 (accessed 7 December 2015).
13 John Ridley, *Stray Dogs* (New York: Ballantine Books, 1997).
14 Linda Ruth Williams, *The Erotic Thriller in Contemporary Cinema* (Edinburgh: Edinburgh University Press, 2005), pp. 97–133.
15 John Ridley, *U Turn: The Shooting Script* (New York: Newmarket Press, 1997), p. xiii.
16 *U Turn*, Rehearsal Papers, Box E-4, Ixtlan Production Files (hereafter I-PF), Los Angeles, CA.
17 Chris Salewicz, *Oliver Stone: The Making of his Movies* (London: Orion, 1997) p. 117.
18 Interview with Oliver Stone, Santa Monica, CA, 7 December 2011. Stone and Richardson almost did reunite in 2007 as plans were well advanced for the shooting of *Pinkville*. However, casting and finance problems put paid to this, and Richardson subsequently worked with Stone's mentor, Martin Scorsese, as well as Quentin Tarantino, winning Oscars for *The Aviator* (2004) and *Hugo* (2011).
19 Oliver Stone, email communication to author, 13 June 2012.
20 *U Turn* Stray Dogs Festivals folder, Box E-1, I-PF.
21 *U Turn* Post Production folder, Early Project (*Nixon*/*U Turn*) Box 80, I-PF.
22 Todd McCarthy, 'Review: U Turn – Stone Rolls in New Direction with "U Turn" ', *Variety* (1 September 1997). Available at http://variety.com/1997/film/reviews/u-turn-stone-rolls-in-new-direction-with-u-turn-1200451234/ (accessed 7 December 2015).
23 Maslin, 'U Turn (1997): A Darker Shade of Noir'.
24 Ebert, 'U Turn'.
25 Eric Bryant Rhodes, 'Untitled Review', *Film Quarterly*, 52, 2, 1998, 44–9.
26 William Glaberson, 'Killer in "Megan" Case Is Sentenced to Death', *New York Times* (21 June 1997). Available at http://www.nytimes.com/1997/06/21/nyregion/killer-in-megan-case-is-sentenced-to-death.html (accessed 7 December 2015).
27 Degen Pener, 'Ted's Civil War', *Entertainment Weekly* (22 November 1996), p. 19.
28 Anthony Lane, 'Lo and Behold', *New Yorker* (23 February 1998), pp. 186–8.
29 Jon Lewis, *Hollywood v Hard Core. How the Struggle Over Censorship Created the Modern Film Industry* (New York: New York University Press, 2000), pp. 293–6.
30 Interview with Oliver Stone, Santa Monica, CA, 18 June 2010.
31 James Riordan, *Stone: The Controversies, Excesses and Exploits of a Radical Filmmaker* (New York : Hyperion, 1995), p. 40.

32 Interview with Stone, 18 June 2010. See also Salewicz, *Oliver Stone*, p. 117.
33 Telephone interview with Moritz Borman, 18 August 2011.
34 Joanna Paul, 'Oliver Stone's *Alexander* and the Cinematic Epic Tradition' in Paul Cartledge and Fiona Rose-Greenland (eds) *Responses to Oliver Stone's Alexander: Film, History and Cultural Studies* (Madison, WI: University of Wisconsin Press, 2010), pp. 15–35.
35 Michael Medved, quoted in Sharon Waxman, 'Breaking Ground With a Gay Movie Hero', *New York Times* (20 November 2004). Available at http://www.nytimes.com/2004/11/20/movies/MoviesFeatures/breaking-ground-with-a-gay-movie-hero.html?_r=0 (accessed 7 December 2015).
36 *Alexander the Great*, Post Production file 7/03-1/04, Box 18, I-PF.
37 Interview with Stone, 7 December 2011.
38 Paul, 'Oliver Stone's *Alexander*', p. 18.
39 Interview with Stone, 7 December 2011.
40 *Ibid.*
41 Interview with Oliver Stone, Santa Monica, CA, 19 August 2013.
42 Paul, 'Oliver Stone's *Alexander*', p. 28.
43 Langford, *Film Genre*, p. 38.
44 Oliver Stone, 'Afterword' in Cartledge and Rose-Greenland (eds) *Responses to Oliver Stone's Alexander*, p. 348.
45 Stone, 'Afterword', p. 247.
46 CNN, 'Same-sex Marriage Bans Winning on State Ballots' (3 November 2004). Available at http://edition.cnn.com/2004/ALLPOLITICS/11/02/ballot.samesex.marriage/ (accessed 7 December 2015).
47 Adam Nagourney and David D. Kirkpatrick, 'The 2004 Campaign: Same-sex Marriage; Urged by Right, Bush Takes On Gay Marriages', *New York Times* (12 July 2004). Available at http://www.nytimes.com/2004/07/12/us/the-2004-campaign-same-sex-marriage-urged-by-right-bush-takes-on-gay-marriages.html (accessed 7 December 2015).
48 Daniel Okrent, 'The Public Editor: Weapons of Mass Destruction? Or Mass Distraction?', *New York Times* (30 May 2004). Available at http://www.nytimes.com/2004/05/30/weekinreview/the-public-editor-weapons-of-mass-destruction-or-mass-distraction.html (accessed 7 December 2015).
49 Carl Boggs and Tom Pollard, *The Hollywood War Machine: US Militarism and Popular Culture* (Boulder, CO and London: Paradigm Press, 2007), p. 2.
50 Lou Lumenick, ''Alexander' the Straight – Stone De-gay-ifies It For DVD', *New York Post* (25 July 2005). Available at http://nypost.com/2005/07/25/alexander-the-straight-stone-de-gay-ifies-it-for-dvd/ (accessed 7 December 2015).

51 Mike Clark, '"Alexander" the Great: Barely even mediocre', *USA Today* (23 November 2004). Available at http://usatoday30.usatoday.com/life/movies/reviews/2004-11-23-alexander_x.htm (accessed 7 December 2015). Nathan Lee, 'All Hail the Conquering Zero', *New York Sun* (24 November 2004). Available at www.nysun.com/arts/all-hail-the-conquering-zero/5358/ (accessed 7 December 2015).

52 Susan Sontag, 'Notes on "Camp"' in Susan Sontag, *Against Interpretation and Other Essays* (London: Penguin Classics, 2009), p. 279.

53 Paul, 'Oliver Stone's Alexander', pp. 21–2.

54 Interview with Eric Kopeloff, Santa Monica CA, 21 October 2010.

55 Interview with Oliver Stone, Santa Monica, CA, 7 December 2011.

56 Helen O'Hara, 'W.: Oliver Stone beats around the Bush', *Empire* (27 March 2008). Available at www.empireonline.com/reviews/ReviewComplete.asp?FID=135529 (accessed 7 December 2015).

57 Manohla Dargis, 'Oliver Stone's Vision Thing: Bush, the Family', *New York Times* (16 October 2008). Available at http://nytimes.com/2008/10/17/movies/17ston.html?_r=0 (accessed 7 December 2015).

58 Kingsley Marshall, 'Oliver Stone's Improbable W.' in Iwan W. Morgan, (ed), *Presidents in the Movies: American History and Politics on Screen* (New York: Palgrave Macmillan, 2011), pp. 177–91.

59 James Riordan, *Stone: The Controversies, Excesses, and Exploits of a Radical Filmmaker* (London: Aurum, 1995), pp. 521–3.

60 Susan Mackey-Kallis, *Oliver Stone's America: Dreaming the Myth Outward* (Boulder, CO: Westview Press, 1995), p. 82.

5
Corporations

Introduction

> You never really know what goes on behind the scenes in corporations, but it was an abrupt cancellation with two, three weeks to go. The decision was made in hours, when I was out of the country. There was no consultation with me. I was simply informed it was cancelled, and it was dead in the water.[1]

In spring 2003, Home Box Office (HBO) abruptly jettisoned its planned and commissioned broadcast of *Comandante*, Oliver Stone's documentary on Cuban President Fidel Castro. As outlined in Chapter 2, the news caused barely a murmur in the US media. The *New York Times* reported in passing in a review of another of Stone's documentaries, *Persona Non Grata* (2003), that HBO's decision appeared to be an editorial one.[2] That Stone's film was too sympathetic seemed to be the reason (or excuse, depending on your point of view). An additional explanation was that there was a need for more balancing material that was critical of Castro, and would throw the 'dictator's' forty-five-year rule into a slightly more complex light. Ever the pragmatist, Stone duly complied when others might have said far more or retreated from the battle altogether and left the project in limbo. In fact, the result of this additional material was a *second* documentary on Castro – *Looking for Fidel* – that *was* broadcast by HBO in 2004. In a review in the *Chicago Tribune* that April, Mark Caro heralded the new film as a 'sequel to the movie that never was', touting Stone as a much more determined prosecutor this time around, particularly in the light of recent arrests, detentions of journalists and even executions of dissidents that had taken place on the island in the intervening time between the two features.[3] 'If *Looking for Fidel* provides few definitive answers, at least this time Stone is asking the right questions,' concluded Caro. Stone's insight certainly gave an alternative persona to the leader few knew about; but for all its handheld edginess and point-of-view camerawork, it still observed the myth and propaganda shining through the fading mystique. *Looking for Fidel* (see also Chapter 2) fulfilled most of its obligations, and yet the cancellation of its companion piece *Comandante* was not rescinded, even though the film was shown on television later in Canada. Stone suspected dirty work at play. The lobbying of HBO's corporate owners, Time Warner, probably by Cuban exile groups in Miami and quite possibly also by the White House, were among Stone's suspicions.[4] The backdrop to this controversy was, after all, the launch by President Bush in March 2003 of full-scale military operations in Iraq backed up by the president's stated post-9/11 ideological conviction that *everyone* was either 'with us or with the terrorists'.[5] The film's cancellation captured the mood of the times and was symptomatic of a country clamping down on any alternative history. However, speculative and beyond easy confirmation these thoughts may have been, they still encapsulated something that Stone had been trying to say about the public accountability of corporate media organisations, and the undue influence (sought or unsought) of government in what gets reported, since he had first locked horns with the media nearly two decades previously.

Corporations – private and public – their activities, and their tenuous accountability were stalking the back corridors of Stone's oeuvre almost from the outset. The script he wrote for Michael Cimino's *Year of the Dragon* (1985) involves the cosy relationship between the New York Police Department and the New York offshoots of the Hong Kong triads. In one scene, Stanley White (Mickey Rourke) outlines to his reporter friend Tracy Tzu (Ariane) where he thinks the real problem lies: 'You want to know what's destroying this country? ... It's TV, it's media, it's people like you – vampires.'

In Stone's iconic glimpse into the morality of Wall Street two years later, individual choices and the moral as well as financial and legal corruption of money are explored further. However, in the central expository speech at the annual stockholders' meeting of Teldar Paper, Gordon Gekko (Michael Douglas) asserts that greed will save the company *and* the malfunctioning corporation called the USA in one fell swoop. Retrospectively, Stone confirmed this scene as being one of the most important in the film. Corporate management was being lauded as some kind of superhero force in these years, and yet in reality it had become weak and self-serving, in Stone's view. However, he also affirmed where the potential for good within American corporations lay, and how the forces of nationalism and patriotism could be countered within their boardrooms and trading floors.[6] It was a hopeful stance that would not last long with Stone. He later concluded that little had changed since the late 1980s; far from countering the forces of America's capitalist behemoth, corporations were, and remained, instrumental in driving those same forces forward.

In 1988, a year after *Wall Street*, Stone returned to corporations, but this time in an entertainment context rather than a financial one. He released the critically well-received but low-key *Talk Radio*, confirming that, in the wake of his comments about *Wall Street*, he had not developed some misty-eyed embrace of corporate America. *Talk Radio* was a carefully worked argument about the cultural and societal dangers posed by the operation and limited accountability of media organisations, with hints towards Clint Eastwood's *Play Misty for Me* (1971) as well as *Network* (Sidney Lumet, 1976) and *Nashville* (Robert Altman, 1975).

Six years later, *Natural Born Killers* (1994) was an all-out assault on the same corporate threat: a critique of the 1990s entertainment and news media industry, and where it was headed if left unchecked. Stone's ability to deliver an on-screen indictment of entertainment news, while at the same time becoming embroiled in an off-screen dispute about the rating of the film, then a running battle with the media, and eventually the Louisiana courts over First Amendment rights of free speech and allegations that the film had precipitated copycat killings, was simultaneously helpful and problematic for his case. Problematic because the legal battle raged on for some years – a result of involvement from the novelist John Grisham, who linked *Natural Born Killers* to the murder of a friend – and because Stone committed personal time and money to his defence while often being characterised as the offending party. Helpful in the sense that Warner Bros. took up the cudgel of defence, contributing an estimated $1 million to see off a case that they and Stone judged as a major infringement on their freedom of creativity and expression.[7] Stone later reflected:

> If Beethoven's symphonies had driven a mild gardener to the point of insanity, the symphonies could be blamed for it. Or a Picasso painting could be the cause of someone's partial blindness or psychotic fractured thoughts resulting during a sex act or something. Picasso would take the fall, and it would be the end of art and culture as we know it. There can be *no* interpretation of any event – it would flatten out society to its extreme. *That* was the issue. If that case had been successfully prosecuted, it would've been a nightmare for Hollywood as well as other industries. It might not have succeeded in the end, and it might also have been overturned at some point by a sane Court. But if it had put its odious morality in place, there would've been a major implosion of our culture.[8]

Warner Bros. and Stone prevailed, and the director's continuing high profile ensured that *Natural Born Killers* and its subject matter were noticed and debated at length. However, was Stone a prophet or a hypocrite on the issues within the film? Even some of his supporters were unsure, and his critics were happy to play along with the caricature of an 'America-hating' degenerate all too willing to cash in while claiming some supposed moral high ground. In time, the film became lauded as something of a cult classic, as well as legally winning its case. The State of Louisiana Court of Appeal eventually concurred with Stone's comment above, and reaffirmed his First Amendment rights – despite condemning the glorification of violence that the court perceived the film to be relishing in all-too-frequently.[9]

A further five years passed once more between *Natural Born Killers* and additional media or entertainment scrutiny, this time with sport as the central motif. *Any Given Sunday* (1999), Stone's first and only foray into 'sports movie' territory was a typically bravado piece, and is often ascribed the much more conservative treatise of masculine, misogynistic mannerisms that better represented other football films. Coming at the end of a self-imposed near-exile from the industry since *Nixon* in 1995 – with only *U Turn* (1997) in-between times – *Any Given Sunday* represented a continuation of the corporate enquiry, but proved a watershed for Stone's own auteur brand. Following personal crisis and professional disappointment, the film was a return to a more complex and intensive production environment, as well as a reconfiguration of Stone's social commentary. He had absorbed some of the hard lessons from the mid-1990s, and had effected a significant reorientation in his personal approach to work and reception: waking up, he said, with the cup half-full rather than half-empty.[10] Part of that reorientation was a much more intricate mix of issues, whereby *Any Given Sunday* carried important anti-corporate commentary into scenarios involving gender, corporate greed and dominant conservative tendencies.

Yet if Hollywood's favourite *bête noire* appeared to be retreating into some kind of safe ideological obscurity, he followed this football film by directing his first two Castro documentaries and the fascinating *Persona Non Grata*, another side-swerve that wrong-footed many of his critics. The move was consistent with wider industry trends, with documentary in the ascendant and less industry appetite for polemical drama. James McEnteer asserted that political documentary filmmaking was becoming a response to the 'corporatization and trivialization of news' in the early 2000s.[11] *W.* (2008), *Wall Street: Money Never Sleeps* (2010) and *Savages* (2012) all reasserted the Stone template of corporate enquiry, but tangentially – reflecting both changes in the director, and the sensibilities of the film industry itself.

Stone himself noted that premium cable TV channels including HBO were offering much greater freedoms to directors than theatrical distribution to tell their tales in more raucous and incendiary fashion.[12] The space for polemical drama contracted for a time after 9/11, and Stone concluded that documentary might offer the best opportunity to make his institutional point.[13] Yet his own experience offered clear evidence of a growing problem for the USA as a functioning democracy: how to service the need for competing views and narratives – the 'marketplace of ideas' – in an environment where news and entertainment executives did not want to appear to be on the 'wrong side' of the administration's 'War on Terror'. Recognising, much less saying something of that post-9/11 change was proving terribly difficult to do. By the time that the *Untold History* project began to form as an idea in late 2007, the fact that the media had so little to say about the condition of the USA galvanised Stone to press on with a series underwritten by the idea that the pursuit of empire was an economic project for the USA as much as it was a political one, and that American corporate interests were invariably the (major) beneficiaries of whatever intervention the government had initiated in the post-Second World War era.

In the light of this career trajectory, this chapter traces two key threads in Stone's exploration of corporations through the films above, and their impact on wider society: one to do with the media, and the other concerning government. In *Any Given Sunday*, Stone returned to some of the themes of media manipulation that he had tackled in *Talk Radio*. The first part of this chapter revisits these two films, exploring how and why the critique of corporations manifested itself in a particular way during this era. Despite less politically insistent dramas in the period after *Any Given Sunday*, Stone continued to give attention to the effects of corporate influence, but channelled these through documentary and an altered feature film dynamic. His Castro documentaries were nothing less than a direct challenge to what he saw as the bias within mainstream media organisations towards anything that might constitute a provocation to dominant national narratives. His third presidential biopic, *W.*, had things to say about corporate and government accountability too, as did *Wall Street: Money Never Sleeps* and *Savages*.

However, Stone's critique was perhaps at its most urgent in the *Untold History* series. His early career embrace of a more benign view of corporate America manhandled by dubious speculators – verbalised up to and including *Wall Street* – shifted towards an increasingly insistent denouncing of the establishment itself and what Stone saw as the folly of empire, corporately driven. As he progressed with the project, it became increasingly obvious to him that 'empire' meant not simply the advancement of US corporate interests in the promulgation of everything from hamburgers to smartphones, but to the corporatisation of the military itself.[14] Indeed, the Edward Snowden story that Stone was drawn to by 2014, explicitly revealed the extent to which the use of commercial contractors had become integral to the emergence of a 'global security state'.[15] The USA had become, in Stone's words, a 'corporate oligarchy', and war was now its stratagem of choice.[16] With its emphasis on the maintenance of empire, the *Untold History* series helped lay the groundwork for Stone's critique of the global security apparatus, and this in turn provided a natural lead-in for Stone to the drama of the Snowden story.

Thus, documentary acted as a counter-view to the corporate infotainment complex, but the *Untold History* series additionally functioned as a source of self-education on the complexities of US history and politics, providing the precursor to an emerging treatise that linked critiques of government with those of business, media and defence corporations. It is a treatise that draws its inspiration ultimately from the roots of American democracy: one dedicated to a less interventionist government, and one where Jeffersonian views of democracy and power predominate.[17]

Talk Radio

Stone's on-screen engagement with the issues of media influence, sophistry and corporate power commenced with his watchable, yet largely overlooked, study of broadcasting, *Talk Radio*, released in 1988. The film was loosely based on the events leading up to the assassination in 1984 of combative radio talk show host Alan Berg by white supremacists in Denver, Colorado. The screenplay credits were shared by Stone and Eric Bogosian, the latter having written an earlier play about the murder, with the story later amplified in a book on Berg by Stephen Singular.[18] The key theme, as Don Kunz notes, is about corruption: the corruption of ambition that destroys personal relationships; the corruption of greed that embraces on-air insult as a legitimate route to corporate revenue, even as it incites criminal activity; and the corruption of espoused belief that reaches its audience segment with references to the Christian creed, while transforming that same creed into undisguised ethnocentrism.[19]

The film opens over Dallas at dusk. A radio station broadcasts a weather warning, anchoring the story in the heartland of America. The visuals and audio then bring the audience into the station, eavesdropping on *Night Talk* hosted by Barry Champlain (Eric Bogosian). His opening monologue rails against 'lying, whoring and intoxication' and closes with an ironic quip: 'Talk Radio. It's the last neighbourhood in town. People just don't talk to each other anymore.' It is immediately apparent how political engagement is being supplanted with a fun-making, yet often callous, mode of entertainment passed off as community spirit within Champlain's manipulative rhetoric. Stone opens the film out to explore the impact, and efforts by local station manager Dan (Alec Baldwin) to sell the show to a media company that would allow national syndication.

Champlain agrees to the deal on-air, but does so by reminding his new sponsor that he will not soften his touch or 'go a little easier'. He already sees himself as speaking truth to power, but now he will be able to address a bigger audience. Champlain's invitation to his audience to join him on this wider stage highlights two contradictions in his stance. First, his personal ambition pushes him to become a part of the system that he seeks to criticise. In making that transition, he fails to recognise the irony of his position: that the 'system' is nothing more than a collection of individuals like him, often doing the same thing. Second, his hectoring style of delivery, predicated on the belief that 'somebody better do something', helps to reify the possibility of direct action to the point where active engagement is substituted for a generalised rage and hatred. The solution he offers is an entertainment medium that plays at being the concerned neighbour, yet really only showcases the prejudices of his audiences and his own invective.

Norman Kagan argues that the underlying message, applying to Rush Limbaugh and Oprah Winfrey as well as to Barry Champlain, is that 'the world is crazy!'.[20] However, the screenplay also suggests a more self-reflective indictment: a collective complicity in the foregrounding of self-loathing as entertainment. While Champlain's 'neighbourhood' is invited to turn to itself for explanation and to outsiders for blame, the result is a mode of destructiveness that leaves unchallenged the agenda of the organisations that directly affect the lives of his listeners: government and media corporations. Champlain's death and replacement at the end of the film highlights this insulation from challenge. His death becomes material that itself can be cycled into the caller narratives. Everything has changed, yet also remains the same.

Talk Radio questioned artistic authenticity: a central theme of the media portrayal to come in *Natural Born Killers*. We are invited to reflect on the role of talk radio, Kunz suggests, as either a legitimate campaign against the disintegration of a certain kind of American culture of respect and integrity, or the pandering to a base interest in demeaning entertainment.[21] In short, the film poses the question: is talk radio part of the solution or the problem? At least some of the negative media response to *Natural Born Killers* was predicated on the conclusion that Stone and his film were prominent examples of the problem about declining media standards, rather than an authentic effort to call attention to that decline. Part of the reason that such a question did not arrive with *Talk Radio* lies in the application of two wildly different treatments.

Talk Radio's set-up allows the issue of entertainment exploitation to be raised in a more abstract, intellectualised form. As the narrative unfolds, we see how the promises that the corporation can offer – fame, wealth – play to Champlain's conceit in a way that gradually undermines his relationship with all of those around him. However, the film avoids descending into a homily about the evils of corporate America by the prominence given to the on-air sequences, where Champlain is taking calls from his audience. The sequences provide a tableau of prejudice that few audience members would register as inauthentic. The intercutting of the on-air sequences with the main narrative provided a ready space for cinemagoers to reflect on the implications of the story. Is Champlain simply the conduit for a wider debate in US society? Or is he an agent provocateur who profits from airing prejudice? How does the relationship between the audience, Champlain and the corporation work, and whose needs are being served?

By contrast, in *Natural Born Killers*, Stone shifted the audience from the position of observer to willing or unwilling participant. The abstraction has been exchanged for a demonstration of the subject matter. The audience is thrust into the bloody carnage, into the midst of the lives of the most deranged of the callers we hear from in *Talk Radio*. While the differences in treatment between *Talk Radio* and *Natural Born Killers* certainly must have contributed to the negative assessments of the latter film, it remains hard to overlook the complicating effect produced by the change that Stone's profile had undergone between the two films. He was judged by his excesses now as much as he had been by his caustic and provocative movies before.

Of course, related to this shift in perception were the changes in the industry and the country. Stone may have become more provocative to some, but the tableau itself against which he was being judged was changing, and his place in it was less clear. In the period between *Talk Radio* and *Natural Born Killers*, Sony had acquired Columbia (1989), Matsushita had acquired Universal (1990), Time had bought Warner Bros. and Viacom had taken over Paramount (1993). The studios were becoming enmeshed in multi-platform global enterprises with interests in music, film, news and entertainment.[22] As Christensen and Haas have noted, the appetites of this global entertainment complex for ideologically controversial content were very limited.[23] Culturally, the USA was in the embrace of a post-Cold War period of self-congratulation perhaps best illustrated by Francis Fukuyama's 1992 publication *The End of History and the Last Man*,[24] with its conceit that the liberal democracies (led by the USA) had reached the pinnacle of cultural evolution.

Adherents of this thinly disguised piece of neo-conservative rhetoric could bask in the afterglow of the first Gulf War and the emergence of a new lone superpower: truly the final word on the emergence of the 'American Century' trumpeted by Henry Luce fifty years earlier. Against this changing backdrop, *Talk Radio* had sat comfortably within an era of film writing and production that had been celebrated for a discreet set of cinematic critiques including *Reds* (Warren Beatty, 1981), *Missing* (Costa Gavras, 1982), *Silkwood* (Mike Nichols, 1983), and of course Stone's own *Salvador* (1986), *Platoon* (1986) and *Wall Street*. By the time that *Natural Born Killers* arrived in cinemas, US audiences were more likely to be savouring *The Bodyguard* (Mick Jackson, 1992), *Jurassic Park* (Steven Spielberg, 1993), *Forrest Gump* (Robert Zemeckis, 1994) and *The Lion King* (Roger Allers and Rob Minkoff, 1994). Only in Quentin Tarantino's *Pulp Fiction* (1994), fêted by the Academy with a Oscar for Best Screenplay and six further nominations, did some of the arguments about violence and media infiltration resonate.

By the mid-1990s, then, Stone was experiencing a kind of brand paradox. His early successes and piercing observations of recent American history had established a bankable brand identity that had been finally able to conceive of Vietnam in a way he wanted to document it, and criticised the consuming greed of the financial system in the manner about which he felt passionately. The controversies over *JFK* (1991) and *Natural Born Killers* did not diminish

Stone's standing, but they had galvanised a new and destabilising aspect to the author brand that was being used by Stone's detractors in the media to redefine him and his work. His own cinematic evolution seemed increasingly to be running in a diametrically opposed direction to the predilections of the industry and, indeed, the country.

Any Given Sunday

Real men drink beer

The National Football League's (NFL) dispute with its players in spring 2011 over sharing revenues may not have set American football apart from other major sporting leagues in the USA and elsewhere, but the sums involved were significant. In 2010, the team owners had drawn $1 billion from the total $9 billion annual revenues to help finance stadiums and the NFL cable channel – but had sought to increase the annual allocation to $2 billion for 2011. Despite a downward revision of their demand to $320 million in the course of meetings in early March, the players were unmoved and the players' union opted to dissolve itself.[25] This 'decertification' was intended to allow players the flexibility to seek an injunction, should the NFL impose a lockout. The NFL duly delivered, immediately proceeding to impose a lockout of players, threatening the annual training camps due to start in August as well as the season itself, due to begin in early September. In April a District Court judge ordered the lifting of the six-week lockout, but the NFL successfully delayed the implementation of the District Court decision in the Court of Appeal.[26] As the clock ticked down towards the start of the new season, NFL Commissioner Roger Goodell and players' leader, Executive Director of the NFL Players Association, DeMaurice Smith, worked towards a compromise agreement which, while it did not increase the overall share of revenues for players, did make additional provision for players in retirement. Agreement was reached in July 2011.

The dispute over revenues is one of two prominent debates within the sport. The other – the long-term health effects of playing – is an issue in its own right, as well as one with repercussions for the question of revenues. The death of NFL wide receiver Chris Henry in November 2009 appeared to mark a watershed in the issue of safety in a contact sport where concussions are commonplace. He was by no means the first player to be diagnosed with Chronic Traumatic Encephalopathy (CTE), but of the twenty-three deaths recorded since 2002, he was the first still to be playing football when he died. The condition, which produces depression and mood swings and eventually leads to dementia, is a recent symptom of a trend towards increasing on-field violence that appears to be linked both to the increasing size of footballers, and the rigours of their training.[27] The revenue dispute broke out against the backdrop of news in February 2011 of the suicide of a former Chicago Bears star, Dave Duerson. The NFL had already acknowledged the longer-term health issues faced by retired footballers with the introduction in February 2007 of a scheme, supported by the NFL Players Association, to fund medical care for former footballers suffering from dementia. Also in 2008, the Chronic Traumatic Encephalopathy Center was established by a number of former athletes in conjunction with researchers at Boston University to study the long-term effects of concussion injuries. Duerson, who had shot himself through the heart, had left instructions that his brain be donated to the Center.

The recent history of, and debates about, the game have leavened the mix of money and safety with other controversies, including questions concerning the use of performance-enhancing and recreational drugs, as well as suggestions of racism in a business world where corporate entities were populated predominantly by older white men running a sport where 60 per cent of the players were African American.[28] In *Any Given Sunday* Stone sought to address the complexities of the game in a way that aired these interwoven issues, while bringing the audience into the intricacies of action on the field of play. The on-field sequences were constructed and filmed in a way that allowed the audience to share the players' perspective on plays, and gain some sense of the confrontation and violence of the tackles.

Stone's interest in gridiron stretched back to an unfilmed treatment he had produced in the early 1980s, titled 'The Linebacker'. The subsequent development of the final screenplay involved a complex mix of sub-projects and collaborations, reflecting the unstable world of studio ownership in Hollywood. A script titled *Not for Long* by Jamie Williams (a former San Francisco 49er) and

Richard Weiner (a correspondent with the *New York Times*) had been rewritten as *Monday Night*, with Cinergi Pictures involved. A second screenplay, written by playwright John Logan and titled *Any Given Sunday*, had been sent to Stone and given backing by Turner Pictures, which hoped to combine it with *Monday Night*. Meanwhile, Warner Bros. had optioned a book by a former football medic Dr Robert Huizenga, titled *You're Okay, It's Just a Bruise: A Doctor's Sideline Secrets*. It was transformed by Dan Pyne into a screenplay titled *Playing Hurt*. Along the way, Cinergi sold its interest to Turner Pictures and the latter merged with Warner Bros., which meant that by December 1996 the rights to all three screenplays belonged to Warner Bros.

Warner Bros. was happy to have Stone on board, and work progressed on *Any Given Sunday* during February and March 1997. The central theme was very much a paean to the traditions of the sport, presented in shorthand as life being a game of inches overlaid with teamwork. However, the screenplay proved not to be to the liking of the NFL, whose cooperation had been sought. Following advice from businessman and talent agent Michael Ovitz in May 1998 on how best to approach the NFL, Stone forwarded a script to Neil Austrian, who was the NFL's president and chief operating officer. Austrian replied on 20 July 1998 that the script 'does not properly represent either the players or the National Football League'.[29] A major concern for Austrian was the representation of drug use, and he wrote to club owners four days later advising them that the NFL would not be cooperating with the production. With encouragement from producer Clayton Townsend, Stone persisted and, for a time, the relationship with Austrian at least appeared on the surface to be improving.[30] However, a rapprochement in November soon evaporated. Austrian wrote to Townsend on 10 December 1998, rejecting a revised script and withdrawing all cooperation with the use of logos and team names in the film.[31] As a result, the fictitious Association of Football Franchises of America (AFFA) and the Pantheon Cup were introduced into the screenplay, along with the strips and logos of the featured teams, including the Miami Sharks, Minnesota Americans, Chicago Rhinos and New York Emperors.

A brief pause ensued in early December, as Warner Bros. assessed the option of shutting down the production. Stone argued for a continuance and pressed on with script revisions, eventually winning the argument. Before the New Year, the project was underway once more, now budgeted at just over $48 million with a sixty-day shoot. The budget included provision for a ten-week football camp – a reprise of the kind of preparatory methodology that had been used on *Platoon*.

With a cast including Jamie Foxx, Al Pacino, Cameron Diaz and Dennis Quaid, plus James Woods, LL Cool J and several former professional footballers including Jim Brown and Lawrence Taylor, shooting got underway in late January 1999. The story focuses on the Miami Sharks football team and the efforts of their coach Tony D'Amato (Al Pacino) to reverse their string of poor performances. In the film's opening sequence we see the team's quarterback Jack 'Cap' Rooney (Dennis Quaid) and his replacement sustain injuries, and D'Amato must rely on the second replacement Willie Beamen (Jamie Foxx). Although the Sharks lose the game, Beamen performs well, and his elevation becomes the vehicle with which Stone explores issues of celebrity, corporate sponsorship and medical ethics. Beamen's unorthodox approach to the playbook and his emerging sense of self-importance as media attention increases, combine to generate tensions with D'Amato. These tensions produce knock-on consequences for D'Amato's working relationship with his boss and team owner, Christina Pagniacci (Cameron Diaz).

On the morning after the game the action moves to Pagniacci's home, where she is in discussion with two of her advisors about how the team might leverage finance from the City of Miami for a new stadium. One of Pagniacci's advisors, Ed (James Karen), comments that Pagniacci should consider leaving the business: 'Start over, start a family. You don't love football.' As her gender credentials in a patriarchal world are questioned, the theme is continued when D'Amato's arrival produces a heated confrontation between the two because Pagniacci wants to sell Rooney and use the money to help rebuild the team, while D'Amato is resistant. The ensuing exchange rehearses questions of loyalty to individuals as opposed to the team, but all the while the mixture of economics and gender is never far from the surface. Pagniacci is positioned as the greedy corporate owner, while D'Amato becomes the bastion of personal integrity. As the discussion draws to a close, Pagniacci intimates that D'Amato's contract may be terminated at the end of the year. His response – that he settled his contract with her father over a beer and a handshake – echoes the paternalistic sentiment that she has heard just a few minutes earlier from her advisor. Thus Pagniacci is confronted with a questioning of her authority that conflates her relative youth and gender: a stereotype that Diaz was sensitive to in the role. In a pre-shooting discussion with Stone in November 1998, she had voiced a concern that her character appeared to be using sexuality as her principal asset. Stone accepted the concern, and spent time with colleagues Dr Robert Huizenga and Lisa Amsterdam working on the screenplay still further. One result was the increased emphasis on Pagniacci having grown up around the business and the team. The removal of any explicitly sexual element in Pagniacci's character served to highlight the ways in which she was being patronised by Ed and D'Amato: a theme that is reinforced later in the film both in her discussion with the mayor about a new stadium, and shortly after her encounter with the Commissioner (Charlton Heston) where he comments, out of her earshot, that she would 'eat her young'.

In Stone's own assessment of the film, one of the key messages is about the importance of channelling individual ambition for the benefit of the team. Stone is concerned with the deleterious effects of corporate culture, some of which is built into Pagniacci's obsession with economics and wider corporate responsibilities. Elsewhere the critique of corporate culture is equally sure-footed.

One of the most powerful sequences in the film concerns the creation of the Willie Beamen brand. This process begins to take shape at the end of the Sharks game against Chicago on the computer screen of sports journalist Jack Rose (John C. McGinley), who is constructing his post-match report. As he lauds Beamen's playing abilities we see the beginnings of a new media persona emerging: 'Beamen is a lethal combination of mobility and escapability ... A warrior poet ...a new breed of athlete.' Later at the Sharks' charity event with Miami mayor Tyrone Smalls (Clifton Davis), the mayor offers his own assessment in an aside to Beamen: 'You are a model for your people now, Willie Beamen. A black man on a parade. Stand tall!'

By the end of the next game Beamen has been anointed 'Steamin' Beamen' by TV announcer Tug Kowalski (Stone himself), and we see shortly afterwards a media montage of sports magazine covers, a soft drinks commercial video and a charity appearance that confirm Beamen's deification. He is becoming a poster boy for the corporate interests that rely on the popularity of the sport. In a television interview with Rose, Beamen becomes dazzled with his own reflection. He begins by calling attention to racial imbalances in the sport, noting that while 70 per cent of the players are African American, very few coaches and no owners are black. However, the thrust of his critique is lost as he segues into a personal assessment that mixes the subjects of race and his sporting ethos together: 'It's all about winning. I mean that's what this country is about, being number one. This whole country was built on kicking immigrant ass – African ass, Chinese ass, don't-matter-who ass.' Beamen is already finding his stride as celebrity pundit. His interview bravado finishes with a description of his special powers on the field. However, these are quickly neutralised in the next game against the Emperors by the other team players' unwillingness to work for Beamen, and he must slowly come to terms with the arguments made to him earlier by D'Amato that success depends on leadership, team play and discipline.

The narrative in *Any Given Sunday* follows a trajectory of growth, crisis and rebirth: for Beamen, his relationship, the team and D'Amato, but not entirely for Pagniacci. The film airs the various tensions between individual success, team effectiveness, media coverage and corporate ambition, but in a way that aligns masculinity with integrity, and femininity with exploitation. Beamen learns the importance of team play from D'Amato; he even learns to accept advice from Cap. Separately he seeks to correct his wayward personal life with a renewal of his relationship with his partner Vanessa (Lela Rochon): she is happy to respond to his overture. D'Amato's traditional paternalism concerning Cap and Luther 'Shark' Lavay (Lawrence Taylor) – concerns that keep Cap in the team, and make Shark aware of the risks that his injuries pose – is presented as the antithesis of Pagniacci's ambition, which manifests itself in her application of pressure on team doctor Harvey Mandrake (James Woods) to drop Cap and conceal the risk to Shark. Her encounter with the commissioner leaves her nonplussed, and her unrelenting pursuit of corporate goals through a franchise bid for a new Los Angeles team is dealt with by the commissioner and his colleagues in typically patrician fashion at a hearing in

New York. That her gender is part of the issue has been exposed in an earlier scene, when she hears her mother tell D'Amato that he was the son that Pagniacci's father really wanted. The real tension between Pagniacci and D'Amato is a symbolic sibling rivalry in which D'Amato's stance is vindicated. In the closing seconds of the Knights game, Pagniacci confides to her mother that things are out of control, and wonders aloud if it is her who is losing perspective. She apologises to her mother for her behaviour. After the game, D'Amato reminds Beamen of the game's ethos: on any given Sunday, you are either going to win or lose. Beamen completes the aphorism: can you win or lose like a man? Finally, during the closing titles, Pagniacci gives a speech at a news conference in which she talks about her father's legacy and the bond with Miami, and then submissively acknowledges the debt she owes to D'Amato for helping her understand what she had forgotten. D'Amato accepts the gesture, but he has one final way of asserting his superiority in this contest. Not only is he leaving for a new management challenge in Albuquerque that will take him back to the spiritual heart of the game, but he has signed Beamen as his quarterback.

The complexities of the screenplay's production, obstacles to access for location shooting, budget questions and casting issues all bear testament to the size and scale of this project and Stone's ambitions for it, as writer and director. Bob Daly, chair of Warner Bros. was pleased with the result, and US audiences – especially those in the mid-west, middle-American brackets – supported the effort with a $75 million gross.[32] *Any Given Sunday* was one of a select few sports movies during the decade that seemed to catch the popular imagination. Tony Scott's *The Fan* (1996) and Sam Raimi's *For Love of the Game* (1999) were big-budget failures, while *Days of Thunder* (1990), also directed by Scott, Penny Marshall's *A League of Their Own* (1992) and most notably *Jerry Maguire* (Cameron Crowe, 1996) all prospered. *Jerry Maguire* shared some of *Any Given Sunday*'s pretentions in pursuing similar 'small is beautiful' anti-corporate themes, but with a more upbeat, romanticised narrative about a plucky corporate hustler reinventing himself in the world of sports agents. The film grossed some $150 million at the US box office, confirming its credentials as part of the raft of 1990s feel-good movies, or 'capitalism capers' that filled screens in that immediate post-Cold War and Gulf War moment.

Any Given Sunday was more complex by comparison, foregrounding personal courage and making the cut-and-thrust of corporatised sport an interloper in on-field politics and conduct. This was a more nuanced commentary on the dislocation between traditional values concerning collaboration and teamwork, and the corporate environment within which the game is played. Thus the critique in *Any Given Sunday* presaged themes of corporate dysfunction picked up much later in *Wall Street: Money Never Sleeps* and *Savages*. The manufacture of Beamen's image by news and entertainment media is seen within the diegesis as shallow and ultimately self-defeating, both physically and spiritually. However, the resolution to this disturbance – the return to a hinterland of more personalised and traditional values – is not entirely a progressive one, even as it seeks to pull against corporate influence. The paternalism directed against Pagniacci early on in the film has a taint of atavism about it, and yet in the denouement Stone appears to celebrate that same response. Pagniacci the woman is the embodiment of the wayward corporation.

This complexity aside, the film's wistful veneration of a smaller, more personal world of local football leagues spoke of a paradox felt by many sports fans, who celebrated tradition while embracing the world of corporate franchise football entertainment. It was a cultural yearning that gave vent to the belated success of NBC's *Friday Night Lights* from the mid-2000s, about a college football team in Texas. Meanwhile, the NFL had risen corporately far from its humble beginnings in the 1920s. Between 1970 and the millennium, under commissioners Pete Rozelle and later Paul Tagliabue, the League developed and exploited both television rights and a highly successful licensing arm. Its own television station, NFL Network, launched in 2003 broadcasting globally, although it attracted criticism at times for its apparent avarice, and has been routinely in disagreement about fees with Time Warner Cable and Comcast.[33]

Forbes magazine's 2009 description of the Dallas Cowboys' new stadium as a 'gold mine' not only turned out to be figuratively true, but could be reasonably used to sum up the finances of nearly all major NFL teams.[34] The average value of a franchise was estimated by *Forbes* in 2012 to be $1.04 billion. Clearly, a key part of revenue is television, and *Forbes* further estimated that the deals with CBS, ESPN, Fox and NBC earned an estimated $3.1 billion annually for the NFL.[35]

Equally contentious has been the question of public money funding stadium construction: an issue that *Any Given Sunday* draws attention to, if only briefly. Bloomberg reported in 2012 that there were, at that point, twenty-one NFL teams playing in stadiums built or renovated using tax-free public borrowing. The accepted wisdom has been that these deals are good for local economies, and indeed cities have vied with each other to attract teams to their locality, despite evidence that the deals bring poor long-term value to the communities and depress federal tax revenue. Paradoxically, a provision in the Tax Reform Act of 1986 – which restricted application of the tax exemption to circumstances where the debt payment from private business revenue did not exceed ten per cent of the total payment – has resulted in city administrations borrowing more tax-exempt funds to ensure that the sports franchise can meet this obligation.[36] Overall, Bloomberg estimated that the total loss to the US taxpayer on $17 billion of debt raised for sports structures since 1986 amounted to $4 billion. The real beneficiaries appeared to be the teams themselves.

In its own way, *Any Given Sunday* spoke to a myth about millennial America, offering up the promise of a return to a time of honour when deals were done over a beer and with a handshake, when the reality was more of a shakedown. In a sense, the film offered middle-American males what it offered Stone: a chance to feel in control again.

Corporate dysfunction

Any Given Sunday sits more or less midway between *Natural Born Killers* and *Comandante*, and in its construction and reception it represents a pause as well as a transition point. In every sense, *Natural Born Killers* was a sign of a director on the edge. From the organised chaos of the production to the arguments over the rating, to the inflamed press coverage after the film's release, Stone had set the entire edifice of his career on fire in the pursuit of a vision of America's cultural descent into on-screen and off-screen violence. Many observers thought that Stone was seeking to have his cake and eat it: profiting from a satire about on-screen violence that itself seemed to break new boundaries in taste and artistic responsibility. Arguably, *Nixon*'s reception was tainted by the fallout. In different ways, *U Turn* and *Any Given Sunday* were signs of gradual recovery from the effects of the mid-1990s: a return to filmmaking, and then to mainstream approval. However, the decision to develop the documentary on Castro brought Stone back to a more studied critique of American media corporations.

Stone was well aware that it was more difficult to reach a wider audience with documentary, but the new millennium added commercial impetus to the genre. As James McEnteer has described, there appeared to be a discernible renaissance in documentary filmmaking: arguably, a passing of the torch within American political cinema from dramatists to documentarians.[37] The work of Michael Moore, Alex Gibney, Eugene Jarecki, Barbara Kopple, Errol Morris, Charles Ferguson, Kirby Dick, Robert Greenwald, Davis Guggenheim and Leslie Iwerks all confirmed this tendency. Yet as Stone's experience with *Comandante* had demonstrated, documentary was not an easy fix for the issues posed by the presence of a small number of companies which controlled much of the distribution space to which filmmakers needed access. Even Moore's success with *Fahrenheit 9/11* (2004) had come only after a dispute between the producer Miramax and its parent company Disney, in which the latter had sought to block release of the film in the USA, apparently because Disney was mindful of its operations in Florida: a state which happened to have a governor who was the brother of the president.[38] HBO's failure to broadcast *Comandante* highlighted the same kind of corporate gatekeeping which had the power to influence the marketplace of ideas. So while documentary filmmakers seemed to be taking up the slack in offering challenges to the corporatisation of news media, they still confronted issues of media ownership and the possibility of censorship.

While acknowledging the problem, Stone pressed on with his critique of news media. In parallel with the work on Castro, he broadened his challenge of what he saw as a wilful lack of balance in the coverage of political leaders who were not regarded as friends in Washington, DC with his retrospective of Venezuelan President Hugo Chávez in *South of the Border* (2010). The reaction in the mainstream press was as Stone might have predicted. Stephen Holden's piece in the *New York Times* caustically reminded readers that this was the same director who had brought *JFK* to the world.[39] The reference back to *that* picture highlighted the point that Stone was trying to make about bias. It also proved that his reputation itself as a challenger of establishment narratives had become part of the establishment response; his criticism of the media could be automatically dismissed as paranoia.

Holden's piece underlined how Stone's antipathy to the media was rooted in his personal experience around the time of *JFK*. Circumstantial while it might have been, questions at the heart of that film about broader institutional accountability had still not been answered. The scepticism that had underpinned *Salvador*'s critique of US foreign policy was grandstanded both in Stone's use of President Eisenhower's farewell address and referencing of the military industrial complex, and in the pivotal scene involving District Attorney Jim Garrison (Kevin Costner) and X (Donald Sutherland) in *JFK*. Banks and the armaments industry were the beneficiaries, it is suggested, of Kennedy's removal, and Stone pushed the suggestion further in *Nixon* by characterising malign forces as 'the Beast', overseeing the phenomenon as a coalition of Cold War interests.[40]

After *Nixon*, Stone set these concerns to one side for a time; but in the aftermath of 9/11, more specific questions about empire and the accountability of the military industrial complex began to gather momentum once again. Some of these themes were rehearsed in *W.*, *Wall Street: Money Never Sleeps* and *Savages*, but it was in the *Untold History* series that Stone refined his thesis and set up the line of enquiry that would lead him seamlessly to an interest in the Edward Snowden story.

In Stone's third presidential biopic, the theme of empire becomes central to the organising narrative of the discussion about invasion of Iraq. In a key scene in *W.* set in the White House situation room, vice-president Dick Cheney (Richard Dreyfuss) highlights for the president (Josh Brolin) and the others present how Iran is the only area in the region where there is no American presence. Cheney spells it out in the following terms: 'Control Iran, control Eurasia – control the world. Empire, real empire.' Stone did not suppose that the scene actually played out as depicted, but he saw it as a piece of drama that allowed him to make a point about the importance of oil in the administration's calculations – both political and economic. While Stone did not have the opportunity in the film to explore Cheney's connections to Halliburton, or the involvement of a Halliburton subsidiary in failed reconstruction projects after the Iraq War had finished, these developments were part of the wider story that he was seeking to reference.[41] Nevertheless, the news media remained a subject for Stone's disdain. In a memorable scene in *W.* featuring two news anchors, Candice Black (Anne Pressly) and Jack Hawk (Jim Garrity), the news item features the arrival by President Bush on the *USS Abraham Lincoln* to give the now-infamous 'mission accomplished' televised address on 1 May 2003. As the aircraft touches down on the aircraft carrier deck, Black marvels at the spectacle: 'He's landing on a boat at 150 miles per hour. I can't think of a Democrat that would do that.' A moment later she adds: 'Perception is reality.' Jack Hawk then chimes in: 'George Bush looks real all right. He didn't fight in the war but he looks like he did, and women love President Bush for this very reason – and women love this war, it's simple.' Stone's send-up underscored his view that Americans were being fed a diet of misinformation and pro-government opinion by all of the major news outlets. The resulting news agenda was becoming an increasingly narrow set of perspectives. The result was a population simply unequipped to hold either their elected representatives, or the business interests whose lobbyists inhabited Washington, DC, to account.

Stone reprised his treatise on corporate dysfunction in *Wall Street: Money Never Sleeps.* Co-written with Allan Loeb and Stephen Schiff, the film at one point showcases an expository speech by Gekko that is, in essence, a reply to the speech in the original film where he had declared that 'greed is good'. Stone – and indeed Michael Douglas – had been taken aback by the veneration that the Gekko character had received. For some at least, Gekko was to become not a salutary warning about the absence of morality or higher purpose, but something of a role model. Who better, then, to offer a riposte than Gekko himself? With some self-irony, Gekko in effect challenges the US embrace of the 'greed is good' mantra and asks his audience to reflect on the unfolding financial crisis. The thrust of the critique is that financial corporations are adding no real value to society. Gekko asserts that the three-letter-abbreviated financial instruments developed by the banking institutions can be categorised under one three letter category: WMDs. He moves on to explain that in the previous year, 40 per cent of American corporate profits came from financial services:

> Not production, not anything remotely to do with the needs of the American public ... It's as clear as a bell to those who pay attention. The mother of all evil is speculation. Leveraged debt. Bottom line? It's borrowing to the hilt – and I hate to tell you this, but it's a bankrupt business model. It won't work. It's systemic, malignant and it's global, like cancer. It's a disease, and we gotta fight back.[42]

It was a striking conclusion. The tide that had helped float all of corporate America in the 1980s and 1990s – deregulation, leveraged debt – had now ebbed leaving a global financial crisis.

Failing banks and dysfunctional business priorities also remained a concern for Stone in the subsequent *Savages*. Themes of police corruption and lack of accountability harked back to *Year of the Dragon*, and the film ends with a press conference in which Drug Enforcement Agency (DEA) agent Dennis (John Travolta) claims that the dismantling of the cartel marks a moment of progress in the efforts to protect (American) children and freedom. The irony runs deeper than the diegesis. Since 1973, when the DEA had been brought into being by President Nixon, the agency has organised itself into an international police force with access to Pentagon materials and support. At the behest of successive presidents, it has engaged in the attempted delivery of some grandiose policy objectives: Reagan's 1988 scheme for a drug-free America by 1995 being a case in point. Despite billions of dollars spent on interdiction (drug seizures in transit), particularly in Central and South America, in countries ranging from Mexico to Peru, the 'War on Drugs' initiated by Nixon remains no closer to conclusion than it had been in 1973.[43] For Stone, this so-called war and its failure to end, as well as the interest of financial institutions that should have known far better, was only part of the story.

The reflections about business that were embedded in *W.*, *Wall Street: Money Never Sleeps* and *Savages* were thrown into new relief as a result of the lines of enquiry that Stone followed in the research for the *Untold History* series. Corporate excess was not just about unscrupulous profiteering, but an alignment of corporate and government interests that were increasingly at odds with fundamental freedoms. For Stone, this all pointed to the unhappy summation that the USA had become a 'corporate-controlled country'.[44] All of the dots – joining war, politics, money and corporations – led Stone to this inexorable conclusion.

Surveillance society

Stone's critique of public corporations – news media and banking – was the most prominent aspect of his commentary on the corporate empires of the post-9/11 era. However, a more far-reaching assessment of the failings of the government – with corporate defence and security contractors in its pay – was already underway. With this investigation came the spectre of Orwellian state surveillance: an apparatus-building exercise that was an obvious concern for Stone.

The *Untold History* series started out with a question concerning the immediate post-war USA, and how it might have prospered without Harry Truman or the detonation of nuclear weapons at the end of the Second World War. This was a challenge to the partisan recording of events that Stone and co-writer Peter Kuznick saw as engraved within the nation's public memory.

Their treatise about these roots of empire was summarised in two programmes that were prepared, but which ultimately failed to make the final ten-part package. In the first of these programmes, titled *World War One: The Russian Revolution and Woodrow Wilson*, government is projected as repeatedly supporting the interests of major American financiers and corporations through military intervention overseas. The chapter charts American expansionist policy under President William McKinley and his successors in the first two decades of the twentieth century.

The narration quotes from a book written by Major-General Smedley Butler who in 1935, at the end of a long career with the US Marine Corps, confessed that he had been a 'muscle man' for big business and Wall Street: a racketeer who, among other things, had made Mexico safe for American oil interests in 1914, and assisted American sugar companies in the Dominican Republic in 1916. Describing himself as a 'gangster for capitalism', Butler's thesis was summed up in the title of his book: *War is a Racket*.[45] Amplifying this theme, Stone and Kuznick argued that the USA was transformed by its financing of France and England during the Second World War from a debtor nation to a creditor: one that, in the aftermath of the war, had been changed radically. On Stone's own evidence the picture is a complicated one. McKinley's 1900 re-election had demonstrated a popular appetite for an expansionist agenda, but there can be little doubt that the channelling of German war reparations back to US finance houses after the First World War played its part in the financial and industrial boom that was to come in the 1920s, and cemented financiers such as J. P. Morgan Jr, as well as a clutch of large corporations at the centre of US policymaking in the interwar years.

In the second programme, *Roosevelt, Hitler, Stalin: The Battle of Ideas,* Stone and Kuznick recorded how industrialists such as Henry Ford, Thomas Watson at IBM, and Alfred Sloan at General Motors profited throughout the 1930s from German subsidiaries that were instrumental in building Germany's war capabilities. Indeed Sloan, among others, would go on to claim compensation successfully for Allied bombing of his German factories. The chapter also recorded the support provided to these companies by US financial and legal companies: noting, for example, that one of Hitler's early financial backers, Fritz Thyssen, himself was supported by US finance house Brown Brothers Harriman through an account managed by Prescott Bush, the father and grandfather of two future presidents. Stone's point was simply that these details tend to be absent from conventional US-authored histories of the era, and he sought to contrast the reality of US business entanglement with the German armaments industry with the sanitised picture of American involvement in the Second World War offered by the US media, and indeed by Hollywood. Brief visual reference is made in the footage to Steven Spielberg's *Saving Private Ryan* (1998), as well as books by Stephen Ambrose and Tom Brokaw – all of which, argued Stone, celebrated the military contribution of the USA while overlooking both the willingness of US industrialists to do business with the Third Reich, and the overwhelming contribution of the Russian people to the defeat of fascism in Europe.

The bulk of the series then concentrated on filling in the ensuing detail from the Second World War to the first Gulf War and the Clinton era. However, in the last chapter of the television series and the final two chapters of the book, Stone and Kuznick did assess the Bush and Obama presidencies extensively. There is much detail here, but two key themes emerge – and both are central to

Stone's critique of successive US administrations. First, the 'War on Terror' remains a racket, both in relation to defence industry expenditure and political mendacity. Second, the ever-increasing costs of surveillance – justified by the need to disrupt terrorist plots – encroached on the freedoms that the 'War on Terror' was supposed to be defending.

Much of the detail in the assessment of Bush revolves around the political preparation for, and consequences of, the invasion of Iraq: an item on the neo-conservative agenda long before the September 11 attacks. However, Stone and Kuznick also draw attention to the monies spent by government and earned by contractors such as Halliburton and Blackwater, and to the ideological fervour – or what in the light of subsequent events one might reasonably call 'hubris' – that underpinned the belief that Iraq could be quickly rebuilt as a model capitalist democracy. In the summary of the immediate aftermath of the invasion, Stone and Kuznick support their thesis that war continued to be a racket for the USA, with reference to a series of measures introduced by the Coalition Provisional Authority under administrator Paul Bremer. These included the privatisation of state-owned enterprises and banks, a provision to allow 100 per cent foreign ownership of companies, and facilities to repatriate all profits from work in Iraq. Of course, things did not quite go according to this plan.[46]

In the assessment of President Barack Obama, Stone and Kuznick begin with a critique of his rejection of public campaign financing and acceptance of corporate election funding, his handling of the aftermath of the 2008 economic crash and the economy more generally, and his grip on healthcare reform. However, while much of the book's finale is devoted to foreign policy and the administration's focus on China as an adversary, Stone and Kuznick do give a closely detailed account of Obama's failure to roll back the expansion of the national security state that had taken place under his predecessor. The account includes details about the handling of the *Bradley Manning* case.[47] Manning had leaked details to Wikileaks, led by Julian Assange, that included what was, for many observers around the world, extensive evidence of US Department of State mendacity, as well as one damning piece of video evidence showing a US military helicopter crew shooting a group of civilians, including two Reuters employees, in Baghdad.

Underlying all the detail in the final part of the *Untold History* assessment was a more profound sense of disappointment in the Obama administration, given the high-profile election promises of change in autumn 2008. When Stone described Obama as a 'snake' in August 2013, it was, as the director himself reflected, not an off-the-cuff remark.[48] It was an expression of deep disappointment in Obama for shifting away from his pre-election promises about transparency in government.[49]

Stone's comment was linked directly to his growing concern about the issue of transparency. Manning proved to be only one of several legal cases that the Obama administration pursued under the Espionage Act of 1917. Thomas Drake's was another.[50] Drake, an employee of the NSA, had been charged under the same Act in April 2010 for retaining national defence documents and obstructing justice. The charges related to information that Drake had revealed earlier to a journalist, detailing a failed surveillance system known as 'Trailblazer' which had cost the US taxpayer more than $1 billion.[51] Eventually, the charges against Drake were reduced on the eve of trial to a misdemeanour offence related to the use of a government computer, and he was exonerated – with the presiding Federal Judge Richard D. Bennett castigating the Department of Justice's behaviour as 'unconscionable'.[52] Drake had followed the NSA's internal whistleblowing protocols to the letter, and his case attracted widespread media attention and seemed to highlight the extent to which the government was prepared to go in covering up incompetence and financial irregularities at the NSA.

The Drake affair drew together two key concerns for Stone related to corporate behaviour and government surveillance, and led directly to the Edward Snowden story. In early June 2013 the *Guardian* ran several stories about NSA collection of bulk data from telephone and internet companies: activities at odds with both previous public pronouncements from the US government and the Constitution. On 10 June, the *Guardian* revealed its source as an NSA contractor, Edward Snowden.[53] In due course, Snowden was quoted in the *New York Times* as having followed the Thomas Drake affair closely, concluding that if he had adhered to the whistle-blower protocols as Drake had done, he and the revelations would have been buried by the NSA.[54]

Inevitably, Snowden's alleged motivations became part of the media appraisal of the story. In Glenn Greenwald's book *No Place to Hide* (2014), Greenwald reveals that Snowden was in no sense a radical.[55] Snowden had enlisted in 2004, intending to fight in Iraq. However, injuries during training and concerns about attitudes within the army had led him to find another way to contribute. Attaining high-level information technology (IT) skills brought him into the orbit of the CIA and then the NSA, where he worked as a systems analyst and security expert. It was during this period, and as a consequence of the access that his security work gave him, that he became aware of the extent to which the NSA was skirting existing surveillance laws. In his interview with the *New York Times*, Snowden indicated that he felt the real issue was the lack of public debate about the reach of the surveillance programmes implemented by the NSA.

Meanwhile, Stone had been alert to the issue of transparency long before the names of Julian Assange or Edward Snowden had begun to feature in the news. In a lecture given in 2006 in London for the David Lean Foundation, Stone highlighted an issue that he and Peter Kuznick would return to six years later in the *Untold History* series:

> Nor should we forget that many liberals in America ... also felt stampeded, as a result of that fear and terror of 9/11, to grant Bush his war powers. That too was a conformist mob. In the name of not being hated for our dissent, we the American people signed off, through our legislators, on our essential liberties without knowing it. I would say to you we don't even have these rights anymore, *they're gone*. Because every American I know, of any sensitivity, has some innate understanding and fear that each and every one of us can be listened upon: our email and bank accounts, our medical records, our sexual priorities known, and that at the end of the day we can be destroyed financially, reputationally, or physically by our own Government and Media, if they so wanted. The right to *any privacy* at all has been sacrificed on the altar of our 'national security'.[56]

As the Snowden story broke, it brought all of these concerns fully up-to-date.[57] The *Guardian* reported in June 2014, and Stone himself later confirmed, that the director had bought the rights to *Time of the Octopus*, a forthcoming novel by Snowden's Russian lawyer

Anatoly Kucherena, and that he would use this along with *Guardian* journalist Luke Harding's book *The Snowden Files*, as source material for a screenplay.[58]

Snowden's story embraced all that Stone had been working on for the previous seven years. Worries about individual freedoms signed away in the post-9/11 embrace of the Bush 'War on Terror' had not only extended the security state out of the reach of congressional oversight, let alone public accountability, but it was an irreversible process that Obama had not even tried to counter, let alone failed in the process of attempting to do so. Snowden's disclosures pointed to the extent to which the government's need to know everything about everybody had been a bonanza for IT and security contractors in the pay of the NSA. Corporate America had become completely enmeshed in the pursuit of empire: equally happy to assist drug cartels, invent get-rich schemes for the already rich that would destroy the global economy and, when called upon, happy to facilitate illegal spying on its citizens. Stone saw a moment to move away from the documentary routine that he felt had contributed to the debate in this area, and back into polemical drama that could be richly contentious, argumentative and solicitous where required.

Conclusion

Not surprisingly, Stone's perspective on corporations has evolved over the decades from a set of questions about the accountability of individual institutions and business sectors – news, television, banking – to a more general philosophy about the accountability and transparency of government towards society. Stone's early engagement with questions about entertainment media, issues of oversight and the independence of news sources in *Talk Radio* and *Natural Born Killers* provided a reflexive commentary on the topic. The measured critique in *Talk Radio* was not appreciated well enough, while the perceived excesses in *Natural Born Killers* became the media story, rather more than the critique of their gaudy mentality towards violence and misery offered by Stone. However, Stone pressed on after this with homilies towards what he saw as the vacuity of the entertainment and news industries in later films such as *Any Given Sunday* and *W.* These pictures came to see performance and politics as linked entities, and ones that drove the director to a more 'pure' form of representation for his own peace of mind: namely, documentary.

The work on Castro and Chávez, together with the *Untold History* series, served as a platform for a widespread critique of corporate entertainment interests and government alike. Not surprisingly, that critique is decidedly anti-corporatist and is dismissive of the global pretentions not just of America's corporations, but of its government. As Stone progressed with the *Untold History* series and the theme of empire loomed larger, it became increasingly obvious to him that the individual lines of critique – media bias, reckless bankers – were simply the more visible elements of a set of shared interests and interdependencies that aligned the government and major US corporations on the one hand, and American citizens on the other. As alarming as the revelations about NSA deception concerning surveillance programmes were to Stone as challenges to constitutional freedoms, of greater concern was that these misdemeanours were underpinned by a wide network of IT and defence contractors whose business prospects and profits had become inextricably linked with a recast 'American Century'. That aspiration now called for a global surveillance and war-making capability. Remarkable as it was dispiriting, the aspiration in the wake of the Snowden affair had been met, shored up and, many argued, expanded by a Democratic Party president who had promised transparency. The drip-feed of revelations about the NSA and global security protocols – the surveillance of personal communications of US citizens, not to mention the leaders of supposed allies, the kill lists, the assassinations, the maintenance of Guantanamo – spotlighted a web of IT and defence providers with ambitions no less extensive than those mainstays of global consumerism, McDonalds and Coca-Cola. The 'War on Terror' was not just a racket; it was shaping up to be the ultimate 'corporate' racket.

For these reasons, the Snowden story represented for Stone much more than a tale of a plucky, Capraesque whistle-blower who had succeeded in exposing the administration's duplicity on matters of national security. Snowden's story was, quite simply, a narrative that drew on everything that Stone had been talking about for ten years, and tapped into a deeper sensibility that had been with him since *Salvador*, if not before, in those dark days as a young man in Vietnam.

Notes

1 Interview with Oliver Stone, Santa Monica, CA, 19 January 2010.

2 Alessandra Stanley, 'A Noted Filmmaker in a Tense Land', *International New York Times* (5 June 2003). Available at http://nytimes.com/2003/06/05/movies/television-review-a-noted-filmmaker-in-a-tense-land.html (accessed 7 December 2015).

3 Mark Caro, 'In "Looking for Fidel," Stone asks the right questions', *Chicago Tribune* (14 April 2004). Available at http://articles.chicagotribune.com/2004-04-14/features/0404140066_1_castro-fidel-dissidents (accessed 7 December 2015).

4 Interview with Oliver Stone, Santa Monica, CA, 19 January 2010.

5 The White House, 'Address to a Joint Session of Congress and the American People' (20 September 2001). Available at http://georgewbush-whitehouse.archives.gov/news/releases/2001/09/20010920-8.html (accessed 7 December 2015).

6 Marc Cooper, 'Playboy Interview: Oliver Stone' in Charles Silet (ed), *Oliver Stone Interviews* (Jackson, MS: University Press of Mississippi, 2001), pp. 59–90.

7 *Byers* v. *Edmondson*, Louisiana Court of Appeal, First Circuit, 2001 CA 1184 (2002). Available at http://caselaw.findlaw.com/la-court-of-appeal/1228410.html (accessed 1 March 2016).

8 Personal written response from Oliver Stone to the authors concerning the *Natural Born Killers* case, 28 January 2015; emphasis in original.

9 Adam Liptak, 'National Briefing: South: Louisiana: Lawsuit Dismissal', *New York Times* (12 June 2002). Available at http://www.nytimes.com/2002/06/12/us/national-briefing-south-louisiana-lawsuit-dismissal.html (accessed 7 December 2015).

10 James Riordan, *Stone: The Controversies, Excesses and Exploits of a Radical Filmmaker* (New York: Hyperion, 1995), pp. 516–24.

11 James McEnteer, *Shooting the Truth: The Rise of American Political Documentaries* (Westport, CT: Praeger, 2006), p. xii.

12 Interview with Oliver Stone, Santa Monica, CA, 19 January 2010.

13 Interview with Oliver Stone, Santa Monica, CA, 8 December 2011.

14 Oliver Stone and Peter Kuznick, *The Untold History of the United States* (New York: Ebury, 2012), p. 564.

15 Interview with Oliver Stone, Santa Monica, CA, 19 August 2013.

16 *Ibid.*

17 Stone and Kuznick, *Untold History*, p. xxvii.

18 Stephen Singular, *Talked to Death: The Life and Murder of Alan Berg* (New York: Beech Tree Books, 1987).

19 Don Kunz, 'Oliver Stone's *Talk Radio*' in Don Kunz (ed), *The Films of Oliver Stone* (Lanham, MD and London: Scarecrow Press, 1997), pp. 150–1.

20 Norman Kagan, *The Cinema of Oliver Stone* (Oxford: Roundhouse, 1995), p. 144.
21 Kunz, 'Oliver Stone's *Talk Radio*', pp. 150–1.
22 Geoff King, *New Hollywood Cinema: An Introduction* (London and New York: I. B. Tauris, 2002), pp. 49–85.
23 Terry Christensen and Peter J. Haas, *Projecting Politics: Political Messages in American Films* (Armonk, NY and London: M. E. Sharpe, 2005), p. 200.
24 Francis Fukuyama, *The End of History and the Last Man* (London: Penguin, 2012; orig. pub. 1992).
25 Judy Battista, 'As N.F.L. Talks Fail, '11 Season Seems in Doubt', *New York Times* (11 March 2011). Available at http://nytimes.com/2011/03/12/sports/football/12nfl.html?pagewanted=all&_r=0 (accessed 7 December 2015).
26 Judy Battista, 'With Judges Silent, NFL Still in Limbo Over Lockout', *New York Times* (11 May 2011). Available at http://nytimes.com/2011/05/07/sports/football/07nfl.html?_r=0 (accessed 1 March 2016).
27 Mike Freeman, 'N.F.L. Preview; A Cycle of Violence, on the Field and Off', *New York Times* (6 September 1998). Available at http://nytimes.com/1998/09/06/sports/nfl-preview-a-cycle-of-violence-on-the-field-and-off.html (accessed 7 December 2015).
28 United States Census 2010. '2010 Census Data'. Available at www.census.gov/2010census/data/ (accessed 7 December 2015).
29 *Any Given Sunday*, Request 29 folder, Box AGS Office Files, Ixtlan Production Files (hereafter I-PF), Los Angeles, CA.
30 *Any Given Sunday*, loose file, Box AGS, I-PF.
31 *Any Given Sunday*, Request 29 folder, Box AGS Office Files, I-PF.
32 Interview with Bob Daly, Santa Monica, CA, 10 October 2010.
33 Richard Sandomir, 'NFL Network Is Counting on Fans to Pay a Lot for a Little', *New York Times* (19 September 2006). Available at http://nytimes.com/2006/09/19/sports/football/19sandomir.html?fta=y (accessed 7 December 2015). Richard Sandomir, 'NFL Is Taking Cable Fight to the FCC', *New York Times* (8 May 2008). Available at http://nytimes.com/2008/05/08/sports/football/08broadcast.html (accessed 7 December 2014).
34 *Forbes*, 'NFL Team Valuations: #1 Dallas Cowboys' (2 September 2009). Available at http://forbes.com/lists/2009/30/football-values-09_Dallas-Cowboys_300988.html (accessed 1 March 2016).
35 Kurt Badenhausen, 'The NFL's Most Valuable Teams', *Forbes* (7 September 2011). Available at www.forbes.com/sites/kurtbadenhausen/2011/09/07/the-nfls-most-valuable-teams/ (accessed 7 December 2015).
36 Aaron Kuriloff and Darrell Preston, 'In Stadium Building Spree, U.S. Taxpayers Lose $4 Billion', *Bloomberg* (5 September 2012). Available at http://bloomberg.com/news/2012-09-05/in-stadium-building-spree-u-s-taxpayers-lose-4-billion.html (accessed 7 December 2015).

37 McEnteer, *Shooting the Truth*, p. xii.
38 Jim Rutenberg, 'Disney Is Blocking Distribution of Film that Criticises Bush', *New York Times* (5 May 2004). Available at http://nytimes.com/2004/05/05/us/disney-is-blocking-distribution-of-film-that-criticizes-bush.html (accessed 7 December 2015).
39 Stephen Holden, 'Oliver Stone, Tour Guide', *New York Times* (24 June 2010). Available at http://nytimes.com/2010/06/25/movies/25south.html?_r=0 (accessed 7 December 2015).
40 Iwan W. Morgan, '*The President Impeached*: Tennessee Johnson and Nixon' in Iwan W. Morgan (ed), *Presidents in the Movies: American History and Politics on Screen* (New York: Palgrave Macmillan, 2011), pp. 151–75.
41 James Glanz, 'Rebuilding of Iraq Pipeline as Disaster Waiting to Happen', *New York Times* (25 April 2006). Available at www.nytimes.com/2006/04/25/world/middleeast/25pipeline.html?incamp=article_popular&_r=0 (accessed 7 December 2015).
42 *Wall Street: Money Never Sleeps* (2010).
43 Matthais Schwartz, 'A Mission Gone Wrong: Why Are We Still Fighting the Drug War?', *New Yorker* (6 January 2014), pp. 44–55.
44 Ed Vulliamy, 'Oliver Stone', *Observer New Review* (23 September 2012), pp. 8–11.
45 Stone and Kuznick, *The Untold History*, p. xxxii. Smedley D. Butler, *War is a Racket* (Los Angeles, CA: Feral House, 2003; orig. pub. 1935).
46 *Ibid.*, pp. 527–32.
47 The guilty verdict in the trial of Manning was summarised in a US Army District of Washington News Release dated 30 July 2013, available at: http://alexaobrien.com/wp-content/uploads/13-31-News-Release-PFC-Manning-Verdict-Announced.pdf (accessed 1 March 2016). A public record of the trial was only produced after a lawsuit. Investigative journalist Alexa O'Brien has assembled a record of the extensive case documentation at: http://alexaobrien.com/manning/official-docket-manning#scroll (accessed 1 March 2016).
48 Matthew Jacobs, 'Oliver Stone Calls Obama a "Snake," Says "We Have to Turn on Him"', *Huffington Post* (8 August 2013). Available at www.huffingtonpost.com/2013/08/16/oliver-stone-obama_n_3767639.html (accessed 31 March 2014).
49 Interview with Stone, 19 August 2013.
50 *USA* v. *Thomas Andrews Drake*, US District Court for the District of Maryland, Northern Division, Case 1:10-cr-00181-RDB, 4 April 2010. Available at http://www.jdsupra.com/post/fileServer.aspx?fName=0f053ecd-c945-4b40-9dec-8ae60275b006.pdf (accessed 1 March 2016). *USA* v. *Edward J. Snowden*, US District Court for the Eastern District of Virginia, Case 1:13 CR 265

(CMH). Available at https://assets.documentcloud.org/documents/716888/u-s-vs-edward-j-snowden-criminal-complaint.pdf (accessed 1 March 2016).

51 Siobhan Gorman, 'Little-known Contractor Has Close Ties with Staff of NSA', *Baltimore Sun* (29 January 2006). Available at http://articles.baltimoresun.com/2006-01-29/news/0601290158_1_saic-information-technology-intelligence-experts (accessed 7 December 2015).

52 Scott Shane, 'No Jail Time in Trial Over N.S.A. Leak', *New York Times* (15 July 2011). Available at http://nytimes.com/2011/07/16/us/16leak.html?module=Search&mabReward=relbias%3Ar&_r=0 (accessed 7 December 2015).

53 Glenn Greenwald, Ewen MacAskill and Laura Poitras, 'Edward Snowden: The Whistleblower behind the NSA Surveillance Revelations', *Guardian* (11 June 2013). Available at http://theguardian.com/world/2013/jun/09/edward-snowden-nsa-whistleblower-surveillance (accessed 7 December 2015).

54 James Risen, 'Snowden Says He Took No Secret Files to Russia', *New York Times* (17 October 2013). Available at http://nytimes.com/2013/10/18/world/snowden-says-he-took-no-secret-files-to-russia.html?pagewanted=1&_r=0%20&hp (accessed 7 December 2015).

55 Glenn Greenwald, *No Place to Hide: Edward Snowden, the NSA, and the U.S. surveillance State* (New York: Signal/Metropolitan Books, 2014).

56 Oliver Stone, 'David Lean Foundation Speech', 6 September 2006 Available at https://facebook.com/notes/oliver-stone/2006-david-lean-foundation-speech/791314950892806 (accessed 7 December 2015); emphasis in original.

57 Shaun Walker, 'Oliver Stone Snowden Movie to Be Part-based on Fictionalised Account', *Guardian* (11 June 2014). Available at http://theguardian.com/world/2014/jun/11/oliver-stone-film-edward-snowden(accessed 7 December 2015).

58 Luke Harding *The Snowden Files: The Inside Story of the World's Most Wanted Man* (London: Guardian Faber Publishing, 2014). Anatoly Kucherena's *Time of the Octopus* was published in Russian in 2015.

Conclusion

> Although we are clearly overreaching, it's too easy to talk about the USA losing its grip because we happen to be rooting for another approach. It's not going to go away that easily. This empire is Star Wars in the 'evil empire' sense of the words ... We are virtually becoming a tyranny against the rest of the world. It's not evident to people at home, because they don't see the consensus in the media and they don't see the harm the USA does abroad. We are not in decline. We are decayed and corrupt and immoral, but not in decline. The USA exerts its will in Europe, Asia, much of the Middle East, and still much of Latin America. The recent revelations that the NSA's and the UK's surveillance programmes are linked is big news.[1]

Oliver Stone has been a fixture in the Hollywood landscape since his Oscar-winning script for *Midnight Express* (Alan Parker, 1978). That high-profile foothold gave him the opportunity to build slowly towards his ambition of capturing on film what he had lived through in Vietnam during 1967 and 1968. The young Yale man who had entered the army was a cerebral romantic in search of adventure; but his experience, not just of combat but also of his return to a country that was already openly divided about the war, altered his perspective and the direction of his life. Enrolment at film school under the GI Bill seemed to offer a way of expressing his anger and disillusionment, and the same determination that had kept him alive in South-East Asia now drove him on to try and tell something of that experience on film. Even as he took his place in the Hollywood firmament, the subject did not need to be

Vietnam to get the fire burning in him. *Midnight Express* started the catharsis, and after this his career garnered praise, admiration and plenty of criticism for the visceral, uncompromising writing in *Scarface* (Brian De Palma, 1983) and *Year of the Dragon* (Michael Cimino, 1985). With the release of *Platoon* in 1986, his ambition to show something of the real terror and confusion of combat was finally realised in a film whose popular reception made Stone Hollywood's hottest property.

In important ways, Stone's auteur brand was constantly evolving during this period. The new wunderkind who penned tales of violent excess in *Midnight Express* and *Scarface,* and who found fame and fortune in the reconfiguring of Hollywood's perspective on Vietnam, also acquired something of a 'Midas touch' when it came to eliciting establishment outrage. By the 1990s, an on-screen homage to Jim Morrison played nicely to off-screen tales of drug-fuelled excesses, although the mixture of professional and personal coverage was eclipsed by the allegation at the heart of *JFK* in 1991 of a state-sponsored *coup d'état*. By this time, Stone's brand identity had traversed the space between wunderkind, *bête noire* and anti-establishment firebrand within little more than a decade, and the story was only just heating up.

In *Natural Born Killers,* Stone pushed the boundaries of mainstream acceptability towards on-screen violence while articulating a caustic critique of the entertainment–media complex. The dispute over the rating for the film highlighted a complex web of incompatible needs that touched on the limits of artistic freedom, the preservation of self-interested studio business, and the effectiveness and extent of industry self-regulation. In the midst of all of this, there were questions of censorship and personal integrity. Stone found himself in the difficult position of trying to explain how a film that seemed to push the boundaries of explicitly violent content also could be a legitimate form of critique of the wider cultural and economic forces that were driving that very same trend in violence. As mentioned in Chapter 5, the fallout from the film brought allegations of copycat killings and a court case that threatened to ascribe a product liability to any film: a move that also threatened the very *raison d'être* of the self-regulatory regime established by the Motion Picture Association of America in 1968. When *Nixon* failed at the box office a year or so later, the harbingers of doom predicted a career decline. Understanding what happened thereafter has been at the forefront of many of the preceding pages.

Studio projects did not vanish in the wake of the cumulative controversies surrounding *JFK*, *Natural Born Killers* and *Nixon*. Like his mentor Martin Scorsese, Stone succeeded in maintaining both a personal vision and a working relationship with the studios. The supposed meltdown and critical decline after *Nixon* – at least in the eyes of some critics – did not materialise. If *U Turn* signposted a rapid descent in earnings potential, Stone's next film, *Any Given Sunday*, actually took $75 million at the US box office for Warner Bros., and the period after *U Turn* accounts for more than 40 per cent of total career earnings. If Stone the iconoclast filmmaker no longer seemed to be at the centre of auteurist discourses that came subsequently, for example, to embrace the works of Paul Thomas Anderson, Darren Aronofsky, Christopher Nolan and the Coen brothers, he still extended his artistic reach, consolidating himself both as a filmmaker that producers and production crews alike are keen to work with, and as a totem for a range of Left-leaning causes and critiques marshalled against the government and media. Indeed, while the veneration of the Hollywood establishment reduced, Stone's auteur brand – strengthened ironically enough by his political credentials – actually increased in some overseas territories.

Nevertheless, the commercial environment within Hollywood did have an impact on Stone in the 2000s. In *World Trade Center* and *W.*, the perspectives on 9/11 and the Bush administration were remarked on for their lack of polemical bite. More visceral and acerbic critiques including *War on Terror* and *Jawbreaker* were developed, but ultimately faltered for want of available funding. This was certainly evidence of what Stone and many other observers saw as the prevailing neo-conservative cultural narrative about the necessity and justification of the 'War on Terror'. However, the mothballed scripts also provided an echo of the kind of studio resistance that Stone had encountered during preparations for *Platoon* at the early juncture of his career, as well as confirmation of an enduring conservatism within the major studios, despite the liberal pretentions of some of the industry's leading spokespeople.

Locating Stone's auteurism within a critical framework always presents challenges for critics, scholars and audiences. These off-kilter projects from the turn of the millennium have made that pursuit no easier. The classic theory of auteurs derived out of the French New Wave, carried through in America by critic Andrew Sarris, and followed on by Peter Wollen and Roland Barthes, offered a range of analytical tools designed to extract meaning from the film text.[2] Sarris argued that an auteur was composed of three components: technical ability; a distinctive signature visible across several films; and some intangible third element; the 'soul' of the director.[3] His model – long since discredited in a number of scholarly circles, although a renaissance of sorts has taken place in recent years – does capture some aspects of Stone's presence as an auteur, but it provides an incomplete picture.

Stone's writing and his editorial eye do provide a 'signature' that has remained relatively stable across all of his dramatic oeuvre. Yet as we have described, other aspects of that signature changed from the mid-1990s, as evidenced by a less realist and more distinct melodramatic aesthetic and, by many accounts, reduced polemical force. Melodrama comes to the fore in *U Turn, Alexander* and *W.*, with all three films foregrounding questions of personal morality. *Wall Street: Money Never Sleeps* and *Savages* also asked moral questions, but locating their respective targets – the failure to grasp any legal oversight facility with regards to financial institutions, and the disorientated, apolitical lifestyle of certain sections of American society – appeared trickier. The absence of real polemic in these films is something that Stone himself has admitted to, and it was one of the reasons he threw himself more steadfastly into documentary work during the 2000s.

The move into documentary reflected a further authorial change. The distinctive editing techniques showcased in *JFK* and *Natural Born Killers* among others were eschewed for a more pared-down palate, visible in the *cinéma vérité* style of the Castro documentaries and the pedagogic techniques of presentation used in *Untold History*. It added up to an auteurist instinct that was almost covering its artistic tracks.

Indeed, post-Sarris, post-structuralism and variants thereof, more recent assessments of auteurism have given added emphasis to the *commercial* aspects of a director's brand. Undoubtedly, this has been a strong dimension in Stone's story too. By the time that *Savages* had completed its tour of cinemas in 2012, the cumulative earnings from films directed by Oliver Stone had topped $1.5 billion, split more or less evenly between US and foreign earnings – a state of financial affairs comparatively rare for a director of his ilk. The details are revealing, not least for what they say about the ways in which media images of Stone as an industry *bête noire* belie a more subtle relationship between the director and the film colony in Los Angeles, of which he is very much a part. Stone's position within Hollywood and his reputation there and beyond as an auteur has remained remarkably stable. His output repeatedly has employed standard industry protocols for auteur commodification – director's cuts, box sets, re-releases – embellished with self-assessments of his work, as well as commentaries on Hollywood and the condition of America. To listen to a director's commentary on one of Stone's films is to be initiated into a series of themes, theories and ideas that are at once challenging, provocative and illuminating. In fact, this added material extra to film embedded in the contemporary technology is almost a lecture series in its own right, detailing everything that Stone set out to be as a director when he returned from Asia in the late 1960s. Yet his auteurism does not quite reside within the 'commercial strategy' described by, for example, Tim Corrigan, any more than it might be said to reside within any particular artistic vision of the kind described in earlier variants of theory.[4]

Stone's interests in social critique and politics have carried him some way ahead of art and commerce into territory that can be best summed up as activism. Each of his films has been a piece of crafted drama with a range of distinctive attributes related to narrative and photography, acting as a baseline for Stone's auteur brand. However, what is striking in the second period of his career is the way in which those core elements of the auteur brand did not merely become retroactive career artefacts for a media narrative that views his auteur heyday as belonging to the past. Instead, Stone's auteurism acted as a platform for a political discourse that retained as much urgency and purpose as films such as *Salvador* and *JFK* had.

The full range of Stone's work does not sit comfortably within the rubric of auteurism any more than it does a commercial entertainment aesthetic. Both elements have populated Stone's career – sometimes at one and the same time – but something more remains. In his journey towards documentary work, Stone mapped out a space for his own brand of political activism expressed in an increasingly strident assault on the political and commercial establishment in the USA. That move was accompanied by both a change in the dramatic work and a shift in personal outlook. In the closing pages of James Riordan's 1995 biography, the author argues that Stone had found in his films a place to both neutralise the pressures of his private life and express the pain he was concealing. Out of this, Riordan suggested that Stone was finding a degree of peace in the realisation that he was not alone; his efforts to find self-enlightenment were shared by many others who were on similar quests.[5] In the book, the portrayal of Stone confirmed a need to redraw the boundaries between himself and the world, reflecting on his previous lack of compassion and a wish to expose himself to more love and understanding. Stone did move on in a way that did not erase his irascible old self, but certainly changed it. The acerbic, combative, guerrilla fighter remained – ready to engage and challenge – but the mix of passion and anger that drove him at the time of Riordan's book became centrally directed at a panoply of establishment malfeasance and mendacity.

An important complement to Stone's broader media presence was his increasing use of social media. Through his Facebook page, established in March 2012, he created a brand that projects himself, his directorial work and his treatise on surveillance, foreign policy, empire, terrorism and drugs.[6] The entries in 2012 were dominated by information on the progress of *Savages* and *Untold History*. However, in-between these updates, Stone referenced a range of his concerns, some longstanding, some new. A plug for the republication of Jim Garrison's *On the Trail of the Assassins*, and a posting of an op-ed piece about *JFK* written by Stone and first published in the *New York Times* in December 1991, were interspersed with entries about Julian Assange and endorsement of Robert Greenwald's 2012 documentary, *Koch Brothers Exposed*. In 2014, Stone continued to use the site to talk about his own work, including the difficulties he had experienced trying to bring a rendering of Martin Luther King's life to the screen. However, he also sought to draw attention to what he saw as failed media coverage of a range of issues, including US complicity in the killings in Indonesia in the 1960s – a topic aired in Joshua Oppenheimer's documentary, *The Act of Killing* (2012) – as well as the political crisis gripping Venezuela in 2014.

Through his developing online presence, Stone's 'brand' has been consolidated in a form quite unlike any other Hollywood filmmaker. Few other directors in Hollywood have attempted to work with both drama and documentary in the way that Stone has, and none have really fashioned a political edge to their work in the manner that he has. Alongside lauded dramatic work such as *Gangs of New York* (2002), *The Departed* (2006) and *Hugo* (2011), Scorsese has assembled documentary work about entertainment industry icons including Bob Dylan (*No Direction Home*, 2005), The Rolling Stones (*Shine a Light*, 2008) and Elia Kazan (*A Letter to Elia*, 2010). However, despite work on a documentary about the Clintons, Scorsese's auteur identity is firmly rooted within Hollywood. With documentaries about Howard Hawks (*Howard Hawks: American Artist*, 1997) and Bob Marley (*Marley*, 2012), UK-born director Kevin Macdonald has assembled a not-dissimilar range of subjects with occasional dramatic forays into politics, most notably with *State of Play* (2009). George Clooney seems to offers a closer mapping in terms of political work. As producer on *The Men Who Stare at Goats* (Grant Heslov, 2009) and *Argo* (Ben Affleck, 2012), and as director on *Good Night, and Good Luck* (2005) and *The Ides of March* (2011) as well as appearances in a raft of other productions, including the ambitious *Syriana* (Stephen Gaghan, 2005), *Michael Clayton* (Tony Gilroy, 2007) and *Up in the Air* (Jason Reitman, 2009), Clooney has established a close association with a range of liberal concerns including media bias, political malfeasance, foreign policy deceit and corporate corruption. Away from the screen, Clooney's political work has combined a critique of US foreign policy and an extensive humanitarian profile. Yet it is Clooney's fame that is foregrounded more often, not least in the celebrity pages and gossip columns, where his Hollywood star still shines brightly. By contrast, what is striking about Stone is that his involvements seem to have no lighter alter-ego side: no musical documentaries, no celebrity partygoing, no whimsy.

Stone's increasing online presence shifted the narrative of his work away from an ordered recital of past projects towards a set of agendas and causes receiving regular updates in the 2010s. Not only did this provide a sense of continuity, but also one of interconnectedness of causes and themes. One prominent example concerned US media coverage of the political protests in Venezuela in spring 2014. In April 2014 the *New York Times* published an op-ed piece by Nicolás Maduro, the President of Venezuela. Stone did not claim credit, but his eliciting of more openness and transparency at the paper bore fruit with the Maduro piece that indicated a greater willingness within the press not to simply tout the official line of the US Department of State – an accusation that Stone had advocated since *South of the Border* first appeared in 2010. It was a small step in advocacy, but clearly one that Stone relished.[7]

The content posted on Stone's social media does not exhibit any personal political pretentions; however, in its commentary it does seem to reflect a desire on Stone's part that the USA find its way back to the kind of republicanism that Benjamin Franklin and the Founding Fathers had sought. On the closing page of Stone and Kuznick's *Untold History* book, the authors conclude that any real hope for the USA 'to regain its democratic, evolutionary and revolutionary soul' lies with the citizens themselves, rather than with President Obama. The book closes with a quote from Benjamin Franklin who, in response to a question about what kind of government had been agreed at the 1787 Constitutional Convention, was reported to have replied: 'A republic, Madam, if you can keep it.'[8] Stone's restorative wish was for an American democracy anchored in political advocacy, and a more personal sense of what it means to be an American. In the wake of Henry Luce's vision of the 'American Century', patriotism and love of country seemed to become the almost exclusive rhetorical preserve of the political Right. As outlined previously, dissenters such as Stone were readily dismissed as 'America-hating'. Thus part of Stone's enduring appeal to some liberals has been in the battle to 'keep' Franklin's republic, and to reclaim a sense of patriotism and love of one's country for all – not just the Right (Figure 10).

In media interviews, Stone continued to use his films to illustrate wider points about the shortcomings of both US foreign policy and the mainstream media coverage of such policy. In some instances, as with HBO's cancellation of its planned transmission

Figure 10 Protest against US military installation, Jeju Island, South Korea, March 2013

of *Comandante*, the critique acquired an extra texture but the message remained consistent. To be an adherent of Stone, one is not merely musing about the evolution of fast editing or acknowledging his position within the industry as a maverick capable of retaining relationships within the studio system; rather, one is embracing a personal worldview: a rebuttal of neo-conservative hegemony, a challenge to government authority, a calling to account of the 'news-for-profit' media, a wider rallying point for Left-leaning disaffection, and the articulation of a variant of the American Dream that is offered as a counter to the myth of global hegemony.

As James Welsh and Donald Whaley have noted, the movement from the supposed macho right-winger who wrote *Conan the Barbarian*, to leftist crusader with *Salvador*, to establishment chronicler in *World Trade Center* has not revolved around some moderate centre-ground with Stone.[9] His politics throughout have been rooted in the foundational myths about America. He is a supporter of still the greatest capitalist nation on earth, but not an unbridled advocate of *capitalism*, much less the continued expansion of corporate power that the particular brand of American capitalism has wrought. (As mentioned previously, there is something distinctly Jeffersonian in this outlook.) He displays an opposition to privilege, corruption and elitism. His production company Ixtlan is relatively modest by Hollywood standards, yet it works unabashedly within the 'system' as well as within its own independent confines. In Stone's lifetime the USA moved from the vision of Henry Luce to the cautionary observations of, in recent times, George Packer and Edward Luce.[10] Stone's leanings as a political advocate have followed a not-dissimilar pattern. His is a view that still sees the possibilities for intervention on the global stage, but which decries unsubstantiated military adventure – and more than anything else, calls for the dismantling of overarching government power.

Such a stance is not without its own difficulties and moral dilemmas, but the direction of travel has been almost as important to Stone as achievement of the aims. If there is one idea that Stone has settled on in his efforts to give airtime to the debate about the failings and missteps of the US administration, it is the tyranny of empire that he sees as knocking at America's door almost constantly now. His choice to pick up on the era's most highly politicised subject – the NSA whistle-blower Edward Snowden – was an obvious decision for someone who had been raising the issue of unwarranted state surveillance since soon after 9/11.

As this new outlook has evolved, Stone has succeeded in neutralising some of the negative aspects of his earlier *bête noire* reputation, replacing it with an establishment figure and talk-show alter ego that has at least as much interest in 'the marketplace of ideas' as it has in referencing and marketing his films. At times, that alter ego has shown signs of impatience, and on occasion has made unguarded comments which then had to be rowed back from, but it continues to command a hearing. Stone the filmmaker, documentarian, political firebrand and American, aided by a news-scape that finally came round to questioning the ideological tenets of the post-9/11 age – through Iraq, Afghanistan, extraordinary rendition, Assange and Snowden – have fused together in a locus of opposition towards Big Government and corporations alike. Stone the Left-leaning libertarian, we might say, his career and his astonishing array of output have been central to that awareness-raising.

Figure 11 Oliver Stone, Sun-jung Jung and their daughter Tara, Berlin, February 2000

> We are in moral decay. The people who broke the law from Bush onwards are in power. The people who decried the breaking of the law are fugitives. Everything is upside down. Most people don't see it. It's a sad world that we are leaving to our children. But we must fight against it – in this [*Untold History*] series, at the end, we say, 'History has shown us that the curve of the ball can break differently.' It's happened several times: with Gorbachev, Khrushchev, Roosevelt, and Kennedy. Hope is still there. Hope is a foundation for action against this empire.[11]

Notes

1 Interview with Oliver Stone, Santa Monica, CA, 8 December 2011. Nick Hopkins, 'UK gathering secret intelligence via covert NSA operation', *Guardian* (7 June 2013). Available at www.theguardian.com/technology/2013/jun/07/uk-gathering-secret-intelligence-nsa-prism (accessed 1 March 2016).

2 Helen Stoddart, 'Auteurism and Film Authorship Theory' in Joanne Hollows and Mark Jancovich (eds) *Approaches to Popular Film* (Manchester: Manchester University Press, 1995), pp. 37–57.

3 Andrew Sarris, 'Notes on the Auteur Theory in 1962' in Gerald Mast, Marshall Cohen and Leo Braudy (eds) *Film Theory and Criticism: Introductory Readings* (Oxford: Oxford University Press, 4th edn, 1992), pp. 585–8.

4 Timothy Corrigan, 'Auteurs and the New Hollywood' in Jon Lewis (ed), *The New American Cinema* (Durham, NC and London: Duke University Press, 1998), p. 42.
5 James Riordan, *Stone: The Controversies, Excesses, and Exploits of a Radical Filmmaker* (London: Aurum, 1995), pp. 521–3.
6 Available at www.facebook.com/TheOliverStone (accessed 1 March 2016).
7 Nicolás Maduro, 'Venezuela: A Call for Peace', *New York Times* (1 April 2014). Available at http://www.nytimes.com/2014/04/02/opinion/venezuela-a-call-for-peace.html (accessed 7 December 2015).
8 Oliver Stone and Peter Kuznick, *The Untold History of the United States* (New York: Ebury, 2012) p. 615.
9 James M. Welsh and Donald M. Whaley, *The Encyclopedia of Oliver Stone* (Lanham, MD: Scarecrow Press, 2013), p. 234.
10 George Packer, *The Unwinding* (London: Faber & Faber, 2013); Edward Luce, *Time to Start Thinking: America and the Spectre of Decline* (London: Little, Brown, 2013).
11 Interview with Oliver Stone, Santa Monica, CA, 8 December 2011.

Interviews

Stone on Stone

Between 2010 and 2014 we interviewed Oliver Stone on a number of occasions, either personally or in correspondence by email. He was always ready to engage with us, quite literally. Stone thrives on the cut-and-thrust of debate about his films, about himself and perceptions of him that have adorned media outlets around the world throughout his career – and, of course, about the state of America. What follows are transcripts from some of those interviews, without redaction. Stone is always at his most fascinating when a question leads him down a line of theory or thinking that can expound on almost any topic to do with his films, or with the issues in the world at large. Here, that line of thinking appears on the page as he spoke, and gives credence to the notion of a filmmaker who, whether loved or loathed, admired or admonished, is always ready to fight his corner and battle for what he believes is a worthwhile, even noble, cause. Oliver Stone's career has been defined by battle and the will to overcome criticism and or adversity. The following reflections demonstrate why he remains the most talked about, and combative, filmmaker of his generation.

Interview with Oliver Stone, 19 January 2010

In relation to the Classification and Ratings Administration

Interviewer: How do you see the issue of cinematic censorship?

Oliver Stone: The ratings thing is very much a limited game. If you talk to Joan Graves, you'll get the facts. The rules are the rules.

They change with societal norms. You can now have a kiss between homosexuals. In *Alexander* you can even have someone go to bed with the man. The only guideline that now exists as far as I know would be the word 'fuck' and various obscenities. It is a limitation. I was told most recently that you can have three or four of them – obviously, context is important – and retain a PG-13, which is an issue on *Wall Street: Money Never Sleeps*. There are occasional curse words in *Wall Street: Money Never Sleeps*, so you need to use each 'fuck' well. Currently, there is a big issue about smoking in films – not sure what the rules are, but they [the Classification and Ratings Administration, CARA] have been very tough. As with any board, they respond to pressure. The movie business is now officially way behind the cable business in terms of freedom of expression. Many filmmakers are now reaching for cable for the freedom to do shows where they can do what they want, including references to penises and any kind of lovemaking. This is a strange development, given that there had historically been such censorship in network television: it was the most hidebound outlet for many years. When my films were released back then, the cuts mandated by the television networks would run to three, four, five pages long. We used to do a television version of scenes while we were shooting. That's to say, we would cover up some of the words where possible to save time and money later in the process. Probably wouldn't do this now.

In relation to cable television

Stone: The television sales market has changed. I'm not up-to-date on it, but cable is now in any case the main purchaser of shows. Network television is much less subversive in terms of sex and language than cable. However, there are still pressures even with cable that can be applied to material. In the case of *Comandante*, HBO came under pressure, I suspect, from various sources, including right-wing Cuban American communities and the White House. I heard about it after the fact – it was really badly done. Promos were already running. HBO is part of a corporate complex at Warner Brothers, and there were a ton of emails coming to that studio, as well as perhaps, I believe, pressure from the White House, so it was cancelled at the executive level only. You never really know what goes on behind the scenes in corporations, but it was an abrupt cancellation with two, three weeks to go. The decision was made in hours, when I was out of the country. There was no consultation with me; I was simply informed it was cancelled, and it was dead in the water. They sat on this film for another year-and-a-half because it was licensed to them, and they didn't do anything with it. Then they returned it to us. It has since gone back to its copyright owner in Spain, who's been very difficult to deal with in releasing the film. We're still working on it, and hopefully it will get out eventually. It is available in England, Canada, and on YouTube for free. Some of the other cable channels will however take more chances to get attention, which means that there is a relatively open market, even though the viewing numbers at these stations can be small. Cable is the best place to work, if you want to get beyond the boundaries of present behaviour.

In relation to personal experiences with CARA

Stone: If you are interested in filmmaking and narrative-making as I am, I have never sought to shock as much as to ask the viewer to consider an alternative – as with the JFK assassination. I have included sex in all of the movies to some degree. I think there was some issues with *The Doors* because of sexuality, but I can't remember – we may have cleaned it up. In *Heaven and Earth* there was a vivid rape scene and CARA made suggestions. We went to see CARA, and tried to maintain a friendly relationship. Heffner was very good at this. CARA would seek to help by making 'under the table' suggestions so as to avoid giving an official rating R, or whatever, which would then get in the newspapers and become an issue. I remember doing this several times, where the issues would be dealt with quietly. Heffner and Graves were both very reasonable. The one occasion where I had no understanding of what I was up against was with *Natural Born Killers*: it was a case unto itself. This was the most negative experience with the ratings board.

As it affected JFK

Stone: *JFK* was only ever considered as an R, probably due to the obscenity and scenes of homosexuality. The film included images of behaviour that I imagine the board did not want young people to see. The censorship that astounded me at the time was in the official media in the country. I think I was relatively naïve; I felt that by 1991 the country was ready to look again at the Kennedy killing, and it seemed like the right thing to do. I felt like someone opening up a cellar. I talked to as many people who had been in Dealey Plaza as I could. The censorship was inflicted early on. When we were shooting, George Lardner was there from the *Washington Post* – he got hold of a first draft of a script. That was eviscerated in the *Washington Post* Sunday Calendar section, in a story about how I was completely perverting the real facts. It was a pretty ugly story. I was furious about this. We engaged Washington publicist Frank Mankiewicz, who had worked with Robert Kennedy, and we demanded fair time on the *Post*; we didn't get it. I did get an article printed eventually.

Newsweek blasted us. The cover story was titled 'Why Oliver Stone's new movie can't be trusted'.[1] It was also much criticised in the *New York Times* – there were more than a dozen articles of different sizes from the editorial board, Tom Wicker, political and cultural critics condemning the film. I would only remind you that the *Washington Post* and the *New York Times* have been extremely rigidly pro-Warren Commission since the beginning. The *New York Times* came out supporting the Warren Commission just as the report was issued, which was several thousand pages long – so they didn't take very long to double think it.[2] For the record, they have never given a good review or much coverage to any book that condemned the Warren Report. They've always given excellent coverage to books pro-Warren Commission; from Gerald Posner 'til way back. There's been a significantly rigid policy in both papers. In fact, probably the *Washington Post* gave me the most coverage as a dissident when they attacked me in that Sunday piece by George Lardner.[3] Bush and Nixon attacked the film. Robert Dole attacked *Natural Born Killers*, so I have been attacked by every presidential candidate except for Clinton!

Jack Valenti [president of the Motion Picture Association of America] lobbied against the film, which was a complete surprise and came out of the blue; the MPAA chairman had never taken a public position on a film previously. Given the level of controversy at the time I was not overly shocked, but I felt it was not Valenti's job. Valenti had said he could not live with this lie – the suggestion that the film had implicated LBJ [US President Lyndon B. Johnson] in the assassination. I do not believe that the film suggests that. I do not believe that LBJ was directly involved, but I do think that LBJ was thoroughly involved in the subsequent cover-up. What people didn't know at that time was that there were significant changes in policy directly after the assassination. Warners [chair Bob Daly] then got pissed off with Valenti. I stayed out of the debate as best as possible, but there is no doubt that Valenti's intervention hurt the film with respect to the Oscars. I met Valenti some years later and made up with him. He was a likeable man, however his position was that when it comes to Johnson, you don't tread there. I think that Valenti's opinion was to some extent shared by some of the other studio heads, who anonymously expressed the view that Warners had acted irresponsibly.[4] Warners took a lot of heat over *JFK*. The combination of that pressure, with the limited success of *Heaven and Earth*, meant that Warners did not back *Natural Born Killers* as well as they might have. They were scared of the film. Warners at that time was becoming more of a stockholding company, with a conservative focus on making movies that pleased stockholders.

On *JFK* I would ideally have put an intermission after the [Donald] Sutherland [X] scene. Tarantino told me that he had seen the film in Holland and the Dutch distributor had put an intermission in at this point, and that it really worked for him because it gave a pause to think about the events of the first half. A lot of information had been given at that point of the film. I recall that when I was making *JFK* I was young and strong-headed, and was on a roll. I had read the books and got to know Garrison, and went for it. I fought with Warners to get the film out in December. The film was shot fast and came to three hours eight minutes. When Warners wanted to preview it in Pasadena, I refused, knowing that such a step would generate calls for changes, and hence delays. Senior execs at Warners really believed in me and [the] film caught the fire and did well, despite the official criticism. It came close to an Oscar win for the [best] film that year. I get letters regularly from researchers who benefited from the availability of material following the set-up of the Assassination Records Review Board [ARRB].[5] There was no acknowledgement in the press of my efforts even after the ARRB was set up.

My experience with *JFK* was part of a wake-up call: I had wandered from being a relative American hero with the Vietnam movies that were respected for telling the American soldier's part of the story. I found later with *Heaven and Earth* that there was no interest in hearing the Vietnamese side of the story. *Born on the Fourth of July* was not universally appreciated. It received several Oscar nominations [eight] and almost won Best Picture, but was beaten narrowly by *Driving Miss Daisy*. I won the Oscar for director, but it became a controversial picture, as Pat Buchanan and the right-wing kicked in with severe criticism of the movie, and of Ron Kovic. Kovic had feinted and run for a House [of Representatives] seat in Orange County against a famous right-winger, Bob Dornan – and when that happened, the Right came down on Kovic and the movie. So we got quite a bit of controversy, and that certainly hurt us. I think we were the early favourite in January to win the Oscar, but *Driving Miss Daisy* did better box office and overtook us. We did very well: it was one of the most profitable I've ever made. It was not as successful financially as *Platoon*, because of the issues of the severe wound and the nature of Kovic's criticism of the United States when he returned. People did not immediately enjoy it, but did come around to liking it. It was not an easy movie for some Americans to watch because of the castration issue, which bothered many young males who walked out of the movie. It didn't connect at all levels. Many veterans could not watch it, and many thought Ron Kovic was belly-aching.

The Doors came out the same year, which made 1991 a massive year for work. I don't recall enormous problems with the board. The band was a shock to the American public because Morrison was that kind of person. He was wearing snakeskin pants, screwing anything in sight and yelling obscenities like 'fuck my mother and kill my father' – I can't remember if that made it into the final movie or not – but it was pretty wild, even for 1991.

As a commercial phenomenon

Stone: *JFK* was the worst case for political censorship, but *Natural Born Killers* was my worst experience with the film board. We hit a wall there. I was supposed to deliver by contract to Warner's an R rating. This pressure for R had arisen in [the] 1970s. The 'X' was a beautiful 1960s concept, but after the *Midnight Cowboy* era, porno films began to displace mainstream films on Broadway. I remember vividly that during my film school years at New York University, main houses other than 42nd Street were playing softcore porno, for example *Devil in Miss Jones, Deep Throat.* Kung Fu films were also very popular. As a result the X rating lost its respectability, and newspapers and TV stopped taking advertising for X movies. Since the 1990s, the 'R' rating has come under pressure from Christian groups, and the current situation is that similar pressure to that experienced by the X is coming on to the R rating. An R rating can only be shown at certain times on television. For the last five to seven years everyone has been under pressure to make PG-13 rather than R. *World Trade Center* was a PG-13, which was a very violent movie about a grim subject. It was however a family-oriented movie with good perceived values. The violence was modified so that the viewer does not see overly crushed limbs. There were heroic true stories, and so the film got a PG-13 despite the violence. This move to PG-13 is driven by commercial pressures. Studios will not make the movie if it has certain threatening elements in it – political and sexual. Also, commercial pressure is driven by rules on advertising: for example, having to use slots on TV after 9pm. Papers and media outlets in smaller cities and towns won't take advertising. There are also big pressures from retailers like Walmart: for example in the 1990s, if a studio was getting 40–50 per cent of its video sales from a retailer who doesn't want to put R on its shelves, particularly in cities in the south of the country. At a certain point it went to 50 per cent or 60 per cent of the business, maybe even more. Now it could be even higher. I think the numbers are really insane. Walmart dominates the market. There is a lot of hypocrisy, because often in cities in the South and the West, and the South-West, despite the presence of Christian groups, there will be demand for more adult materials. At one time you would often find that small towns had an alternate video store with all of the juicy materials. Walmart had a 'Christian' aura of sanctity and a clean image, and this affected what the studios did. A provocative movie just can't make as much money because you can't get the broad base for financial success, including the kids and the 'right thinkers'. You can only get the 'free thinkers' – and they are in limited numbers in any society.

In the old days the audience base didn't have to be so big. A movie could gross $5 million to $20 million to $30 million and be a success, with merchandising costs being relatively low. Therefore, you could successfully appeal to the smaller audiences off the dime, and take chances: for example, with people like [Roman] Polanski or with *Midnight Cowboy* [John Schlesinger, 1969]. However, people did start to get greedy. Actor costs have gone up, driven by agents. The costs of production have not gone up dramatically since I first started in 1980s. Crews are still very hardworking, and costs have never been excessive. The real growth has been in the costs of 'above-the-line' people – the actors and the advertising. The television business drove the advertising change, where for example a $30 million movie might cost $20 million to advertise. That is a disconnect. This brought with it a move for conglomerates to own film studios with an anchor in television stations. The dynamic between these two businesses has been fascinating, because now the film studios seem to have reasserted their profitability, whereas in the 1990s it was looking like television was going to dominate strongly; but then television ran into strong competition from cable, and lost its easy profitability. The movie business seemed to have gotten away, lost its soul when the television advertising took over. Adverts had to work in prime time, be provocative but not go too far abroad. In Ang Lee's R-rated *Brokeback Mountain* [2006] the positive critical comments and the fact that it was Oscar-nominated allowed it to be advertised on television, despite the homosexual theme.

There is a whole level of hypocrisy in the Oscar aspect. Films can be uncommercial, but the Oscar label allows it to be advertised extensively. This still may mean that Americans will not go to see films like *Brokeback Mountain* or *Milk* [Gus Van Sant, 2009]. There were several producers who did change the business radically and pervert the meaning of the Oscar by chasing after it. Independent producers who use a large amount of money and illicit contact to campaign for Oscar success for their films – that changed the nature of the game. By time I attended the Oscar event for the *JFK* nominations, campaigning for awards had become very hostile.

The ratings board doesn't play a role now. Everyone is making a centrifugal movie to meet criteria of social responsibility and acceptance. If you do a *Doors* movie, you go against that grain.

This reflects great conservatism in the industry and in the country. The presentation of news to the American public is in similar vein. It's OK to give aid to Haiti, but not OK to criticise efforts in Iraq or Afghanistan, where we are destroying countries. This is an issue of political correctness. Movies critical of Iraq have not done well. In *Platoon*, I had a mix of dead stone killers and heroes which allowed me to attempt a reassessment of Vietnam. The film did show Vietnamese being killed and it did become a subject of discussion, yes. I was called a 'baby killer' and so forth, and people said that I should be tried for 'baby killing' and for 'war crimes'. It was mentioned, but it was not the prominent mention. It was overlooked in general, because the film was seen as an homage to the American tragedy in Vietnam at that time. America was ready for it in the mid-1980s, and was tired of the cliché of *Rambo*. Similar issues reflected in *South of the Border*. I talked to seven South American presidents about Chávez. They all said positive things about Chávez, but none of this is known in the USA, where he is regarded as a clown and a demon – as is Castro. That is true censorship: in a way, it's an unofficial censorship of the mind arising from the way that our news is presented to us. I believe that we live in the most controlled society with the exception of the Soviet Union, which went under, and I suspect that the USA is paralleling their history to a similar conclusion. The news is ethnocentric: America first. Generally speaking, America is never to blame: 'Terrorists v US'. There is no concept that we partly created Osama [bin Laden] or [Saddam] Hussein, or that many US businesses and individuals supported the Hitler regime. We have started so much shit in the world. We are constantly labelling others as the enemy. The education system contributes to this: high schools are very conformist, and books reflect a pro-American interest. Colleges are more open but also more fragmented. We are not really in a people's democracy where the majority control policy. Obama was elected by the people, yet he still has finished up doing what the joint chiefs and the military complex want. Kennedy was the last president to really challenge the system, and say this is insanity – and he was killed. We are really in a gridlock like the Soviet Union was, and we can't get out of it. The only possible end was indicated in the 2008 financial crisis: that we would go broke, and could not afford to continue with the rigid control of the world that we are seeking.

As it affected Natural Born Killers

Stone: In 1994 *Natural Born Killers* was an essay about these issues of unofficial censorship, about the replacement of values with media and its love of violence. At that time the O. J. Simpson trial was the staple of American news, and might well have made close to $10 billion for the networks. News used to be a non-profit activity, but that changed in 1980s with Larry Tisch buying CBS and declaring the news division for-profit. Whereas up until that point, to the best of my knowledge, all the licensing on television was done on the basis that news was supposed to be non-profit. That changed the game at CBS. This is to the best of my knowledge. For me, *Natural Born Killers* was a satire, but others saw it as violent, gory garbage. The Board informed me that the film would get an NC-17, which was a no-go that meant that it could not play at certain theatres and advertising would be limited. It would have been treated similarly to a porno film. Bob Daly at Warners told me that they needed an R, that Bob would help, but that Warners wouldn't release the film in that form. The film is finally available now in its original uncut form, re-released on DVD last year, although it received little attention. In 1994 I had to fight and went back to the Board with my editors six to seven times to work things out, without it becoming a scandal. I made a lot of cuts – about 150 – and the film was released as an R. I didn't lose anything essential except the rhythm and the savagery and brutality that I wanted. At one stage it was difficult to understand what the Board wanted to have cut because even they weren't sure; it was just the air of general chaos that they didn't like. The film did moderately well and made money; however, it was seen by some as not satire, but garbage with a flimsy excuse of satire. That was the end of my relationship at that time with Warners, although I did subsequently make two movies over the next ten years with them, *Any Given Sunday* [1999], and 50 per cent partnership with them on *Alexander* [2004], but essentially the relationship was fractured.

Natural Born Killers was not an easy movie for this town to accept. I had been in a similar position with *Scarface*, although I was only the writer. In 1983, *Scarface* likewise was abhorred and got very bad reviews, although it went on to become a cult classic. At that time it hurt our careers – Pacino, De Palma and my own. *Natural*

Born Killers had a harder time. The independent producer Arnon Milchan was looking to make money, and was not interested in fully promoting the film.

As it affected Nixon

Stone: *Nixon* was rated 'R' for language, but there were no particular rating issues. However, on the day the film came out it was attacked by Diane Disney [Miller], who said words to the effect, 'How can my father's studio make this film?' – clearly calculated to damage the film. However Michael Eisner, then head of Disney, told me that he felt it was the best movie they had made that year. From my perspective it was a defeat, losing $35 to $40 million. I think any portrayal of Nixon was probably not destined to make a lot of money. Even *Frost/Nixon* [Ron Howard, 2009], with enormous advertising only took around $19 million box office. Nixon was a man of great talent, but his own worst enemy. Nixon did make some progress with the Soviet Union and China, and in that respect he may, like Kennedy, have crossed a line – and it has even been suggested that Watergate might have been a response from the establishment to that development.

As a continuing phenomenon

Stone: *U Turn* was a story about incest and was released as an R; but by 1997 things had started to loosen up a little. However, by the time of *Alexander* I discovered that the gay relationship with Hephaestion was still a shock – certainly for the studio. As a result I did not at that time use the relationship with Bagoas – a eunuch. In the 2007 DVD version, this relationship is restored. *Alexander* was an explorer and went beyond all boundaries. The intermission which is only in the 2007 version was valuable to allow people to breathe. After *JFK, I* continued to get negative press for *Heaven and Earth, Natural Born Killers, Nixon* and *U Turn* which was deemed to be too violent. *Any Given Sunday* was also lightly regarded because it was about football.

I worked with Warners as a partner on *Alexander*. There was a change of administration at Warners. We had made a lot of money with Warners DVD division on *Any Given Sunday*, and they were willing to take *Alexander* and quietly release it again in 2007 [*Alexander Revisited*]. In the USA, the representation of homosexuality was a big issue; no one came to even sample it in the south of the country. Newspapers played with the title: 'Alexander the Gay', 'Alexander the Not So Great'.[6] The idea of a gay military commander was just unacceptable to Americans. If *Brokeback Mountain* had been a story of soldiers rather than cowboys, it would not have succeeded! The strength of reaction to *Alexander* may suggest an insecurity in the American psyche, linked to our aggressiveness and love of war. We have fought seven wars since World War Two, and none of them were necessary. War ramps up spending and provides a means of control, but it doesn't have to be so.

Comandante drew criticism, although the television programme, *Persona Non Grata* about Palestine, was balanced and not easy to criticise. It was released by HBO that year, but without much fanfare. It was 67 minutes long, and does exist in the Oliver Stone DVD Collection. I also returned to Cuba after *Comandante* to do a second documentary for HBO, which was released, called *Looking for Fidel*. It was my second interview with Castro, and this is a hard-hitting Q&A, but does not have the broad, portrait-like feel of *Comandante*. The documentaries on Castro came up as a result of me being approached by Spanish and Argentine producers with good contacts in Cuba. I had done *Salvador* and had a liberal's desire to help, but I never really had a thing for Castro until going there. I have also now done a third documentary on Fidel. We finished shooting in August, and are now slowly editing it. It's a farewell to Castro. *South of the Border* is also due out this year. I am currently working on *Secret History of the United States*. This has taken two years up to now off and on, and will probably take a third year to complete. It's proving to be very exhausting work. The recent press announcement again drew criticisms related to my comment about Hitler – it doesn't seem to let up. The *Guardian* report was probably the most accurate.

W. was a well-respected movie; however, by the time the movie came out Bush had lost his bite. If the movie had come out two months earlier, while the debate was still about national security, the film would have done a lot better. By the time of release in October 2009, the debate had moved on to the economy. There was no participation or input from any of Bush's close associates who were – and are – very secretive. There is still a lot that is still unknown about Bush and that era.

Wall Street finished shooting in New York last month and the studio is looking for an April release, but this is still to be agreed. *World Trade Center* did good business around the world. Ixtlan is often approached with interesting stories, but from a movie perspective they are lost causes. I cannot follow the news, films take too long to make. In any case, I want to focus on the things that really interest me, given the time it takes to make a movie. I don't get any approaches from the studios, they are not interested in making those kinds of movie. The official line is that 'dramas are dead': the project either needs to be a comedy, or a big-pull teenager film. *W.* was an effort to fill that gap. It was financed with independent money, with 55 per cent from Hong Kong, plus Australian, French and German finance and a small amount of US equity. It was essentially a foreign production. There is a strong economic aspect to censorship, with the rule being 'don't rock the boat too much'.

As evidenced in media coverage

Stone: It's exhausting to go through all of these debates when you make a movie, because the debate is not about the movie, but about whether you are telling the truth or not, what a fraud you are, or what a liar you are. It becomes personal, and those attacks do wear you down – they beat the shit out of you, frankly.

I don't think anything could have prepared me for what I was going to get into in my life. My father always used to say to me when I was a kid: 'Kiddo, don't ever tell the truth – keep it to yourself.' I always tried to be a truth-teller because I was a bit of a rebel. Unfortunately I didn't realise the implications of that. I say that because it's very much a part of my life and I find that it goes on to this day; I am often criticised. As an only child, I do have a problem with criticism, but there is something beyond my own ego, and that is the truth. Some of the great people I admire probably had to learn the same lesson: for example, Martin Luther King. I believe that in an Anglo-American culture – it's the same situation in England as in the USA – what happens is that if you defend yourself in the press, you get attacked harder. Should one take a *noblesse oblige* approach and let most things pass? Generally I have taken this approach, but as a result a lot of scandal and false rumours pass unchallenged.

Interviewer: Love appears in many of your films, but is little remarked upon?

Stone: With the exception of *U Turn*, all of my films have an aura of optimism about them. In *World Trade Center* it is feelings of family that help pull the people out of the hole. In *W.*, Laura Bush is a binding force. In *Wall Street*, love is also important. *U Turn* demonstrates the problem of isolation.

I think *Natural Born Killers* connected with young people because it is essentially a love story. The theme is: love beats the demon. The theme is used on t-shirts and is used on projections: for example, in the scene with the 'Indian'. Mickey and Mallory are monsters in a sense, but they reflect better because they are surrounded by greater monsters – people who completely corrupt the system, and kill and murder in their own way – people such as the policemen represented by Tom Sizemore, the warden represented by Tommy Lee Jones, and the media represented by Robert Downey Jr. I shot two versions of the ending: in one, Mickey and Mallory get away; in the other, they are killed by someone who is in fact worse than them. I didn't like the latter ending, but it was shot in case there was a censorship pressure not to have Mickey and Mallory be seen to have gotten away. Certainly there was some bluenose reaction to the ending that was used. Some people were fearful that young people would model themselves on Mickey and Mallory. The movie was done in the spirit of asking how crazy has our culture become. Janet Maslin wrote in the *New York Times* about the edits in the film – some 4,000 – but not about some of the other cultural aspects.

Interview with Oliver Stone, 18 June 2010

Interviewer: How did *U Turn* develop as a project?

Stone: I did a lot of rewriting on *U Turn*. Also at that time Richard Rutowski [was] also involved in the rewriting. I didn't claim writing credit for *U Turn*, as I judged it below 50 per cent of the total, which is the WGA [Writers Guild of America] threshold. I think that a 25 per cent threshold would be more appropriate. The whole thing is screwed up. The WGA rules tend to favour the first writer, who is often the most incompetent. I adopted a hands-off approach over writing credits on *U Turn* perhaps because of the reaction of Quentin Tarantino over the *Natural Born Killers* script. I had bought the screenplay wholly and legally and paid him very well, but he later got very upset with my rewriting it. The screenplay had been lying around for some years and he admitted that he did not have any intention of directing it. My view when I saw it was that it was a primitive but interesting idea. I talked to associate producer Janet Yang and I saw it on her desk, and said that's a great title. I had seen *Reservoir Dogs* [1992] and I was very impressed with his work. I loved *Reservoir Dogs*. I thought the original screenplay for *Natural Born Killers* would have also made a great first movie, but as it stood, it was shallow. I then bought the screenplay from Jane Hamsher and Don Murphy. What I didn't know was that there was bad blood between these two producers and Quentin, a long-simmering feud – they said they'd discovered him, blah blah blah. So I plunged in. Quentin then came to see me about the rewriting of the screenplay. I tried to explain to him that I had been there before too, in films like *Scarface* and *Year of the Dragon*, where I had written the screenplay and then changed it towards the director's vision. He was very bruised by it. He believes that the writer has to have the integrity of the material; I said I don't think we can do that. Writer integrity is important, but movie-making is a collaborative one, and singly-written screenplays don't always make for the best movies. My view on reflection is that the rewrite made a more interesting movie in that it went into the sociological issues and created real characters.

However, at the time Quentin was very pissed off. Quentin made his version of the screenplay more than available to everyone he could – available to various fan magazines – so it's possible to look at the final version and see how it was developed. The point was, Quentin was very upset. I had never seen such a campaign of vilification. *Natural Born Killers* opened, coincidentally, at around the same time as *Pulp Fiction* [1994]. In fact *Pulp Fiction* had been screened at Cannes and from my perspective, the timing of *Natural Born Killers* just after *Pulp Fiction* was unlucky. We were in his shadow. Both the timing and the controversy hurt *Natural Born Killers* during its opening. It has subsequently found its way to success as a cult film. I had said at the time that Quentin was suable for his comments. When you take money from the producer you agree certain conditions. We have since made up, but it was a very painful period. I don't think to this day he had admitted to seeing it. I admire him as an artist and have enjoyed his later films. It's a tough business. I came from a tradition where as a screenwriter if you didn't like what the director did, you shut up or you waited until he died at least – which is what I did with Hal Ashby.

In *U Turn* the original book was a great set-up, good dialogue; however, it didn't go far enough – it wasn't crazy enough. Sometimes, great thrillers need to be made more crazy for movies. I was working on the script even during the shoot. It was a real down to the wall job. Richard Rutowski had been scouting in Arizona, looking for somewhere that would work as the location for the film – a hole-in-the-wall kind of place. As we looked for a suitable location in out-of-the-way places, the idea of incest came up. It is a chilling concept, but there are many products of incest in rural America. I hate to tell you, but it's true. Richard told me about an experience he had had during scouting on the back roads. During one of these visits he came across an ideal out-of-the-way place and pulled up to a shack – a big shack – with a guy sat on the porch with a shotgun. He said 'What do you want?' Richard bullshitted him a bit that he was a scout. Out of the shack walked a nymphet with shorts, cut-offs and all that. She looked, according to Richard, exactly like him, but the guy was not behaving towards her as if she was his daughter. This reminded me of a previous scouting experience in Mississippi near Parchment, where there appeared to be evidence of incest among some of the people that I came across. I suspect that Mississippi was famous for it. I think probably there's a lot more goes on than is admitted, possibly more so in the USA than in England. In the USA, rural communities are very physically isolated and insular, and people get away with it. They don't cooperate with the census. These people are off the map. They don't want to fuckin' know. In any event, these personal observations prompted me to weave incest into the narrative of *U Turn*. It is my darkest film, the idea was to go as black as possible. *Natural Born Killers* is a love story, but there is no possibility of love in this universe in *U Turn*: they are like scorpions in a bucket – nobody could get out alive.

It was one of the darkest spaces personally that I had ever been in. I had just finished *Nixon* and my book. I was turning 51 years old, and for some reason it was a dark period. Fifty is a very dangerous age – a mid-life crisis. I wanted to make a film that was deliberately low-key. I had been attacked so much for making big films. This was an attempt to return to my roots and make something low-budget, quick and dirty – really dirty. I feel I got killed for it. It went too far. Even Mike Medavoy, the Chairman of Phoenix Pictures, said that I hadn't given him the film that I wrote. Mike also said that I had made it too brutal. From recollection, I think Janet Maslin said something similar which probably put off some more respectable viewers. Mike and I have no luck together! We worked together on *The Hand* [1981] and also on *The People vs Larry Flynt* [Miloš Forman, 1996]. A lot of my weirder friends really love the movie. I think *U Turn* has some surface similarities with *Red Rock West* [John Dahl, 1993], but it's not the same kind of film. I found that kind of accusation demeaning – that I would make a copy of another film. All film noir films today are cheats – people live at the end. *U Turn* is a true film noir – the key people all die. Only the two weirdest people – the blind 'Indian' and Darrell – survive. I think Billy Bob Thornton is great in the movie. He was scared of flying, and every time we needed to get him on set they had to take a van from Arkansas.

Bill Paxton dropped out of the shoot with just two weeks to go to shooting. He called me when the crew were in Arizona at a production meeting, to say that he just couldn't perform that role. After I took the call from Paxton, I returned to the production meeting and pretended for the next two hours that all was well. Sean Penn had passed the initial offer to be involved, but after Paxton's departure Penn was available and took the role. There was some tension in the relationship between us, which Penn later expressed in a David Letterman interview; there had been an incident related to Penn's loss of temper on set. Certainly the work schedule for the shoot was tough, and this may have contributed to Penn's attitude. Despite the pressure of the shoot, I did stop production for two days so that Penn could return to Santa Monica to open his nightclub. There were some bad feelings that persisted after the film was completed, but these have healed over the years.

In addition to the personnel change there was also a change of title. We attempted to agree with Akira Kurosawa to use the *Stray Dogs* title, but Kurosawa was extremely litigious. Kurosawa wanted to avoid confusion with his own *Stray Dog* [1949]. As a result, a replacement title was needed. I did run a competition during the shoot for a new title, but eventually I settled on an idea I had had on a trip to Morocco.

In *U Turn*, I was able to take the story and give it a deeper meaning. I had a similar experience in *Alexander*, where I had been able to focus on questions that historians had previously overlooked. I asked the question why *Alexander* never got back to see his mother. The movie also raises questions about Roxane. I recently met Paul Cartledge, who did a book on the movie, on a trip to the Cambridge Union. He said that the film had given him cause to re-examine the role of Roxane in the story of Alexander, and the connections with Olympias. Angelina Jolie has had some issues in her personal life, and she was up for the challenges of Olympias. I'm not sure if Jennifer Lopez fully understood what was going on within the screenplay in *U Turn*. I think Lopez was a little disturbed by some of the nudity. Bob Richardson [cinematographer on *U Turn*] was also disturbed by the sexuality. Sean Penn was also not happy with the direction the movie took. I saw this role as similarly hopeless to that of Dix, played by Humphrey Bogart in Nicholas Ray's *In a Lonely Place* [1950]. There is no love in the world. The woman he thinks he loves doesn't know what love is. The theme of emptiness is reinforced at the end of the film, both by the blowing of the radiator hose and in the lifting helicopter shot. I recall that the production did not get any positive coverage from the local paper in Phoenix.

As to why *U Turn* didn't find its audience, I think that certainly one reason was to do with not getting to Cannes. That really hurt us. The film had a terrible opening weekend. It opened against *Kiss the Girls* [Gary Fleder, 1997], which was an entertaining murder story. I also have the sense that Mike Medavoy, who didn't like the portrayal of incest, didn't fight with TriStar to keep the film in theatres after the first weekend. TriStar didn't put any further effort into promoting the film. I also suspect that incest, and indeed homosexuality, are both issues that Americans don't really want to hear about.

Interviewer: Was television censorship an issue?

Stone: On the general question of censorship, it becomes very difficult to monitor and keep control of what happens to a film after its theatrical release. The offering of films for television transmission does provide a means by which the studios can recover their money, but it does involve edits to the film. *U Turn* was probably one of the worst examples of a film getting chopped up. In the case of Turner [Network Television], their need to work with advertisers necessitated the cuts. I hope that at least if people see the film in some form, they may return and seek out a version that is accurate – for example, on DVD – but it is a far from ideal situation.

On the question of news priorities in the USA and the limited reporting of the war in Afghanistan, I think that the USA is a funny place. When you are in the madhouse, it's hard to judge. England has pretentions to civility but is one of the most aggressive countries in the world, and are partners in crime with the USA. I think that the BBC has played an important role in the UK's 'cold warrior' stance, particularly against the Soviet Union. The sanctions in Iran are yet another march to war, with many of the same perpetrators still involved.

Interviewer: How is *Wall Street* progressing?

Stone: As regards *Wall Street*, I was pleased with the overall reception of the film at Cannes. It was offered as a non-competitive entry. Several Wall Street traders made the journey to Cannes to see the premiere. There has been some discussion of the issues raised by the film at Cannes but the film is intended primarily as entertainment – in contrast say, to *South of the Border*. *Wall Street* was viewed by Fox earlier today and they were happy. Some minor tweaks are still required – not by the studio – but by me.

Interview with Oliver Stone, 7 December 2011

Interviewer: What impact did Robert Richardson's departure have on you?

Stone: Bob departed after *U Turn*. His departure had a tremendous impact on me. I sort of think he had a younger brother–older brother sort of issue. I can't drill into his psyche, but I think he felt I was too strong and too much of a dominant factor in his life, and it was time to move on. It certainly hurt, the whole thing. I miss him. I don't think we'll get together again.

Interviewer: How did you get into making *Any Given Sunday*?

Stone: I would agree that while *Any Given Sunday* did not do badly at the US box office, it would it be fair to say that its failure to attract a wider audience was in no small part due to its failure to adhere to some of Hollywood's conventions of narrative simplicity.

It took a lot to make this movie, including buying these freighted scripts that were no good. There were a lot of junk scripts. I wanted to make the movie. The vision I had was a combination of what I saw in the doctor's [Robert Huizenga's] book, what I got from my own observations, and what I was getting from [screenwriter] John Logan, so I took it upon myself in this period [late 1998] to try and unify the scripts and get everybody on board with the same script. We were prepping in Miami, and the actors didn't know what script we were doing, and the studio head [Terry Semel] didn't know. That was the problem. They [Warner Bros.] had hesitation because we were spending money to get ready. I succeeded in getting the script finalised two-and-a-half weeks before the shoot. Al [Pacino] and Terry saw the script at the same time. Without the script, that would have been worse than any disaster; would have been what poor Francis [Ford] Coppola went through with *The Cotton Club*, I guess. I didn't have a green light on any script until two-and-a-half weeks before the shoot. That's pretty wild!

The 11 November 1998 memo from Neil Austrian at the NFL to the production, which suggested the NFL would have final script approval, was a kind of a fake, in that Clayton [Townsend] was the whole time trying to keep the NFL in the mix. I said on our first meeting that this will never happen with these guys. They are assholes – just another culture, another world, billions of dollars, Disneyland. They said we couldn't have the language in the screenplay, or talk about playing to the death or about the corruption. Clayton's attitude was, let's play them along because we've got an issue with the stadiums. He put up with meetings and meetings. They did eventually send memos out to tell the coaches not to cooperate. I would never have given final script approval. On reflection, perhaps Clayton's approach was right. We did ultimately get the Miami and Texas stadiums because the guys were rebels.

I had extensive talks with George Clooney because he was coming up, and I knew he would be great as a quarterback and he loved football. We talked and he thought that I was going to make certain changes in the picture that would make him bigger in the movie. I thought they [the changes] were good, but they were not up to what he thought, so he pulled out.

Tensions were very high throughout the shoot. There was a dust-up between LL Cool J and Jamie Foxx, kind of semi-comic. Al got in the middle of the fight and almost got his head taken off. It was a macho film with a lot of real footballers involved, including the entire second unit. [Production designer] Victor Kempster resigned three-quarters of the way through, and we finished [the film] with his art director, Derek Hill. He did a great job. I don't know that Victor was right for the movie because he didn't like football and made that evident to me on several occasions. His attitude was, 'Why the fuck are you making this kind of movie? You should be making something more important.' I resented that. I thought it was important. It wasn't just about football but changes in the culture and of the corporations involved. It is clear that the corporations were changing in the late 1990s and becoming more and more what they are now – risk-free and liability-averse. A lot of the fun has gone. Making the movie was a bit like learning the truth. It is an ugly game in some ways. Sports movies tend to be nostalgic and don't go to the underlying corruption. I didn't seek out the corruption as a theme. It came to me gradually as I read the books.

There was very little attention from the sports media when the film came out, almost as if they had got a memo from the NFL reminding them of how much money comes from the NFL!

Interviewer: Why are there three versions of *Alexander*?

Stone: Thomas Schühly is a lover of classical film. He proposed *Alexander*, but he didn't know how he wanted to do it. I hired other writers (it's a dirty story relating to the WGA, not worth repeating). An Italian company then claimed that Schühly had sold the rights to them; it was very confusing and I just didn't feel that Schühly was the right guy to be in business with. I later spoke to Moritz Borman. He had a big company called Intermedia, and he asked me what I would like to do, and I said *Alexander*. He said, oh shit! However Intermedia raised the money, mainly through independent sources via Cannes. Various markets were sold and then the USA. We then reinstated Schühly as exec. producer. He was around, but not a significant factor.

I wish to God I'd had the courage to tell Warner Bros. that I needed more time, but it would have been a scandal. It was sold to them on the basis that it was the son of *Troy*. However, the little that we know indicates that *Troy* distorts history. We know that the relationship between Achilles and Patroclus is not just man-to-man.

That was the most rushed film we ever did. We finished shooting in January [2004] and were out in November. It was just too tough. They wanted a less than three-hour film. The film was number one in many countries, but the reception of the film in the USA and the UK was devastatingly bad. I can only blame myself. The [original] script actually resembled the third version [*Alexander Revisited*, 2007] more than the first two. Warners were upset with me. I promised them a sanitised film. I saw a list of their cuts and we went back and forth. There was no way I was going to make all of those cuts. They wanted all the homosexuality out. They hated Bagoas. There was also huge problems with blood.

Looking back, Rodrigo Prieto did a good job as DP [director of photography] on *Alexander* – as good a job as he could have done under the circumstances, on three continents and a very tight schedule. The flaws in the film have more to do, if anything, with my editing process at that time. The second version was done immediately as a DVD, as I was still chomping at the bit. This was the director's cut. It was shorter but didn't deal with the essence of the problems, and that gnawed at me for two-and-a-half years.

The next reworking was for me, and thank God I had one ally with Warners Home Entertainment who gave me a shot: they gave the chance to put out my version on Blu-ray. *Alexander Revisited* did well as a catalogue sale – about one million copies – but I couldn't get the critics to look at it again. It was the best I could do, and I think it does explain a lot about that world. There is also a lot about my feelings about life in there. *Alexander* had a point. It wasn't clear in the first two, but it was clear in the third. I would like to see this version shown on TV, but I think the chances are thin. I would be in your eternal debt if you guys could get the two-part with intermission, 3 hour 48 minute version *Alexander Revisited* on TV. I could go to my grave feeling good. I grew up with long movies – they work.

Interviewer: What happened with the proposal for *Pinkville*?

Stone: [Bruce] Willis pulled out because of script issues. Mikko Alanne had been an intern in my office and wrote the script. There were problems, but nothing that couldn't be fixed. There was a New Year's break coming up, and I had the intention to fix it before we were due to start in January, as I had done on *Any Given Sunday*. We had a great cast lined up, including Woody Harrelson and Channing Tatum.

We had the village built, we had the whole thing set up. Unfortunately Bruce got cold feet and he pulled out. I was surprised when he pulled out. *Lions for Lambs* [Robert Redford, 2007] had opened, and [producer] Paula Wagner received a lot of criticism for doing the movie. She used the Willis excuse to pull support for the film. We got Nick Cage to replace Willis a month later, but Paula was grateful to be off the hook. The issue was that Willis felt he didn't have enough to do. We could have solved it because I was aware of the issue in rehearsals, but he didn't have much patience. It's a great story. [Robert] Richardson came back for that, he wanted to work on it, but it didn't go through.

Interviewer: What cinematic options did you consider in relation to 9/11 and the 'War on Terror'?

Stone: Prior to 2006 I did work on *War on Terror* and *Jawbreaker*. *War on Terror* was going to be about the mistake we were making at a domestic level. It is about a dentist who gets lifted and just doesn't get back home. The script needed work but I just didn't have the time. *War on Terror* was not financeable at that time. In those days, to open your mouth to criticise the USA drew a lot of criticism. I was criticised in the press when I spoke out against Christopher Hitchens at a *New Yorker* event at the Lincoln Centre in 2001, where he was talking about bombing Muslim countries.

Jawbreaker I bought. It was written by Gary Berntsen, who had been on the ground in Afghanistan. He was at Tora Bora and was a real hardcore, right-wing operative. It showed the facts as he saw them. At Tora Bora the Pentagon let the CIA down. They refused to commit the necessary troops; the focus was already on Iraq. It was a classic government fuck-up. I would have made a hero out of this guy B., and perhaps I would have been faulted for it. In hindsight, I think if the USA had cooperated with Iran and Pakistan, it would have been possible to bring pressure on the Taliban to get rid of Osama [bin Laden]. We didn't need to fight that war, but we bombed right away and then let him go.

Jawbreaker was a doable deal with Paramount. Cyrus Nowrasteh wrote a script, but it didn't work yet. Nowrasteh also wrote and directed *The Day Reagan was Shot* [2001] and wrote the *ABC* mini-series *The Path to 9/11* [2006].

Michael Shamberg and Stacey Sher brought me *World Trade Center*. It was a chance to work with the studio. It was a script that Michael and Stacey had developed and had been worked on by Andrea [Berloff] for a year, and I tried to respect that. However, the more I got into preparations for shooting the script, the more it became clear to me that we really couldn't shoot that script, and it needed restructuring. I worked on it before, during and after, trying to solve the structural problems and also trying to add some spirituality to the dialogue – it was their spirit that kept them alive. I didn't go for co-credit: it was Andrea's first script. It was a difficult script to shoot. We had to alternate light and dark to prevent the viewer having to look at too much content in darkness. It was also hard technically shooting in the holes because of breathing problems, and it was personally difficult standing on the side of a rubble heap for many hours.

John McLoughlin and Will Jimeno were happy with what we were doing. We also had fifty of the rescuers come from New York to Los Angeles to help us on the film because they liked what we were doing. It wasn't any kind of false patriotism on their part. They were just doing their jobs, and wanted to help us show that in the film. The marine was a patriotic right-winger who went back to Iraq. He did say those things. Some people assumed that I was saying we have to go and bomb Iraq, which was the farthest thing from my mind. I wanted to look at a micro-level; I didn't want to bullshit anybody about what happened down there. I felt that by honestly dealing with fear and hysteria you can come to grips with what happened that day, rather than running around saying we can't let any of the Guantanamo people come to the USA, and spending $50 billion protecting ourselves from ghosts.

Interviewer: *W.* pulled its punches in the eyes of some critics. How do you see it?

Stone: In 2006 there was very little information about Bush. It's living history, and it's hard to piece it out as we go. This was

Bush in 2008: he was the least popular president. In some ways the movie was too late, people were saying: 'Who gives a shit about George Bush?' That made financing difficult. I think we had a story. We took the tack of national security. [Senator John] McCain pulled even in the polls in August 2008, and then the economy became the main issue in September. This became the one issue in the election, and at that point our movie became irrelevant to the debate that ensued between Obama and McCain.

So the economic woes hit me in two ways. On *Pinkville*, the hedge fund that was funding Paula Wagner pulled out on her, and then a year later it did me in on *W.* I am a victim of that fucking economic crash! We all were.

One scene that didn't make it into the movie was the ghost of Saddam talking to George Bush. I didn't think it was interesting enough. It seemed like an oddball tone, and it was on the edge of silliness. The Oval Office finale, a showdown between Bush *père et fils*, was shot with a swing lens, and the office was completely stripped to signal that this was not intended to be taken literally.

The film picks up the administration's story in 2002 after 9/11, and before its entry into Iraq. It might have been possible to start earlier with Bush's first year and the response in the immediate period after 9/11 – but that would have meant going into the Patriot Act as well, and we already had a long movie.

On Dreyfuss let's just say he was impossible to work with. It was one of the worst experiences of my life. Let's just let it go at that.

We did talk about a possible end-scene with Bush in an orange jumpsuit at the Hague – that's funny! – but I don't think it was in the script. Everyone was attacking Bush, and I felt we did not need to hammer him. It's a little bit of a whimsical movie. He grows delicately. He arrives at this very tender moment with his wife, and asks 'What have I done wrong?' When he goes upstairs after the news conference and slams the door, he knows he has fucked up. He just doesn't know what to do about it. But that's the first sign of a consciousness: that's how delicate the movie's representation of him is. It ends with the hopeful note that someone might learn from his mistakes, and then of course he's in the outfield, but the ball never comes down. It's a lighter movie, but it's made about a man who is a lighter man. He is a two-dimensional man. He's Peter Sellers in *Being There* – he just doesn't belong.

Interviewer: You passed on *Wall Street 2*?

Stone: I did pass the first time on directing *Wall Street 2*, but after the crash it was too important to ignore. The banks had become the Gekkos.

Interviewer: How was working with Fox?

Stone: We live in a world where we need patrons. We are all artists. I may work with Fox another day.

On media coverage

Stone: Frank Rich wrote last week in praise of Stephen King's new book *11/22/63*, about how right he was about [John F. Kennedy].[7] King claims that he is 99 per cent sure that Oswald did it alone, based on the fact that he [Oswald] took a shot at Edwin Walker.[8] Just shows you that he has done a lot of research. Aside from that, Rich goes out of his way to call me that 1 per cent crusader-type. That's a cheap shot, he's a smart guy. Problem with my generation, all the smart ones, they didn't get it – they missed it. People like [the journalist] Bill Keller.

The world is run by madmen. They are completely deluded – and it remains for us, the 'V for Vendettas', to tell the truth. We had the WMD story in Iraq, now we have it in Iran. Some crazy stories about Iranian plans to kill the Saudi ambassador. The same cast is back – who did the WMD story – and the newspapers are providing the same drumbeat. We kill their scientists and we blow up their installations, and we are the good guys.

What annoyed me was how little coverage the HBO–*Comandante* dispute got in the US media. That's another aspect of the media game: they hype what they want. The idea of the artist being censored by the studio is a great story – it always plays well – but they didn't play it. The same thing was true in the *Natural Born Killers* case in the fight with Grisham. There was no sense of challenge to Grisham's claim that artists should be sued for their statements – that they could be sued as if they were products.

On writing and work

Stone: Finding a good writer is like finding a wife or a husband. It's a very hard thing to do. You can sit here and you can babble all you want, and you can produce hours of transcripts and the guy or the girl goes out and writes, and it has nothing to do with what you fucking talked about. I mean, you have wasted hours and then you say, 'Why didn't I write it myself?' But I can't do everything. I depend on partners, on the kindness of strangers. A lot of Hollywood deals don't go bad for any one reason. Sometimes it's just that the chemistry isn't there between the writers, or between the writer and director. That's why I cut back. I was expending energy on a lot of projects that were not getting done.

Heaven and Earth, *Nixon* and *U Turn* were my three greatest failures in terms of money. However, it's not a business only of money, it's a business of impression. As far as keeping within budget goes, I have never been in trouble on that point. When people ask me which of my movies I like better, I say it doesn't matter. It's a year of my life.

Interview with Oliver Stone, 8 December 2011

Interviewer: Media coverage of you and your work and career is seldom tepid in tone. What kind of perspective do you have on the often hostile appraisals of you and the work?

Stone: Well, the piece written by Camilla Long in *The Sunday Times*[9] is a case in point. There is no goodness in this and articles like it, it's all negative. It doesn't matter how tough you are, it does wear you down. It makes filmmaking so impossibly difficult. You reach the point where, as David Lean so eloquently said: 'What's the point?' The curse of my career, but it was also a blessing – it works both ways – was that I won Academy Awards young and unknown. It was a great surprise to me. Richard Brooks said to me backstage at the Academy Awards for *Born on the Fourth of July*: 'It will be a long time before you get another one.' With few exceptions there is a point where a man's life reaches a zenith and he doesn't know it, and no matter what he does after that, he can never approach that again. That's not to say I don't try and do my best work, but the way other people see your life is determined by these Greek drama perspectives.

So if you wrote the life of me, Oliver, you might see it that way, but as you have suggested, I think I have matured. I'm still doing the work. It's not like all of a sudden I couldn't say the same things, it's just that I said them differently. The Bush movie [*W.*] and *World Trade Center* were cases in point. On each occasion I tried to respect the story. The climate changed after 2001, but for me it changed after 1995. *Nixon* was one of my best films, but it was received in a very niggardly manner, partly due to my earlier success, and partly due to the scandal associated with *JFK* and with *Natural Born Killers*. By then people were exhausted with scandal. Lars von Trier got away with it twice and he ended up talking too much and making a fool of himself, but that doesn't make him any less of a filmmaker.[10] Anybody put under the spotlight is bound to have flaws in the public eye. I reached that place in 1995. I think it was one of my best films, but when *Nixon* came out there was a giant thud of silence. There was a lot of quibbling about the film. Hopkins didn't look like Nixon, but anyone who understands drama knows that this can work. There were Oscar nominations for Anthony [Hopkins], Joan [Allen], John Williams for the music and one for the script, but not for directing. The message I got from that was there was quite a bit of antagonism around town, because if anything, it was very much a director's film. The film only took $13 million at the US box office, and not that much abroad. It wasn't as if I collapsed, but I gave in a little – got demoralised – and concluded that people no longer wanted me or these kinds of films. After that I did a low-budget film [*U Turn*] just to escape the wrath. It was different, low-budget film noir that would be fun for me. It was compared to other film noirs, and dismissed and also compared unfavourably to *Natural Born Killers* by the constituency who liked that movie. The poor performance of *U Turn* was also a demoraliser. I then wrote a book to get away from it all. It came out and sold 20,000 copies in hardback. These messages come along. I then made a supreme effort on *Any Given Sunday*. It was dismissed as a football movie. On 31 December 1999 we were the number one film in America, but there were no Oscar nominations. Then I moved to documentaries which didn't get attention, and then to *Alexander*, which also received poor reviews – for example, in the *New York Times*. So I could say that I was working as hard, but the critics were not in a mood to receive. There was a different story for journalists to tell, about someone who had received this early praise, and was now on the fucking bonfire. It's a hard place to come back from. I'm still the same person and the work endures, and I hope that people will eventually notice it. The truth endures. It's on film, thank God. If I had done theatre, it would be impossible now to function.

Interviewer: How have your media profile and political interests affected your relationship with the studios?

Stone: People have kept employing me from different places – for example, *W.* was funded out of Hong Kong. I have also worked inside the system on *World Trade Center*, *Wall Street* and *Savages*, and I have managed to maintain my freedom within that centre. *Pinkville* was a horrible setback. As for loyalty to the system and the studios, I tried to be loyal but gave up with *Nixon* at the point at which Warners dumped me. I bought the rights back from Arnon Milchan, and made the film with Anthony Hopkins and the independent Cinergi [Pictures], distributing through Disney.

Warners did get re-involved with *Any Given Sunday* and with *Alexander*, where they became involved reluctantly. That was then the end of my relationship with Warners. With *World Trade Center*, Paramount were very happy. *World Trade Center* was their ideal movie: serious, Oscar-worthy and made money. However, there was no recognition from the Academy. After that, Paramount would not make *Pinkville* – and that's when they supposedly liked me. So you have to be a gypsy, you have to take your banjo and try to move on and get another patron. I was offered *Wall Street* because Michael Douglas thought I should have first refusal; however, the studio would have happily moved on to another option. I realise that I am an older director and memories are not so long. I bought the material for *Savages*, and then Universal came on board in March of this year, but who knows where Universal will be in a year. They have been bought by a company called Comcast, who are relatively conservative. So I think we all work on the basis that any relationship is a one-picture thing. If a picture takes $100 million at the domestic box office, that will make a difference to the kind of relationship you have with the studio – but otherwise, no.

Interviewer: How successfully do you think other leading directors are at working with the studios?

Stone: I admire Spielberg. He has the technical ability. He solved the issue by becoming the billionaire moviemaker; his approach is, however, different than mine. [George] Lucas, [Peter] Jackson, [James] Cameron, [Ridley] Scott are all really good at what they do.

I think for some, I am perceived as crude or excessive. There is also still a stigma about my association with Vietnam, that I am in some way lecturing them because they didn't go to Vietnam. I still don't think the younger moviemakers really see the bullshit in our foreign policy. They are ready to celebrate World War Two, but they are not ready to look at the root causes of why we are such a militaristic country. Writers like Stephen Ambrose have been happy to celebrate the 'Greatest Generation', but a lot of those people were not so great. They moved on to become our commanders in Vietnam, but they didn't see clearly. Eisenhower was a grandfather figure, yet he built up our nuclear capability to the hilt and he intervened in foreign countries repeatedly. At the time of making *JFK* I admired Eisenhower for the speech he made about the military industrial complex, but it later shocked me that he was more responsible than anyone else for building it. He gave us Cuba and Guatemala. In a way, *Saving Private Ryan* [Steven Spielberg, 1998] is a celebration of the same kind of thing, a glamorisation of that generation. There is no doubt that D-Day was a big deal, but the timing of *Ryan* in the late 1990s coincided with US remilitarisation. The sentiments that saw *Platoon* and *Born on the Fourth of July* become hits had all gone out of the window by '98 when *Ryan* came out. Ridley's film [*Black Hawk Down*, 2001] did the same thing. Here we have a depiction of slaughter with American technology. Jerry Bruckheimer received an award nomination for the film [AFI Movie of the Year].

Interviewer: What is your assessment of the national political direction taken in recent years by Bush and Obama?

Stone: It was a terrible time in 2003, it was a strange time. There was a false patriotism. We need to react to terror like the Europeans had done – Spain, Britain. They respond with covert work, intelligence gathering, police work. The Americans have insisted on militarising the response. We are now a militarised state. We have people in America who are talking more and more about the military undertaking police work, while the police look more and more like military. It's out of control. Michael Moore's movie [*Fahrenheit 9/11*] helped a bit in 2004 because it brought out some truth, but Bush got re-elected. The media response to Moore was focused on him rather than his film. Anyone who questions too much from the Left gets the same kind of treatment. Ralph Nader received a similar hearing.

The problem in America is that we don't apologise, and we don't learn. The protests against the Iraq War worldwide were enormous. I don't think Americans got a sense of the protest or the damage in Iraq at all. The protests were not that big a story in the USA. The American press report on every story from an American viewpoint: it is what comes naturally to them. It's not done out of malice, they don't know any better – they find it hard to become more international. A British journalist, perhaps because he comes from a smaller country, goes out and sees the world. I don't believe the American journalist does that – certainly the ones that belong to the mainstream. Even the *New York Times*, which is supposed to be the most liberal, is pro-empire. American interests come first. In the handling of stories like Iran and even Cuba, you never get the full historical background. We never go back to look at what Castro was fighting against, to the earlier period of American control of Cuba from 1898 onwards. The three documentaries provide some counter to that. He's a tough guy, but I don't see him as a monster. The American media's perspective is always ethnocentric; it sees the world from the perspective of American interests. This is noticeable now in the reporting of China, where the focus is on whether the US is slipping behind China. As to why Obama has not managed to reach out more and change this balance, I think that in the two to three months between election and taking charge, the security state frightened him with stories about threats. The guy was probably brainwashed with these stories. Kennedy, by contrast, had served in World War Two in combat. Obama, like Clinton, had never been in the military. Both were probably in awe of the military people around them. The quality of our intelligence has also suffered from attacks from within. The fiasco involving our counterintelligence chief, James Angleton, and the disastrous paranoia from his reign, resulted in the wiping out of any kind of an informed Soviet bureau, with the result that we went to war with the Russians in Afghanistan. That in turn led us to encourage the zealots there. What happened to the peace dividend after the end of the Cold War? When Obama gave that acceptance speech [12 October 2009] for the Nobel Peace Prize about America's service to the world for the last fifty years, I felt like vomiting. It's like he has bought into a doctrine of endless war. It is a crazy time. It's almost an end time. Holy shit, what a way to go out! I hope there is some better news on the way.

Interviewer: Has your shift to documentary work been in part at least a response to the changing political climate?

Stone: My film business travails, although they have been painful personally, are not as significant as the travails of the world. So if I can do something as a filmmaker – as a documentarian – maybe to bring some benefit, then that is a good thing. I believe there is a core of resistance, of good people. I like *V for Vendetta* [James McTeigue, 2006]. There are intelligent people around who know what's going on; I applaud people like Julian Assange. The move to documentary work is an effort to put pressure where I can best put it, even if it's a reduced impact. The *Untold History of the United States* documentary work has taken up a lot of time and energy, almost four years now. It may not have immediate impact, but perhaps students will see it in due course, say on YouTube. *Comandante*, for example, is available on You Tube but is not available commercially in the USA.[11]

As to whether the move towards documentary work says something about a reduced appetite on the part of the studios for more controversial dramatic content, there are always exceptions. *Savages*, which is backed by Universal, is not a conservative movie. It has a lot of violence and sex. It is, however, not a political movie, although it does criticise the drugs war to a degree. I am putting more of my political passion into the documentary work at this time. The studios have been reduced into a position of fear, where the corporations are more dominant and the profile of the individual filmmaker is reduced. The old concept of turning out money-making films from a factory is back, but they are making too many and hurting themselves.

Interviewer: What scope is there for political expression and creativity within the current studio structures in Hollywood?

Stone: Some filmmakers can come and go to some extent within the studio structure. George Clooney, for example with *Syriana*, received studio support for a film that did critique the oil companies and the administration. [James] Cameron, however, was more reticent about any kind of explicit political commentary in *Avatar*, but it seems pretty clear what we were looking at. Who were those guys? The fucking American army – but no one could say it. Ironically, the film that won the Oscar [*The Hurt Locker*, Kathryn Bigelow, 2009] exonerated the American troops, saying it doesn't matter what the political situation is, you guys are courageous for doing this. I do admire Clooney for what he is doing. He's not saying exactly what I am saying, but he is using the platform he has, to say what he has to say; at the same time he has got to survive. I enjoyed *The Descendants* [Alexander Payne, 2012], and *Michael Clayton* [Tony Gilroy, 2007] was a very good movie. George is a serious, committed man, like Warren Beatty. I do admire creativity, and there are people in the system doing that – but I'm not interested in making movies for myself. I find too many independent movies bore the shit out of me. They are depressing, with a closed view of the world. I want an expansion. My father used to say to me, 'A lot of people don't give a shit about your problems.' He was exaggerating, but I do think there is too much self-indulgence. You have to find a way to take your own observations of self and put it together in a way that is entertaining and exciting for others. People like [Federico] Fellini managed this with *8½* [1963], [François] Truffaut with *The 400 Blows* [1960]; [Jean-Luc] Godard and [Luis] Buñuel likewise have managed this transformation. My favourite of Terry Malick's movies is *The Thin Red Line* [1998] – not everyone agrees, but I think it captured something very accurate about war, and it is also a poetic movie. To take five or six years to make a movie, well at one level there is nothing wrong with that, but you have to be careful about becoming lost in your own thought processes; like Theseus but without a thread – and the Minotaur gets you. [Stanley] Kubrick did a wonderful job on his movies but he agonised a lot, and you wonder sometimes if he hurt himself. *Eyes Wide Shut* [1999] is a movie I don't understand. However, Kubrick did a wonderful job on *Full Metal Jacket* [1987] and captured something about Vietnam, even though it was shot in England.

Charlie Wilson's War [Mike Nichols, 2008] did not work so well. I think it was a lie on many levels. It sets up Wilson as a hero for taking on the Soviet Union, but the CIA were already involved. The film doesn't deal with the results of that intervention. In many ways Charlie Wilson is what's wrong with this country, and not what's right. I don't think Mike Nichols examined the values of the man. He represents the vigilante, the bully. Interestingly Hanks' most famous film is Forrest Gump – a guy who doesn't know any history.

Interviewer: What persuaded you to do the cameo in Ivan Reitman's film, *Dave* [1993]?

Stone: Well, I was right in the piece, wasn't I?! I don't think I would have done it if I'd been wrong! No ... I did it because it allowed me to make a little fun of myself at a time when I was getting a lot of flak. It was one day's work with Larry King, and was fun. It was a well written piece by Gary Ross.

Aaron Sorkin's writing is also good, although I do think he is something of a pessimist. I think that feeling is in the air at the moment, it has become something of an art form at the moment. I feel a little more optimistic than that. If you end on a potentially happy note, say with Gekko wanting to enjoy becoming a grandfather, you become suspect. It's like everybody must be cynical about everything. It's not how I was raised. Cynicism is a virtue now in this society, we're Orwellised. It's fucked up – I mean, the culture is fucked up. People must find their way in a very complicated world where there is no hope for government, or no mercy from government or the media. People must lie to survive.

Interviewer: Did you always have a sure and steady sense of what makes good drama?

Stone: No, not at all. Every screenplay is its own struggle. Every screenplay has been difficult. I'm wrestling with *Savages* in the editing room at the moment. I did a lot of rewriting and I just changed something in the structure yesterday, and it's much better now. How come I didn't see that in the fucking screenplay? I worked and slaved over that. I don't know the answers. As a dramatist I have no confidence: I feel like every movie is a truly humbling sport. You learn over every time. I used to have a little more confidence, but my screenplays were never noted. It's true that I did win the Oscar for *Midnight Express*, but in the critics' minds it was regarded as a crude film.

A lot of my characters are martyrs, but I don't want to be a martyr. I'd love to have the business acumen of Spielberg, to put together my own studio and do exactly what I want – but it takes acumen and you have to make deals, and where do you make your deals? You try to soften the edges because you are not looking to fight, but you don't want to run from a fight. I once took money to write a P. D. James novel, *Innocent Blood*, years ago – I spent a month and couldn't fucking get there. I took the money and then returned it to the producer.

Interviewer: As an artist, do you have a vision from the outset, or do you see new possibilities as you make the movie?

Stone: Kubrick and [David] Lean spent a lot of time in the editing suite: that is part of the excitement of movies. You see it one way as a writer, then you shoot it and it morphs into something else, and then you edit the movie and it changes again. It's like a chemical experiment where by the very act of measuring it, you change it. Kubrick said something that I love: I can't quote it exactly but I think he said, 'When I am editing I am not a director.' I feel the same way – I am only looking at whether it works. No love of a scene – no matter how difficult or how painful, or how much fun it was to shoot – makes any difference. The director wants to expand the vision and be generous to the actors – expand, expand! The editor's job is the opposite – restrict, restrict! In every movie I have done, a lot has changed structurally during the course of making the movie. I can't believe that [Alfred] Hitchcock was so arrogant as to say that after the first day of shooting, it was over. I remember Billy Wilder once told me – I don't know if he was bullshitting me or not – but he told me he had *Double Indemnity* [1944] in a Pasadena theatre for a preview three weeks after he finished it! I mean, I know they wrote them tight in those days – but still ... I love structure. Logically, something belongs before something else, but when you make the movie – no! It should have happened before you figure it out. I like three-act structures, but there are a few four-act plays that work.

Interviewer: How far will *Savages* look beyond the issues of the drug war to the wider critique of southern California offered at the end of Don Winslow's book?

Stone: I'm still not sure how much we will go into that. I don't believe the southern Californian culture is as bad as Don makes out. There is a lot of great things that have happened here. I'll find my way to my own expression. I don't want to make a value judgement about the journey of the three youngsters until I have lived longer with the film. The girl in the book is a tough chick. The girl we used – Blake Lively – is different again. So right there, we are into a slightly different world. She is a woman with two men. Why is she with two men, and what does it mean to her? So we have to come to a new understanding. The character in Don's book is perhaps closer to how Jennifer Lawrence, the original choice, might have played the role. My choice of Blake changes the whole nature; the choice of star absolutely changes the nuances of the story. I looked at a lot of gamine actors for the role, including Emily Browning; however, there is something special about Blake that I wanted. Benicio [del Toro] also changes the nature of Lado – he makes a moment out of nothing. So as a dramatist you then have to wrestle with how the choices of actors bring new meanings to the story. Movies work differently than novels.

Interview with Oliver Stone, 19 August 2013

Interviewer: What prompted you to describe President Obama as a 'snake'?

Stone: My reason for calling Obama a 'snake' is because I am very upset, as are many people, by the latest revelations from Ed Snowden, and I've been upset for a while about Bradley Manning and about Obama's attitude to whistle-blowers and to Wikileaks. You also have to reference what I remember of him in 2008 as a reform candidate: a candidate for transparency in government. So when I say he's a 'snake', it's a fully considered comment – it's not off-the-cuff. I don't mean to belittle reptiles, but I do mean it negatively about Obama: he has not only made legitimate the illegalities of the Bush administration, but has made a point of attacking the people who have tried to expose the war crimes and horrors that this government has visited on other countries. It's one thing to say that all countries seek control of the diplomatic world, but we are the dominant country, we are the Roman Empire – and we are totally obsessive about it. Obsessive – and we're bugging allies as well as enemies – and when I say 'snake', it references the Garden of Eden. We always thought we had a chance to get democracy back after the 2000 debacle. The 2008 election was that chance. It was – if you can remember that slogan – a very important one, it was: 'Change we can believe in.' Change we can believe in! It's been the opposite of that. He delivered no change. He's kept it the same – status quo, 'War on Terror'. So what he has done is actually beyond me. His actions have undermined the faith of young people who voted for him, and the root organisations that went out there for him, and he has basically laughed in their faces and said there is no change, and democracy doesn't work. That's what's really fucking depressing. Everyone I know who is a progressive person – and even average guys with no particular politics – are depressed at where this country is at, and feel powerless to do anything about it.

Interviewer: What prompted the editorial choices in *Untold History*?

Stone: The intention was to make history dramatic. I realise it's a lot of material, and we cut and recut so many times to make that 58-minute limit per segment. That produced an enormous amount of reworking of the documentary texts. It had to be done like a movie: how do the pictures and the script work together? For me it was very hard work. [Film editor] Alex Marquez and I in the last year really twisted our brains to get it finished, and we went down to the wire in January of this year. We finished on 9 January, and the last episode aired on 12 January. The style is certainly 'headlong'. I don't know of any documentary that has ever delivered this much information, this fast – we had to do it that way. I knew nobody could quite keep up all the time, but I went with the idea that someone who was really engaged would go back and look at it again. What is amazing is that we had equally good ratings from Showtime for week ten as we did for week one. Some people on my social media sites did say that they had to tune out because it was just too much information, but I think they will come back to it. There are some opportunities to pause, but not for long. There are music breaks, we used as much music as we could: [composer] Craig Armstrong really opened the series very well. I worked with him on *World Trade Center* – beautiful score. However, after five hours of the series we were beginning to overuse those pieces. I don't know what it is. I guess it's a five-year movie, and it required two composers. So I needed Adam Peters, who also worked on *Savages*, to come in and provide some fresh music. They both contributed about the same amount of work. We used Górecki and also Beethoven and Brahms. In addition we used movie clips to offer breaks in the monologue. It was very important to put those in, although we were rushed for time. [Visual effects artists] Christina and Paul Graff did a great job, especially on the maps, which helped nail a few issues.

We tried to hone the events down to their essence, the pattern, the big picture. The aim was to avoid boring people. I tried to do that, although I'm sure there are a couple of sections I could redo.

There are only ten hours to cover World War Two to the present, and two additional hours [released as part of the series DVD set] to reach back to the turn of the century. The book had much more material and grew out of the series. After about two years in we decided to validate the detail with a book to deal with the questioners, the haters, cynics, etc. Peter [Kuznick] and his research students – some ten people – really did the hard work on the book. My problem was getting each episode down to 58:30 without going too fast. It's a balance. The target audience was really a seventeen-year-old studying American history who had already studied some history, and who would be open to an alternative view.

The only talking head I did for the series was an interview with Tariq Ali for a thirteenth hour to be included in the October DVD release: we used new archive footage for this. Otherwise, no talking heads were used: it would never have worked; we would never have made the 58:30, it would have slowed the pace down totally. With a talking head you are affirming points more slowly than can be made in a narrative flow.

Overall, we were trying to make the case that after the Second World War, the United States became a national security state of over-burdensome proportions, and after 1991 and the fall of the Soviet Union, continued on to become a global security state – and now Obama has activated the Asia pivot. We are helping create this fear of China to promote our own interests. There is no going back on empire. We are a bad force in the universe, we heighten tensions in every part of the world. It's not good for anybody – it's going to backfire on us eventually. We are not interested in pacifying, except under our own conditions: it has to be done our way.

The launch has taken about three-quarters of my time. Peter and I went everywhere we could. We were accepted readily by the progressive press. We had a mainly indifferent mainstream press. None of the network shows like *60 Minutes* dealt with it; I don't think we appeared on one public broadcast show. We were saying to the American people: look, we didn't have to drop the atomic bombs. If we can't get even that message out on PBS, I think we're fucked. I think Showtime were pleasantly surprised with the 1.1 million viewers per week without any major advertising. There was no Emmy campaign. The British were much kinder to us: we got more media attention in Britain than we did in the USA. There was also enormous attention in all the newspapers to the launch in Japan: even the right-wing press was fair in its coverage; they were, however, less open on the issue of Japanese barbarism in World War Two, that's a sensitive issue still. Their leaders still worship at a shrine where there are thirteen or fourteen class-A war criminals. The Japanese have never understood these crimes because they have no official history of it. I went to a small privately funded museum in Nagasaki which is the only one that really covers this issue. It's not in the school books. We hear about the 'comfort women' now! These stories only started appearing fifty years after the war ended. The Japanese had sex stations in Burma, Indonesia, Saigon – it wasn't just Korean women. The crimes in China were huge. We made the point that after the war, Germany made a conscious effort to deal with the legacy of Nazism. The Japanese never dealt with their past.

So the message in Japan was complicated: to talk about the atomic bombs and the barbarism and to plead with them to rethink their United States strategy. The US has controlled Japanese politics for sixty-eight years – it still does. When the prime minister of Japan, Yukio Hatoyama, three or four years ago, tried to do something about the US bases in Okinawa and change things, Obama ate his lunch. He lost the confidence of the electorate and was outed. And now we have a right winger in Shinzō Abe, who I'm sure Obama likes. He takes the US line on China.

The twelve-hour DVD will be aired in San Sebastian in September. The DVD launch in October will be big here. It will be the last effort – I'm really putting everything I can into that.

Interviewer: Given the depth of the critique of the American administration in *Untold History*, is that critique now part of your ongoing agenda?

Stone: This critique of the establishment is part of who I am. When I was younger I would have shied away from it, but now that I'm 66, going on 67. The *Untold History* work has broadened my horizons, and in some ways has returned me to that *JFK* thing – reminding people what I stand for. There is hope. When things look depressing that's when the curve of the ball can break differently.

Hey, it was a dream project, but I paid a price for it. It took me out of the film business because I wasn't developing projects. I wasn't thinking about film – every spare moment was here. Yet

I did manage to make three films during that period and two documentaries – *South of the Border* and *Castro in Winter.*

This critique may affect my film career, I don't know. I don't want to make a silly movie. I don't want to make it for the wrong reasons. I have a storytelling sense and a sense of drama, and I want to continue.

Each film I've done has been a growth, and the *Untold History* pushed things to a new level. For the time being, I've done all I want to in documentary work and said all I want to say. Financially I can't really do it. It's punishing, it's been five years. We still haven't broken even on *Untold History*. I guess its *pro bono* work. If I thought about purely commercial work I guess I'd be further ahead.

Interviewer: What is your assessment of other documentary filmmakers who have sought to explore aspects of US statecraft?

Stone: I think Michael Moore set the standard with *Fahrenheit 9/11*. I don't like Gibney's new film on Wikileaks [*We Steal Secrets: The Story of Wikileaks*, 2013]. It seems to be motivated more by personal animosity about not being able to get an interview. [Eugene] Jarecki's *Why We Fight* [2006] was a classic. [Errol] Morris' *Fog of War* [2003] was well done and it got a lot of play in this country, but I think it has a fundamental flaw in that the discussion about Cuba does not really give the Cuban point of view. As a result you form the impression that the United States was being aggressed upon by Cuba, which is one of the commonest flaws in our history of the dispute with Cuba. The focus was on what they did, as opposed to what we did to them.

Interviewer: What drew you back to make another cut [*The Ultimate Cut*] of *Alexander* at this point?

What draws me back to it is my dramatist's idea of what a film should be. I did sign off on the new long cut in 2007 [214 minutes], but then later when I saw it screened three or four times at festivals, I realised that I could make it shorter without sacrificing the essence of the film. In *Alexander* there is a tension between the inner and outer world. As Alexander goes to the outer world, he must keep returning to the inner world. The parents' story is the key to the inner world. I wanted to find that rhythm between inner and outer all the way through the movie. Also, I saw that one of the key parallel scenes with the mother was too late in the movie. It belonged earlier – after the assassination of Philip – we went to the original French negative to get some footage that we wanted. I think it sets up the ending better.

Ptolemy says that Alexander should have died in India: that's true for dramatic reasons, but I like the ending we have because it touches on the nature of history. Ptolemy changes his story. He first admits to the assassination of Alexander, and then goes into why – because dreamers cannot exist, dreamers exhaust us all. He then removes this version for another more sanitised version of history. Later, of course, Ptolemy's writings are lost. I appreciate the way that history plays games on us. There is a line at the end of *Savages*: 'The truth has a mind of its own.' I think that pertains to all things, including my life and yours.

What kept Alexander going is the same as what keeps me going – the tension of trying to find out who you are. I came back to Alexander because I'm an explorer. I didn't have to go back, but Warner Bros. was pleased with the 2007 results of *Alexander*, and out of the blue offered me the opportunity to do another version. I am now signed off on it! I'm finished! I can't do more. I do still see flaws, for example with Colin [Farrell], which are partly my fault, but I believe the film truly works, and that it's a kind of miracle to have rediscovered this ancient time and place.

Interviewer: In the light of Spielberg and Lucas' recent commentary on the impending economic disaster awaiting studios who continue to depend on $300 million franchise movies, do you see any evidence of studios being interested in shifting their emphasis to supporting more $30 to $50 million projects?

Stone: No – on the contrary. They continue with this neo-economics. It is senseless. People have always responded to ideas in films, no matter what the cost – so if the ideas are good, it will work. There is a kind of 'neo-think' in operation, an assumption that everyone thinks alike. The position does make it harder to make controversial films.

Interviewer: In both *Nixon* and *W.* there is a definite sensitivity in your portrayal of inner conflict and the search for recognition. Does the ability to empathise with these men draw on some degree of recognition of a similar struggle within yourself?

Stone: I always worked at drama from the inside out. For example with *Nixon*, it doesn't matter if I don't like the man: you have to learn to eat the soup; you wear a hair shirt to some degree. Spend a whole year of my life on a movie about Nixon? Come on! There's no sex, no action, all talk – but that's moviemaking, you have to plunge into it and see the world as they did. Although I despised Bush, I tried to put myself in his shoes. His father was a giant to him. He had a younger brother who was getting all the attention. You have to use your feelings to get at these things. Bush's father was, in my opinion, an awful president,[12] and in the movie James Cromwell and I discussed making Bush senior an uglier figure, but I felt in the end we needed a foil for Bush Jr. With Bush [G. W.] the issue was that he was around power his whole life. When that happens you smell it, you want it. For Bush, the only way to be strong was to be stronger than his dad. In that sense, Bush's best moment is when he decides to invade Iraq – show his dad that he can finish the job! That's the way he saw it.

Interviewer: How did the deal for *Savages* get set up?

Stone: I liked the book right away, and purchased it myself from Don Winslow. He attached conditions that he would write the screenplay with his partner Shane Salerno. It was a very difficult writing process, and I eventually did a lot of work on the screenplay. It took almost a year. I had other things on my plate, including *Untold History*, and it took longer than it really should have.

We finally went out to several studios in March 2011. All passed except Universal. We never know what goes on, we live like mushrooms on our side of the equation. In any case, Universal liked the screenplay, and made the deal for $48 million – and we turned it in for about a million dollars less and returned the money. They were very impressed by that: they told me most people lie about budgets. Universal wasn't scared of the violence or the drugs – the others didn't like it – anyway, Universal was happy. They didn't want to hamper me, they wanted me to unleash myself, but it was a tough schedule with penalties if we ran late. We couldn't shoot down in Laguna until after Labor Day. There were all the usual problems of actor schedules. Blake Lively had a TV series, it was painfully difficult to work her into the schedule.

Looking back at the last two films, Universal felt a freer working experience. Fox was more controlling on *Wall Street: Money Never Sleeps*. That was Tom Rothman's approach at Fox, but it is just their way of working under Rupert Murdoch.

Interviewer: Is there a wider critique of government running through *Wall Street: Money Never Sleeps* and *Savages*?

Stone: Yes – I would tie both of those films together. *Wall Street: Money Never Sleeps* was a complex film to make. We were very professional and open with Fox. There was a script by Allan Loeb and a previous one by Stephen Schiff, plus I did a lot of rewriting. One of the constraints was that Gekko was no longer the Gekko of 1987. You can't go back to that kind of movie, but Michael Douglas was where the money was. The studio was less interested in the Shia LaBeouf character, and we had a new villain played by Josh Brolin, and of course the Frank Langella character at the beginning, who was very important within the story. So from a story perspective, there were a lot of different balls in the air, including the intimate relationship of father, daughter and her new boyfriend. Perhaps I tried to do too much with the story, but I still like it. I know there has been some degree of criticism of *Wall Street: Money Never Sleeps*, about it not being as vituperative or visceral as the first one, but to me it's not about that. It's about a man getting older and actually finding some degree of humanity.

It didn't catch the pop wave, but a lot of Wall Street professionals saw an accurate portrayal of their world. In *Wall Street: Money Never Sleeps*, the banks have taken over Gekko's job. I was shocked when I went back to this in 2010. In *Wall Street*, Gekko had been the outsider, the inside trader guy, the thief, the blackmailer – and that's what the banks do now. In the old days the banks would never have done that – it was considered immoral – but by 2010 the whole thing had shifted because of deregulation. I think perhaps some of the critics' response missed the irony of that change.

Savages, to me, is about the art of negotiation. The drug cartels are enterprises which, like banks, have slipped free of all effective regulation. It is also about our 'War on Drugs'. The drug thing is so ugly because it creates such a false bureaucracy. We have a 'War on Drugs', a 'War on Poverty', a war on this, a war on that, a 'War on Terror'. Now we have so many wars we can't keep track any more. Now we have a border war on immigrants. So we have drugs, immigrants and terror, and we have now built into our system a huge budget for ICE [Immigration and Customs Enforcement]. ICE submitted a $5.3 billion budget request for 2013 to the [US] House Committee on Appropriations. ICE was overlapping responsibilities with other functions in homeland security, and with the FBI and with the DEA. So you have so many departments. It's like the same problem we had with the US army in Vietnam: we stepped on our own dicks so often. We have the same issue with our intelligence agencies, we couldn't even get the story on the Bin Laden 9/11 attack straight. The real problem with the 'War on Drugs' is that wars generally don't work. We need to get back to common sense.

Interviewer: The double ending in *Savages* is not in the book. What prompted you to introduce it?

Stone: The ending in the book was a different kind of ending – with the double suicide. I never bought that, and certainly when I rehearsed it with the actors and saw the relationships, I just couldn't buy that those two young people would kill themselves because their third partner had been killed. Certainly they would grieve, but I don't think they would kill themselves. It was romantic, we had that touch of *Butch Cassidy* [*and the Sundance Kid*], but in *Butch Cassidy* Katharine Ross disappears at the end and it doesn't quite work dramatically. All the way through the rewrites I was always thinking about another ending.

As you get into it and really think it through, it's clear that the [John] Travolta character is much brighter than the guy in the book: there are too many opportunities for him. As good as Don is, and as good as his previous book on the drug wars was, I look at this book as a rather whimsical view of California. It's not likely that the big cartels would get involved in Los Angeles; they make far more money by shipping huge vats of marijuana and other stuff north to big terminus points. Why would you fuck with the legal system in California? A boutique business is not really the kind of thing they are going to go into – they make too much money the other way. It's possible that a small cartel which was under pressure might do this, but it is an unlikely fantasy. Don has written a very hardcore previous book called *The Power of the Dog* which really deals with the whole issue more realistically. So I looked at the book more as a poem.

Jennifer Lawrence was going to be O. When she left to do *The Hunger Games*, yeah, it hurt. She was looking after herself – and she was right, I guess – although I didn't care for the picture at all. It made her life. At that point it didn't matter to Universal, they didn't mind who was in the role. They liked Aaron [Taylor-Johnson] because they had worked with him on *Kick-Ass*. They liked Taylor [Kitsch] because of *Battleship*. They liked Salma [Hayek] and Benicio [del Toro] and John Travolta but they were veteran actors – supporting cast from their point of view, they weren't the money behind the picture. It's funny because those three got the best reviews, as you know. I liked what A. O. Scott wrote in the *New York Times*, he was accurate about the film. It's a bit like *Wall Street: Money Never Sleeps* in that there are a lot of balls in the air – a lot of actors.

The DEA agent has got to be smarter than in the book, so that makes Travolta very interesting. He has a double role: he is a spy from the beginning. He gives everybody up, including himself. When you play out the negotiation it seems to me that the DEA agent is going to win. Once he figures out that Elena is in country, he has got his fly trap. If you follow the logic, the whole thing is set up when Elena goes north.

The DEA, as you know, always come out OK in the news, no matter what. It's still fucked up, and the drug war goes on and on. It's a racket. On both sides of the fence, and in prison. It makes the prison industry bigger.

That's the realistic ending; the other one was the romantic ending. So the idea was to have the romantic ending and then top it and turn it around. It's been done before, not often. Fritz Lang did it twice: *The Woman in the Window* [1945] was extraordinary. I liked the idea of the double ending. Yes, preview cards revealed some people didn't like this foreign concept. 'What's real?', they wonder. Most were happier with the second ending, and those people hated the first ending [the suicides]. It was far too nihilistic. I liked the idea of the kids going off to a desert island and getting a second chance – not that they would stay together. O says something about her two men, but that won't work over a period of time – a few weeks or a year maybe. I don't think O was ever realistic in the movie or the book; I think she was a dreamer, and she would have grown up and the boys would have grown up or changed. The idea at the end of the voiceover was that life goes on, and that each of them will go their own way. I went to all of the pre-release screenings, apart from England. I knew that there was resistance. Universal was very helpful: they asked me to reconsider. I went back to [Universal Pictures executive] Donna

Langley with my recuts, after a Woodland Hills [California] screening that took us to a place where the cards were good enough to go with.

When it finally came out in theatres, the scores were lower. Adam Fogelson, the head of Universal at the time, liked the movie so much he moved it up to July – it was originally slotted for the fall, which I preferred – but they rushed it, and I think we took a hit there because we had *The Amazing Spider-Man* [Marc Webb, 2012] one week ahead of us, with *The Dark Knight Rises* [Christopher Nolan, 2012] opening one week behind us. There was also an unforeseen hit for Universal – *Ted* [Seth MacFarlane, 2012], as well as Channing Tatum's huge hit – *Magic Mike* [Steven Soderbergh, 2012] one week ahead of us. So we had three fucking hits in front of us, and one right behind us. That was really bad timing. The 4 July weekend is a frivolous weekend: you wouldn't release this kind of relatively complex film on a 4 July weekend. So we didn't do as well as we had hoped, and the picture panned out at $48 million in the USA. I think if it had come later in the summer or in the fall, it would have been higher.

The voiceover about 'in the end we worshipped only ourselves' is Don's version, and yeah, it's in the earlier screenplays. It's the romantic version, it's like he is blaming all of them for being so selfish. I just didn't want to end on that kind of note.

Interviewer: Aside from *Savages, Wall Street* and *Natural Born Killers*, where else have you shot two endings?

Stone: There were two endings shot for *Wall Street*. The romantic one had Daryl Hannah on the steps waiting for Charlie Sheen at the end, and I went for the one now in the film. In *Natural Born Killers* I liked the ending where they meet their fate at the hands of another serial killer – a just retribution, I suppose. But this time I went with the romantic ending because I wanted to see them live! Which, by the way, really pissed off a lot of people who condemned the movie for its violence.

In *Platoon* we shot a version where Chris [Taylor] does not shoot Barnes, possibly to soften the verdict at the end – that he was a killer – but we didn't use it. Also, on *Any Given Sunday* where Jamie [Foxx] and Al [Pacino] walk off the field after the game: that was the ending. Then there was a news conference during the titles where there was a further twist, where Al leaves the team, having signed up Jamie Foxx. It wasn't quite two endings, but I guess we added on an extra bit – the twist. That's it for second endings.

Endings are always difficult. Even in *JFK* – where do I end it? Do I end it in the courtroom, or do I have them walk out afterwards? In *Salvador*, there was the same question in my mind. Should I go all the way and show Maria being arrested by US immigration authorities at the end? I did.

Interviewer: Are you expecting to become more involved in the JFK assassination debate as the 50th anniversary approaches?

Stone: No, I don't think so. I think the Assassination Records Review Board did a fairly good job – exhuming millions of pages of data, some significant reaffirmations that much more was going on than meets the eye – but the government cut the money for the time needed to pursue. That Act also led to accidents. Things came out you wouldn't have expected – for example, the Pentagon's Operation Northwoods, which involved secret proposals for the CIA to carry out terrorist acts in the USA and blame them on Cuba, in order to foment public anger and the invasion of Cuba.

Numerous people ask me to attend events. I did some significant TV, but expect to be edited in ways appropriate to their conventional message. I may attend a couple of conferences if I feel up to it, but I don't want to be used as some kind of symbol. I am more interested now in talking about the material in Chapter 6 of the *Untold History* – how I see the presidency of JFK overall, rather than focusing on the assassination. There is a lot of evidence of changes in his thinking during his presidency, and it's clear his re-election would have been a threat: it would have made a difference. Based on his three-year record and his standing order to withdraw, I don't believe for one moment Kennedy would have gotten involved in the kind of debacle in Vietnam that Johnson did.

Interviewer: What is your prognosis for the American empire?

Stone: Although we are clearly overreaching, it's too easy to talk about the USA losing its grip because we happen to be rooting for another approach. It's not going to go away that easily. This empire is Star Wars in the 'evil empire' sense of the words. We do have an incredible shield – full spectrum dominance. The game is now not about nuclear bombs. Obama can look like a good guy, cutting infantry strength and so forth, but we still have 'lily-pad' island bases all over the world. We have 700–1,000 foreign bases, and are ringing Russia with NATO. As to China, with a new assortment of allies, treaties and bases, we have declared a new 'Asia pivot,' which brings us right back to World War Two days, Korea, Vietnam – we're still there, never gave up an inch. We are developing a new generation of drones, all kinds of intelligence and cyberwarfare capabilities. We have used these against Iran. We act like the underdog, as if China is overwhelming us in cyberspace, yet we have been working on these capabilities for years and have developed the most advanced techniques. The question is: how quickly will we have space fully weaponised?

So this is a serious issue. Although we may be hurting economically, we definitely have become a corporate oligarchy. It is still getting crazier. We are virtually becoming a tyranny against the rest of the world. It's not evident to people at home because they don't see the consensus in the media, and they don't see the harm the USA does abroad. We are not in decline. We are decayed and corrupt and immoral, but not in decline. The USA exerts its will in Europe, Asia, much of the Middle East and still much of Latin America. The recent revelations that the NSA's and the UK's surveillance programmes are linked is big news.[13]

Hillary Clinton talked in 2011 about America's 'Pacific Century' and how the USA would be at the centre of things, echoing Henry Luce's comments in 1941 about the 'American Century'. All of the countries affected reacted to that news supportively: Philippines, Australia, Taiwan, Vietnam, South Korea and Japan. It elevates the tension. China is being portrayed as a threat to this world, yet they do not have 700 to 1,000 bases abroad like we do. They have one foreign base! They build an aircraft carrier, and all of a sudden they are the enemy of mankind? The perception of China, as it was of the Soviet Union, is magnified way out of proportion to justify continuing US empire.

We are in moral decay. The people who broke the law from Bush onwards are in power. The people who decried the breaking of the law are fugitives. Everything is upside down. Most people don't see it. It's a sad world that we are leaving to our children, but we must fight against it – in this series, at the end, we say, 'History has shown us that the curve of the ball can break differently.' It's happened several times – with Gorbachev, Khrushchev, Roosevelt and Kennedy.

Hope is still there. Hope is a foundation for action against this empire.

Notes

1 'Twisted History', *Newsweek* (23 December 1991). Available at http://newsweek.com/twisted-history-201132 (accessed 7 December 2015).

2 The *New York Times* reported on 25 September 1964 that the Warren Report had been delivered to President Johnson the previous day. On 28 September the paper published its assessment, which began: 'The Warren Commission's report is a comprehensive and convincing account of the circumstances of President Kennedy's assassination. The facts – exhaustively gathered, independently checked and cogently set forth – destroy the basis for the conspiracy theories that have grown weedlike in this country and abroad'. *New York Times*, 'The Warren Commission Report', 28 September, 1964. Available at http://nytimes.com/1964/09/28/the-warren-commission-report.html?_r=0 (accessed 1 March 2016).

3 George Lardner Jr, 'On the Set: Dallas in Wonderland; How Oliver Stone's Version of the Kennedy Assassination Exploits the Edge of Paranoia', *Washington Post* (19 May 1991). Available at https://www.washingtonpost.com/archive/opinions/1991/05/19/on-the-set-dallas-in-wonderland/0c958035-3fc2-48a7-a108-da0855c92a94/ (accessed 7 December 2014).

4 Warner Bros. President Bob Daly confirmed in interview that he (Daly) had intervened and asked Valenti to stop criticising the film prior to its release. Daly shared Stone's concern that continued sniping would affect the film's chances at the Oscars that year. Interview with Bob Daly, Santa Monica, CA, 18 October 2010.

5 For example, James Douglass; Douglas Horne on autopsy and the Zapruder film, and James Bamford, who wrote the book *The Puzzle Palace*, about the National Security Agency.

6 Wesley Morris, 'Stone's 'Alexander' turns out not so great', *Boston Globe* (24 November 2004). Available at www.boston.com/ae/movies/articles/2004/11/24/stones_alexander_turns_out_not_so_great/ (accessed 1 March 2016). Olga Craig, 'I have let Alexander down', *Telegraph* (3 January 2005). Available at: http://telegraph.co.uk/culture/film/3634344/I-have-let-Alexander-down.html (accessed 1 March 2016).

7 Frank Rich, 'What Killed JFK?' *New York Magazine* (20 November 2011). Available at http://nymag.com/news/frank-rich/jfk-2011-11/ (accessed 1 March 2016).

8 Part of the Warren Commission case against Oswald relied on an FBI firearms expert who testified that when shooting the rifle found at Dealey Plaza (Mannlicher-Carcano) at less than 100 yards with a telescopic sight, 'you should not have any difficulty in hitting your target'. (Ch. 4, p. 190). Despite this, the Commission concluded that Oswald had used the same rifle in a failed attempt to assassinate Maj. Gen. Edwin Walker on 10 April 1963. (Ch. 4, p. 187). According to the Dallas Police report of the incident, Oswald had rested his rifle on the fence at the back of Walker's house and missed Walker, who was sitting at his desk by the window. The police report estimated the firing distance was 35–40 yards, with a clear view and no window shutters (Commission Exhibit CE 2001, p. 6). National Archives, *Report of the Presidents Commission on the Assassination of President Kennedy*, Ch. 4. Available at www.archives.gov/research/jfk/warren-commission-report/chapter-4.html#walker (accessed 1 March 2016). Commission Exhibit CE2001 available at www.history-matters.com/archive/jfk/wc/wcvols/wh24/pdf/WH24_CE_2001.pdf (accessed 1 March 2016).

9 Camilla Long, 'Oliver Stone: Lobbing grenades in all directions' *Sunday Times* (25 July 2010). Available at http://thesundaytimes.co.uk/sto/newsreview/features/article352668.ece (accessed 1 March 2016).

10 See *Melancholia* (2011).

11 Although it is available in the UK.

12 See Chapter 9 of *The Untold History*.

13 Nick Hopkins, 'UK gathering secret intelligence via covert NSA operation', *Guardian* (7 June 2013). Available at www.theguardian.com/technology/2013/jun/07/uk-gathering-secret-intelligence-nsa-prism (accessed 1 March 2016).

Bibliography

Ali, Tariq and Oliver Stone, *On History* (Chicago: Haymarket Books, 2011).

Bach, Steven, *Final Cut: Dreams and Disaster in the Making of Heaven's Gate* (London and Boston, MA: Faber and Faber, 1985).

Bamford, James, *The Puzzle Palace: A Report on America's Most Secret Agency* (New York: Penguin, 1983).

Beaver, Frank, *Oliver Stone: Wakeup Cinema* (New York: Twayne, 1994).

Bernsten, Gary and Ralph Pezzullo, *Jawbreaker: The Attack on Bin Laden and Al-Qaedda: A Personal Account by the CIA's Key Field Commander* (New York: Crown Publications, 2005).

Boggs, Carl and Tom Pollard, *The Hollywood War Machine: US Militarism and Popular Culture* (Boulder, CO. and London: Paradigm Press, 2007).

Bookman, Milica Z. and Aleksandra S. Bookman, *Economics in Film and Fiction* (London and New York: Rowman and Littlefield Education, 2009).

Brent Toplin, Robert (ed.), *Oliver Stone's U.S.A.: Film, History and Controversy*(Lawrence, KS: University of Kansas Press, 2000).

Brooks, Stephen, *American Exceptionalism in the Age of Obama* (New York and London: Routledge, 2013).

Brownstein, Ronald, *The Power and the Glitter* (New York: Vantage Books, 1992).

Butler, Smedley D., *War is a Racket* (Los Angeles: Feral House, 2003; orig. pub. 1935).

Cartledge, Paul and Fiona Rose-Greenland (eds), *Responses to Oliver Stone's Alexander: Film, History and Cultural Studies* (Madison WI: University of Wisconsin Press, 2010).

Christensen, Terry and Peter J. Haas, *Projecting Politics: Political Messages in American Films* (Armonk, NY and London: M. E. Sharpe, 2005).

Churchill, Caryl, *Serious Money* (London: Methuen, 2010; orig. pub. 1987).

Collins, Jim, Hilary Radner and Ava Preacher Collins (eds), *Film Theory Goes to the Movies* (New York and London: Routledge, 1993).

Couvares, Francis G. (ed.), *Movie Censorship and American Culture.* (Amherst, MA: University of Massachusetts Press, 2nd edn, 2006).

Davies, Philip John and Paul Wells (eds), *American Film and Politics from Reagan to Bush Jr.* (Manchester: Manchester University Press, 2002).

Douglass, James W., *JFK and the Unspeakable: Why He Died and Why It Matters* (Maryknoll, NY: Orbis Books, 2008).

Fiss, Owen M., *The Irony of Free Speech* (Cambridge, MA: Harvard University Press, 1998).

Fukuyama, Francis, *The End of History and the Last Man* (London: Penguin, 2012; orig. pub. 1992).

Galeano, Eduardo, *The Open Veins of Latin America: Five Centuries of the Pillage of a Continent* (New York: Monthly Review Press, 1997; orig. pub. 1971).

Garrison, Jim, *On the Trail of the Assassins: My Investigation and Prosecution of the Murder of President Kennedy* (New York: Institute for Media Analysis, 1990).

Gianos, Phillip, *Politics and Politicians in American Film* (Westport, CT: Praeger, 1998).

Grainge, Paul, *Brand Hollywood: Selling Entertainment in a Global Media Age* (London and New York: Routledge, 2008).

Greenwald, Glenn, *No Place to Hide: Edward Snowden, the NSA, and the U.S. surveillance State* (New York: Signal/Metropolitan Books, 2014).

Hamburg, Eric (ed.), *Nixon: An Oliver Stone Film* (London: Bloomsbury, 1996).

Hamburg, Eric, *JFK, Nixon, Oliver Stone and Me: An Idealist's Journey From Capitol Hill To Hollywood Hell* (New York: Public Affairs, 2002).

Hamsher, Jane, *Killer Instinct: How Two Young Producers Took on Hollywood and Made the Most Controversial Film of the Decade* (New York: Broadway Books, 1998).

Harrison, Colin, *American Culture in the 1990s* (Edinburgh: Edinburgh University Press, 2010).

Heffner, Richard D., *A Documentary History of the United States* (New York and Harmondsworth: Penguin/Mentor, 6th edn, 1999).

Holloway, David, *9/11 and the War on Terror* (Edinburgh: Edinburgh University Press, 2008).

Hollows, Joanne and Mark Jancovich (eds), *Approaches to Popular Film* (Manchester: Manchester University Press, 1995).

Horne, Douglas P., *Inside the Assassination Records Review Board: The US Government's Final Attempt to Reconcile the Conflicting Medical Evidence in the Assassination of JFK*, vols. 1–5. (Falls Church, VA: Douglas P. Horne, 2009).

Huizenga, Robert, *You're Okay, It's Just a Bruise: A Doctor's Sideline Secrets About Pro Football's Most Outrageous Team* (New York: St. Martin's Press, 1994).

Johnson, Haynes, *Sleepwalking Through History* (New York and London: W.W. Norton & Co., 2003).

Kagan, Norman, *The Cinema of Oliver Stone* (Oxford: Roundhouse, 1995).

Kean, Thomas (ed.), *The 9/11 Commission Report: Final Report of the National Commission on Terrorist Attacks Upon the United States* (New York and London: W.W. Norton & Co., 2004).

King, Geoff *New Hollywood Cinema: An Introduction* (London and New York: I. B. Tauris, 2007).

Knebel, Fletcher and Charles W. Bailey, *Seven Days in May* (New York: Harper and Row, 1962).

Kovic, Ron, *Born on the Fourth of July* (New York: Pocket Books, 1977; orig. pub. 1976).

Kunz, Don (ed.), *The Films of Oliver Stone* (Lanham, MD and London: Scarecrow Press, 1997).

Langford, Barry, *Film Genre: Hollywood and Beyond* (Edinburgh: Edinburgh University Press, 2005).

Lewis, Jon (ed.), *The New American Cinema* (Durham, NC and London: Duke University Press, 1998).

Lewis, Jon, *Hollywood v Hard Core. How the Struggle Over Censorship Created the Modern Film Industry* (New York: New York University Press, 2000).

——, *The End of Cinema as We Know It: American Film in the Nineties* (New York: New York University Press, 2001).

Luce, Edward, *Time to Start Thinking: America and the Spectre of Decline* (London: Little, Brown, 2013).

McEnteer, James, *Shooting the Truth: The Rise of American Political Documentaries* (Westport, CT: Praeger, 2006).

McLean, Bethany and Joe Nocera, *All The Devils Are Here* (London: Portfolio Penguin, 2010).

Mackey-Kallis, Susan, *Oliver Stone's America: Dreaming the Myth Outward* (Boulder, CO: Westview Press, 1995).

Madison, James, Alexander Hamilton and John Jay, *The Federalist Papers* (London: Penguin, 1987).

Maltby, Richard, *Hollywood Cinema*. (Malden MA and Oxford: Blackwell, 2nd edn, 2003).

Marrs, Jim, *Crossfire: The Plot that Killed Kennedy* (New York: Basic Books, 1989).

Marx, Karl, *Early Writings* (Harmondsworth: Penguin, 1980).

Mast, Gerald, Marshall Cohen and Leo Braudy (eds), *Film Theory and Criticism: Introductory Readings* (Oxford: Oxford University Press, 4th edn, 1992).

Mill, John Stuart, *On Liberty* (London: Penguin, 1974; orig. pub. 1859).

Morgan, Iwan W. (ed.), *Presidents in the Movies: American History and Politics on Screen* (New York: Palgrave Macmillan, 2011).

Morton Blum, John, *Years of Discord: American Politics and Society, 1961–1974 (* New York and London: W.W. Norton & Co., 1991).

Packer, George, *The Unwinding* (London: Faber & Faber, 2013).

Palmer, William J., *The Films of the Eighties: A Social History* (Carbondale, IL: Southern Illinois University Press, 1995).

Pepper, Andrew and Trevor McCrisken, *American History and Contemporary Hollywood Film* (Edinburgh: Edinburgh University Press, 2005).

Phillips, Kevin P., *Post-Conservative America: People Politics and Ideology in a Time of Crisis* (New York: Random House, 1982).

Ridley, John, *Stray Dogs* (New York: Ballantine Books, 1997).

——, *U Turn: The Shooting Script* (Newmarket Press: New York, 1997).

Riordan, James, *Stone: The Controversies, Excesses, and Exploits of a Radical Filmmaker* (London: Aurum, 1995).

——, *Stone: The Controversies, Excesses, and Exploits of a Radical Filmmaker* (New York: Hyperion, 1995).

Rollins, Peter C., *Hollywood as Historian: American Film in a Cultural Context*. Revised Edition (Lexington, KY: University Press of Kentucky, 1998).

Rollins, Peter C. and John E. O'Connor (eds), *Hollywood's White House. The American Presidency in Film and History* (Lexington, KY: University Press of Kentucky, 2003).

——, (eds), *Why We Fought* (Lexington, KY: University Press of Kentucky, 2008).

Salewicz, Chris, *Oliver Stone: The Making of his Movies* (London: Orion, 1997).

Schatz, Thomas, *The Genius of the System* (Minneapolis, MN: University of Minnesota Press, 2010).

Scott, Ian, *American Politics in Hollywood Film* (Edinburgh: Edinburgh University Press, 2000).

Shaw, Tony, *Hollywood's Cold War* (Edinburgh: Edinburgh University Press, 2007).

Silet, Charles (ed.), *Oliver Stone Interviews* (Jackson, MS: University of Mississippi Press, 2001).

Singular, Stephen, *Talked to Death: The Life and Murder of Alan Berg* (New York: Beech Tree Books, 1987).

Sontag, Susan, *Against Interpretation and Other Essays* (London: Penguin Classics, 2009).

Stone, Oliver, *A Child's Night Dream* (New York: St. Martin's Press, 1997).

Stone, Oliver and Peter Kuznick, *The Untold History of the United States* (New York: Ebury, 2012).

Stone, Oliver and Zachary Sklar, *JFK: The Book of the Film* (New York: Applause Books, 1992).

Toobin, Jeffrey, *The Nine: Inside the Secret World of the Supreme Court* (New York: Anchor Books, 2007).

Vaughn, Stephen, *Freedom and Entertainment: Rating the Movies in an Age of New Media* (New York: Cambridge University Press, 2006).

Wallace, Henry A., *The Century of the Common Man* (New York: Reynal & Hitchcock, 1943).

Warner, Marina, *Managing Monsters: Six Myths of Our Time* (London: Vintage, 1994).

Welsh, James M. and Donald M. Whaley, *The Encyclopedia of Oliver Stone* (Lanham, MD: Scarecrow Press, 2013).

Wheeler, Mark, *Hollywood: Politics and Society* (London: BFI Publishing, 2006).

Williams, Linda Ruth, *The Erotic Thriller in Contemporary Cinema* (Edinburgh: Edinburgh University Press, 2005).

Williamson, Edward, *The Penguin History of Latin America* (London: Penguin, 1992).

Winslow, Don, *The Power of the Dog* (New York: Vintage Books, 2006).

——, *Savages* (London: Arrow Books, 2010).

Wolfe, Tom, *The Bonfire of the Vanities* (London: Vintage Books, 2010; orig. pub. 1987).

Index